W⟨orld Business⟩

Cu⟨ltures:⟩

A H⟨andbook⟩

Comp⟨...⟩

Third

Barry

With 12 key market culture profiles and more on our website: Arabian Gulf, Brazil, China, France, Germany, India, Italy, Japan, Russia, South Korea, The United Kingdom and The United States of America

Thorogood Publishing Ltd
10-12 Rivington Street
London EC2A 3DU
Telephone: 020 7749 4748

Email: info@thorogoodpublishing.co.uk
Web: www.thorogoodpublishing.co.uk

A CIP catalogue record for this book is available
from the British Library.

ISBN:

Paperback (10) 1854188119 (13) 9781854188113

Ebook (10) 1854188127 (13) 9781854188120

Printed and bound in Great Britain by
Marston Book Services Limited, Oxfordshire

Table of Contents

Chapter 6

How to negotiate internationally.....................127

Chapter 7

What not to do and what not to say...............149

Acknowledgements

The authors would like to acknowledge their enormous debt to Richard D Lewis, Chairman of Richard Lewis Communications, for his enormous research, thought leadership and support over thirty years of work. His Lewis model remains one of the most practical and influential ways of understanding how business cultures operate.

Acknowledgements are also due to HarperCollins for the sections on business language, presentations, meetings and negotiations developed in 'Key Business Skills' by Barry Tomalin, HarperCollins, 2012.

Thanks too to our colleagues at the London Academy of Diplomacy for their support, especially Professor Joseph Mifsud, its director.

Special thanks are due to close colleagues and experts in the field, including Michael Carrier, John Farrer, Jack Lonergan, Susan Stempleski, Ulla Ladau Harjulin, Rob Williams and Debby Swallow.

But most important of all are our families, Mary and Paul Tomalin, Carole Nicks and Tracy, Gary and Jessica.

The authors

Barry Tomalin, MA is an international business consultant, specialising in international communication and cultural awareness. He lectures at the London Academy of Diplomacy and is Director of the Business Cultural Trainers Certificate at International House, London. Barry's career has been mainly in international education. Trained initially in African Studies at the School of Oriental and African Studies in London, he has worked as a language teacher, Overseas Development Authority adviser to the Government of Benin, Editor and Marketing Director of the English Language division of the BBC World Service and is the author of a number of books on language and culture. Barry speaks French and some Spanish. Barry's website is www.culture-training.com.

Mike Nicks is a journalist and author, media coach and language enthusiast. He has worked on the launch or development of around 40 magazines and newspapers in the UK, France, the USA and Australia and has written for national newspapers in London including the *Guardian*, the *Independent*, the *Sunday Times*, the *Daily Telegraph* and the *Observer* on topics as varied as motorsport, business cultures and language learning. He has worked as a special projects editor in Paris, and as an editorial director with Emap USA in Los Angeles and with Bauer Specialist Media in the UK. He is the co-author of John Surtees: *My Incredible Life on Two and Four Wheels*, a photo-autobiography of the motorsports legend. Mike speaks Spanish and French.

Introduction

Since 2010 and our second edition the world has changed. As the Chinese proverb says, 'We are living in interesting times.'

The international banking system is in the process of reorganisation and consolidation. Traditional markets are weakening and new markets are becoming more powerful. Trends that forecasters predicted for 2020 and 2050 are occurring much sooner. In 2013 China overtook the US as the world's largest economy by manufacturing output. We are years ahead of trend.

Why do cultural differences matter in business? Many say they don't. However the majority who realize that culture in business is critical have often learned the hard way. Differences in culture manifest in differences in ways of working. Failure to spot these and to plan for them means slippage in deadlines, failures in quality assurance, management poor relations and non-co-operation, poor performance, financial penalties for delays or non-completion penalties, and even withdrawal of contract or the agreement leading to protracted lawsuits.

Culture isn't soft. It's essential. It is one of your key defences against international business and financial disaster.

The impact on the world's exporters is clear. We need to think beyond our traditional markets to the new emerging markets. This radical change affects manufacturing, financial services, and commerce – in fact, every aspect of international trade.

But there is another area that is just as important: the internal internationalisation of companies. Middle managers in international companies are now in regular communication with managers in other countries, and often their direct reports both senior and junior are based overseas. Yet the two sides may never actually meet: they communicate by telephone conference call and occasionally by videoconference. They know little about their colleagues' or managers' cultures or working conditions, and often they can't travel because travel is either too expensive or the company is very security conscious. Yet in many cases these overseas senior managers, who their subordinates never meet and only contact remotely, are responsible for their progress in the company and are responsible for their appraisals and even bonuses.

There is a third characteristic of our contemporary world: migrant workers. These are not just the seasonal fruit pickers who may come and go, but workers who arrive from other countries, integrate into a company and rise to higher management positions. There are now large communities of workers from abroad living in our cities and working in our companies.

How do we respond to them? Migrant workers have always been a part of local manufacturing and business, but the number of migrant workers is increasing exponentially. To take just one example, some 400,000 French citizens live and work in the UK, most of them in London. This fact prompted a former French president, Nicolas Sarkozy, to dub London France's fourth largest city (statistically, it is now France's sixth largest city).

These three factors – export imperatives, the internationalisation of companies and the increased migration of labour – are complicated by a fourth, a trend that we can call globality.

For the last ten to fifteen years, Western companies have increased margins and reduced costs by outsourcing and by absorbing companies in emerging countries into their own organisations. Now we are beginning to see the reversal of that process. Indian companies, in particular, are setting up branches in Europe and the US and competing with their former employers.

The most powerful aspect of this phenomenon is the way that Indian companies are beginning to absorb Western organisations. India's most iconic company, Tata, is now the proud owner of many Western brands (such as Jaguar and Land Rover vehicles in the UK) and steel and manufacturing enterprises. China is investing heavily in Africa and Latin America to access the raw materials it needs to boost its manufacturing, taking on part of the role traditionally played by the US in Latin America, and Britain and France in Africa.,

In short, globality means that everyone is competing for everything everywhere. In this new environment, we need to get to know each other much better. That means understanding the cultures – and particularly the business cultures – of our partners. That's what this book helps you to do. The secret is to know what to look for, and we offer simple guidelines to help you unlock any business culture in the world.

In our experience culture can be complicated. When you look at a colleague's or partner's business culture there are many things that seem to come into play: values and attitudes, customs, folklore, climate, food and drink, entertainment, classical and popular culture, traditions, ways of communicating and ways of doing business, etiquette – and sport. What you need as an international business person is a clear focus – you need to know what to look for.

That is why in this book we show you what to look for and we demonstrate it in our profiles of 12 key business cultures. We've called the process, RADAR, a laser that allows you to tune in instantly to other business cultures. We have identified seven key tools:

1. **RADAR EXPECTATIONS** – what are the features of a business relationship that create trust across borders?

2. **RADAR COMMUNICATION** – what are the six key ways that people communicate across borders and how can you adapt?

3. **RADAR ENGLISH** – English is the language of business but not everyone uses it in the same way and to the same level. How can you adapt your English to make it clear for everyone you deal with, wherever they may be?

4. **RADAR MANAGEMENT** – What are the key management style features that differentiate business cultures? What problems can these differences cause and how can you overcome them?

5. **RADAR PROFILE** – What is your management profile? How can you compare it with colleagues or JV and M&A partners in other business cultures?

6. **RADAR SYSTEM** – How can you spot and deal with problems before they arise?

7. **ECOLE** – an acronym to help you identify the key differences in another business culture.

RADAR© shows where to look for differences and shows you how to deal with the differences when you identify them. It is the best and most effective methodological tool you need.

We've divided the book into two parts. Part One (Chapters 1-10) presents those guidelines with lots of examples of how to deploy them, and summaries to help you refer back to them quickly. Part Two (Chapters 11-20) profiles the world's key markets, most rated by the investment bankers, Goldman Sachs, as among the world's top ten economies. For countries not in the book, please visit www.worldbusinesscultures.com, where you can download additional cultural profiles, or contact us and ask. We also include a list of the sources that have influenced us, and an index to the book for ease of reference.

Between us we have lived and worked in over 60 countries in every continent of the world. We've always believed that a knowledge of local cultures was both important and enjoyable. Now we know that it's essential.

Barry Tomalin & Mike Nicks

Part One
Chapter 1
Culture is about perception

In 2013 the traditional rivalry between France and Britain was re-ignited by food. Complaints arose that meat food products sold by certain supermarkets contained horsemeat. One problem was that the use of horsemeat was not listed on the package ingredients. However, the other problem was cultural. The British don't, on the whole, eat horsemeat. The very idea is repugnant to many, but this is not the case in France.

To be fair, the products complained about didn't originate in France although they were packaged and distributed there. But different attitudes to the acceptability of horsemeat and other animals as food are deep-rooted. Why do we get upset about these things and what does it say about our culture? The French have a prejudice that British food is inferior (it isn't). However, British and French attitudes to what is tasty do vary.

The horsemeat scandal was ultimately about trading standards but what the fuss was really about was cultural attitudes, and culture, to a degree, is about perception. It's often not what you are really like but what I think you are like that determines my initial view of you.

Perception is a sensitive subject. Culturally, it describes the recognition that what I hate about a social behaviour may be what you accept. The point is that what we register about another community is the differences and if we don't like those differences, the perception may well be negative.

David and Sarah are friends of ours. They are teachers and they love France. So what did they do when they retired? They bought a house in a small village in the Dordogne (a region in west central France). They love cheese, wine, good food and the good life, but were frustrated by French bureaucracy, by what they perceived as French rudeness, and by the apparent lack of interest shown by their neighbours in anything that was not French. They became quite lonely and eventually sold their house and returned to the UK.

Their experience isn't common, but it illustrates an important point: culture is about perception. It is not what you are like, but what I think you are like that determines my opinion.

There's more. Our cultural perceptions are often negative. And the negative often outweighs the positive. Jack is director of a UK sales company dealing with Sweden and Italy. He likes the Swedes: they're calm, methodical, organised and on time. He enjoys the feeling of working in a 'no surprises' culture.

By contrast his Italian colleagues give him nothing but surprises. They're always charming, friendly and hospitable. He loves that. But they don't reply to emails, are often late, tend to be overemotional and volatile and, when they are in contact, don't address the issues he needs to discuss.

We asked Jack which business community he prefers. It's a no-brainer: Sweden good, Italy bad, although he finds that the Italians are lovely guys personally. By the way, the Swedes and the Italians probably have their own problems with Jack!

We need to avoid this tendency to treat culture comparison like a football score, as in Sweden 4, Italy 0. Why? Here is the first rule of culture.

Trust is the key

When we work in our own cultures we know how people operate, more or less. We have shared professional standards that we may or may not live up to, but we know what they are. However, when we work with different cultures the rules of engagement change. We need to learn their conventions regarding behaviour. Business partners and clients in other countries may have different attitudes to time, communication, teamwork and management styles, and we need to respect them.

More importantly, what makes a good impression in country A may have no effect in country B, and might even create a bad impression. Take Spain, for example. First, we need to understand that Spain, like most other countries, contains several cultures – Castilian (Madrid), Catalan (Barcelona) and Andalusian (Seville) being just three of them. However, there is a Spanish way of doing things, and one of them is emphasis on character.

In the US, for example, as long as you produce to specification, on time and on budget there is no problem. If we do a lot of work together we may become personal friends, but only so long as the work goes well. In Spain they do things differently. Your business partner or colleague needs to get to know you, not just as a business partner but as a person. That's why character matters, as well as organisation and efficiency.

In many countries in Asia, building relationships takes time. George Renwick, a noted American consultant, has a telling anecdote. He was asked to advise an American company on what looked like a failed merger attempt with a Chinese company.

'We've been talking for four years and nothing's happened,' the president of the US operation said. 'Should we pull out or what?' 'Mr President,' Renwick replied, 'you've only just started!'

So what builds trust with a foreign partner or colleague? Two things – rapport and credibility.

Build trust with rapport and credibility

Rapport means building good relations. To do that you need to understand what your client expects. What they consider relationship-building may seem like wasteful socialising to you. Do it anyway. It will be the foundation of your business partnership and will protect you when times are tough.

Credibility means you are who you say you are, and you can do what you say you can do. The important word in that sentence is 'say'. The key to successful credibility is communication. This is the single most difficult aspect of building good business and social relations. You need to understand how the other side communicates, and be prepared to adapt to it.

The TRUST triangle

We can present these elements in the TRUST triangle:

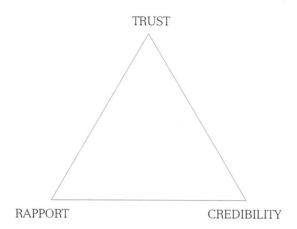

TRUST

RAPPORT   CREDIBILITY

Multinational corporations: one size fits all

Omar is an Arab diplomat, and works at the London embassy of a leading Middle Eastern country. One day after a seminar he came up to us holding a trade magazine, *The Diplomat*. 'Tell me,' he asked, 'internationally, don't you think we're all the same?'

We leafed through *The Diplomat*. It was what you would expect: photos and descriptions of social events – receptions, ceremonies and sporting occasions. The photos were of diplomats and their partners, mainly dressed in Western fashions, with a very few wearing national dress. Everybody had a glass and food in front of them. The drinks were mostly champagne, but there was also orange juice and soft drinks. The food was primarily standard Western buffet snacks, with a few national specialities such as Chinese spring rolls or Lebanese falafel.

So it's true, isn't it? We're all the same.

No. The glossy photos mask a host of differences, both personal and cultural. The personal differences may be to do with family background, social environment and education and may involve considerations of faith. It is dangerous to assume that belonging to a common professional community means you have a common set of beliefs or behaviours, or even that you will all get along.

Kimo Sasi, Finnish diplomat and former Minister of International Trade, once said that before he meets any foreign counterpart, he checks their biography and learns about their family background and the culture they grew up in. He also finds out where they were educated and whether they have lived or worked in other countries, including his own. He doesn't assume people are the same. He assumes people are different and he takes the trouble to find out how.

He explores and accepts the differences, both personal and cultural, and prepares himself to adapt, if necessary. But he also does something else. He looks for something that he and the person he will meet might have in common. This includes personal interests, people they both know, and places they have both visited. He also looks for areas where Finnish customs and interests and those of the person he is meeting come together – but also where they might collide. The first is to be exploited. The second is to be avoided. Armed with this information, he's in a far better position to get the most out of his meetings and to achieve cooperation.

The lesson? Never take superficial similarity for granted. It can cause you minutes of discomfort and years of anguish at lost opportunities.

There is one area where a common culture needs to exist, however, and that involves multinational companies. Rahul is general manager of a leading international bank: he's based in Chicago, but his background is Indian. One of the challenges he has had to overcome in his own country is the Indian relaxed attitude to time. 'There's a saying in India,' he tells us. 'You (in the West) have the watch, but we have the time.' In other words, time for many Indians is flexible. He also reinterprets IST (Indian Standard Time) as 'Indian Stretchable Time'.

As Indian multinationals themselves know, you can't run a business across international time zones with 'stretchable' time. Local businesses, not just in India, may hold to local 'time tolerance', but it doesn't work internationally and causes immense frustration at missed deadlines and poor communication. There are certain areas of international affairs where you just have to conform, simply in order to get the business done. Time is the most important, and we will examine attitudes to time in detail in Chapter 9.

In the meantime, we are back to the same question. Are people actually that different?

Isn't it all about stereotypes?

'OK, we accept that individuals are different. But do they all conform to national stereotypes? Whatever you tell me about a culture, I can always tell you about someone I know from that culture who doesn't conform to the stereotype at all.'

That was said by a teacher that we know. Very experienced internationally, and very cynical about what she calls national stereotypes. We don't believe in stereotypes either. We agree that labelling everyone from the same country with the same characteristics is just wrong. Stereotypes fix people, and they don't allow for variety.

According to popular national stereotypes, Americans are loud, the British are stiff and formal, the Japanese polite, the Chinese inscrutable (hard to read, which should make them good poker players), and Italians emotional, while Africans dance all the time and Arabs are volatile. And so on and so on. But it's just not true.

It's interesting to ask where these stereotypes come from. Immediately, our old friend perception comes into play. An unfortunate historical encounter, maybe centuries old, may have caused a perception of a race or culture, and the image has stuck.

Why a false stereotype can remain is also interesting. Very often the stereotype represents an element of truth about a culture, but one which has been misunderstood and misinterpreted by foreigners. Take Chinese inscrutability, for example. Chinese people are much more open with their emotions than you would expect but they also believe in maintaining face. Face, or *mianzi*, means personal dignity. In practice it means that you don't show your feelings under pressure and you don't lose your temper in public, because to do so would represent loss of face. Those who know the Chinese are familiar with the 'long face', which indicates disapproval or displeasure. So perhaps that's what outside observers once called 'inscrutable'.

However, national characteristics do exist. We prefer to describe them as generalisations. We can say that a majority of people behave or think in a particular way – but it's important to allow for variations. An interesting example is the United Kingdom. A government survey in 2007 identified Britain as a community of commonly held values. These included the rule of law, tolerance and fair play. Not everyone in Britain believes that these values matter, but most people do. So we can say, for example, that most people in Britain believe in fair play. That's a generalisation.

We can make generalisations about a culture at national level, but that's just a start. If I say that Asians are concerned about not losing face (their personal dignity in the world), you can show me lots of Asian people you know who don't care about face at all.

That's because national characteristics are just the surface. We use them as a platform to dig down to the personal level. But as we do so, we go through a number of levels or types of experience. Take Nelly: she's from the north of China, from Harbin, close to the Russian border. It's where they hold an ice sculpture festival every winter. Nelly is 25 years old, and an administrator in an electronics firm. So as well as being Han Chinese, she's a Northern Han Chinese, which means that she has a regional experience different from that of the Chinese in Beijing, or further south in Shanghai.

Electronics and computers are important growth industries in China as elsewhere. So Nelly has the experience of being a young executive in a young and rapidly expanding industry. This gives her a professional experience very different from that of a poor country farmer, for example.

Nelly is the only child in her family, a product of Premier Deng Shao Peng's 1979 one-child policy, which was introduced to restrict China's rapidly expanding population. As a girl in a country where the majority of single children are boys, she is much in demand, so she has a particular kind of social experience.

The reason we know Nelly is that she studied in London for her MA and then did an internship in a leading electronics company based in London. So we know that she has a very special experience of living, studying and then working in London.

We can represent these different levels of experience in the following way:

NATIONAL EXPERIENCE
REGIONAL EXPERIENCE
PROFESSIONAL EXPERIENCE
PERSONAL EXPERIENCE

When we're trying to assess someone from another culture, we need to start at the national level, but we should not stop there. We have to dig down to the deeper levels of regional, professional, social and personal experience. These experiences don't invalidate a person's national experience, but enrich it.

There are questions we can ask to elicit these experiences. Here they are:

- **NATIONAL:** Where are you from?

- **REGIONAL:** What part are you from? What's it like there?

- **PROFESSIONAL:** What did you do before you worked here? How was it different?

(The form of question is important. By asking about a former workplace you can neutrally elicit opinions of the current workplace. This may in turn alert you to cultural issues the person is facing.)

- **PERSONAL:** Have you travelled abroad much? Where to? (This may indicate a more open-minded approach to cultural differences, but not always).

When do you need culture?

When things are going well you can argue knowledge of cultural differences is not necessary. The danger is when things start going wrong; when there is mis-communication or there is deadlock over a contract or agreement. Maybe deadlines and milestones are missed or specifications are not adhered to.

When there are problems or disagreements the tendency is for each side to revert to their own cultural norms and prejudices and blame the other for not adhering to them. This is when you need cultural awareness.

The trick is to understand what the real needs of the person or company you are dealing with are. These may be rooted in national cultural ways of doing business.

Mick is a manager who needed statistical information from a country in central Europe. He sent an email. No reply. He sent another email. Still no reply. Then he sent a third, stronger, email. Still no reply. 'Why didn't you call them up, Mick?' we asked.

'I don't like phones,' he replied. 'I prefer emails. It gives me a record of what's going on.'

This was a perfect example of two cultural ways of doing business in conflict, creating delays. Mick likes emails. He feels it is safer, more impersonal and creates a 'paper trail' of the transaction. His colleague in Central Europe finds the phone more efficient, more effective and more personal. Once Mick got on the phone and explained his position, the problem was solved – and the Central European company replied to his emails, because they felt they knew and could trust him.

Why didn't they trust him before? Because for sixty years they had been under a system of Communist government where the wrong document could lose you your job and worse. Older managers, and this was one, still remembered and were affected by the old days. Old habits and old cultures die hard!

This is a small example but vital to everyday business efficiency. The message is, don't blame the other for non-performance. Put yourself in their shoes.

Three ingredients of culture

The secret of unlocking a business culture is knowing where to look for the evidence. Is it in the music, the literature, the dance traditions, theatres and art galleries? Is it represented by their movies and pop music? Or do you seek the key simply in their daily life?

Susan Stempleski is a much-travelled American. She has spent years as a language teacher at Hunter College and Columbia University in New York, has written books about language and culture and worked on teacher training missions all over the world, many for the United States Information Agency (USIA). In a book, *Cultural Awareness* (which she co-wrote with Barry), she distinguishes between the Big C and the little c. What was she talking about?

The Big C is all about the cultural icons – art, architecture, theatre, that kind of thing. The little c is about the small things – everyday lifestyles and customs, including business customs.

We're not saying that the Big C isn't important. Increasingly it's what most of us do on special occasions, such as celebrations, or when we notice a particularly beautiful building, monument or public space. The little c is what we do every day. It determines what we think about, what we say to each other and how and what we do.

That's why in this book we've taken the little c a bit further and divided it into three areas – expectations, communication and behaviour. These are the three things you look for in another country's business culture. So if we're working in any new market we will ask three questions:

1. What are their expectations of the business relationship?
2. How do they communicate
3. How do they behave?

We can present the three ingredients like this:

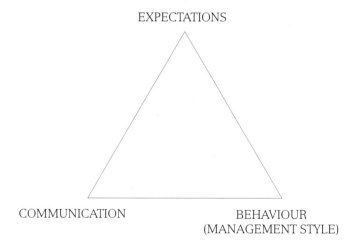

EXPECTATIONS

COMMUNICATION

BEHAVIOUR
(MANAGEMENT STYLE)

What are their expectations?

Their expectations are what they think about business relationships. Do they want you to be their friend or just a colleague or
customer or provider? Believe it or not, countries differ radic-
ally in this respect and it affects the whole process of building
business relations. We'll examine this in detail in Chapter 2.

How do they communicate?

Take English, first of all. Communication styles can be complicated. What we do know is that apart from talented international
English speakers, most speakers' use of English is influenced by
their mother tongue and by the communication styles of their
own culture.

And how these vary! Some communities prefer to talk to you
face to face or on the phone and others prefer to write. Some
communities are informal and others formal and respectful.
Some communities like to show their human side and expect
you to share your personal life; others prefer to reserve conversation about their personal life for their family and close
friends. Some communities use their eyes and hands to illus-
trate what they say; others prefer to keep their arms tightly by
their sides and their eyes neutral. Some people like to touch you
when they talk; others don't. Some communities are happy to
interrupt you when you are speaking; for others, it's extremely
impolite.

Only one thing is common to all styles. Get it wrong, and you
risk losing credibility in the eyes of the person you're dealing
with, so it's worth knowing how to match a particular culture's
communication style. We show you in detail what to look for in

Chapter 3 and give lots of examples in our key market profiles in Part Two of the book.

How do they behave?

Once again different business communities have different management styles, and different approaches to teamwork, time and business organisation. They run meetings differently to what you are used to, they negotiate in different ways and treat women in the business environment with different degrees of respect and importance. One size definitely doesn't fit all. All these things you need to learn about and understand. We'll disentangle it for you in Chapters 4 to 9 and give masses of examples in Part Two.

RADAR Five Alive

So, here you are in a foreign country or dealing with a business group you have never met before, and suddenly everything seems different. The use of English (or another language), the communication style and the way people are behaving simply don't match your expectations. You're here to do business but the way that people seem to be responding feels like anything but: sometimes you feel like you're on another planet. How do you proceed?

The answer, as the Chinese philosopher advised, is 'one step at a time'. And that's where the Five Alive tool is useful. It's simply five things you need to do to keep your sanity and your business hopes alive. The Five Alive tool is based on a 2007 European Union project called Uniting Europe Through

Culture. The project conducted surveys in various countries, and identified five things you can do when you encounter an unfamiliar situation, not just in business but in any area of interaction with a different culture.

The five steps are:

1. Identify
2. Compare
3. Empathise
4. Manage
5. Reflect

Let's unpack them.

IDENTIFY

This is when you see or hear something you are unfamiliar with. It may be odd. It may even be upsetting. However, unless it's related to personal security (i.e. you're in danger), the best thing to do is to stop and observe what's going on and don't react.

COMPARE

The reason you've noticed something is odd is because it's different from what you do at home. So compare it with what happens at home. How is it is different? Be as precise as you can. But still, unless it's dangerous, don't react.

EMPATHISE

Ask yourself, why are they acting like this? This simple thought allows you to move from opposition (I'm surprised or shocked) to understanding (a more positive frame of mind). You're still reactive, but now you're in a better position to decide how to respond.

MANAGE

Now you're ready to decide what to do. Ask yourself, 'What skills do I need to manage this situation?' Remember that one of them might be just to do nothing. Another might be to ask what's going on. A third might be to ask for advice. A fourth might be to assert your own will and make it clear what you need in order to proceed in a harmonious fashion. As long as you're polite, your position will be respected.

REFLECT

This is probably the most important tool. Ask yourself consistently, 'What have I learned from this incident about my colleagues' expectations, communication style and behaviour?' And most importantly, 'What (if anything) will I think, say or do differently in the future?'

After a while it becomes second nature to do this, but to begin with you need to make it a conscious, if at times slightly painful, process. You'll make mistakes, of course. Everybody does. But the fact that you're able to reflect and learn will earn growing respect from your foreign colleagues and clients. And you'll build up a library of experiences and ways to behave that will support you in the future.

Don't forget the fun

Talking like this, it's easy to make dealing with different cultures a difficult and slightly forbidding affair. Sometimes it is, of course, but you're dealing with different people with different backgrounds, customs and ways of enjoying themselves.

We've been treated to brilliant meals, wonderful drinks, great company in exotic surroundings, the chance to dance samba in Rio or salsa in Havana, see temples and palaces that are out of this world and some of the most famous landmarks. We've been to concerts, theatres and art galleries housing masterpieces we would rarely or never see in our own countries. We've attended cultural events we never knew existed, but which are highlights of the local year. And we've been enriched by being allowed to enter, even for a short time, the lives of local people who have invited us home and shared their hospitality with us.

And we've learned. We've learned about new books, new movies, new sports and teams and we've learned about and from the people we've come across. Working across cultures is a moving and unforgettable experience that deepens, spiritually enriches and broadens anyone who comes into contact with it.

There's a tendency on a foreign visit to sit in the hotel room or office and just work. After all, it's what you're there for. Then you race for the train or the plane and get back - home. But never forget that the chance to work internationally that more and more of us are now experiencing is not just a work opportunity. It's a life opportunity. Grab it!

Five things to remember

1. Culture is about perception, so beware of creating false perceptions of foreign cultures.

2. Remember the TRUST diagram – cultural relations depend on building rapport and credibility.

3. In multinational corporations, a common attitude to time, delivery and operating systems is essential.

4. Think generalisations, not stereotypes. Use the levels of experience to dig down from the national culture to the person you are dealing with.

5. Use the Five Alive tool to help you analyse, and manage cultural differences – identify, compare, empathise, manage, reflect.

Chapter 2
What do they expect?

What did they expect? The book *Beijing Jeep* tells the story of how America's Jeep company invited its Chinese merger partners to their sales conference in Las Vegas. The Chinese dignitaries doubtless expected excellent accommodation, good formal and relaxed discussions, excellent food. And maybe a trip to the famous gambling tables for relaxation.

What they got was something else. A US corporate-style sales conference, with everyone celebrating successes, and letting their hair down and letting off steam. Drinking, sex shows and loud partying were the order of the day. The Chinese sat there, dignified and largely silent. Then they left early.

Deal over.

They didn't get what they expected. Should they have adapted? Should Jeep have scheduled a different time and place? Should they have provided their Chinese guests with a more comfortable environment? Difficult to decide. After all, it could have gone so differently.

A large UK insurance company was visited by representatives of a new Indian agent. As part of the social programme, the UK sales director took the visitors to a strip club. According to him, they loved it, and it certainly didn't do the business any harm. But, as he admitted, it was a risk. It just happened to pay off.

Now, don't get us wrong. We're not advocating strip clubs, or gambling for that matter. What we are saying is that if you want to do business internationally, finding out your client's or colleague's expectations is the key.

Here's an example of another company that got it right. A British advertising firm heard that its Spanish equivalent was selling out, so they decided to go for the business. Their plan was simple: invite the Spanish management team over. Meet them in the office. Show them round the plant. Have lunch in the canteen. Hold a meeting in the boardroom. Then order them a taxi back to the airport. Simple, no?

No. Luckily, the British company called us in. We found out two vital pieces of information. The company's offices are on the edge of the Yorkshire Moors, not far from where the Bronte sisters lived and where Emily Bronte wrote *Wuthering Heights*. We also discovered that the former company chairman knew the managing director of the Spanish company.

So here is what we recommended. First, invite them to stay overnight in the nicest hotel in town. On the day of their arrival, go to the East Midlands airport and collect them, but don't take them to the office – take them to their hotel instead. Then invite them out to the chairman's house for cocktails and maybe dinner. Finally, back to the hotel.

The following morning, receive them in the office? Hold on. After breakfast, a car took them for a drive across the moors to Haworth to experience the beauty of the landscape and the richness of the heritage. Then lunch, in a Michelin-starred fish and chip restaurant. Yes, they exist. Finally, to the office for a quick look at the plant, an opportunity to meet and greet key operational staff, and then back to the airport and home.

What – no business meeting? No PowerPoint experience? No detailed review of technical processes? No – the Spanish knew all that. What they didn't know is what kind of people the British company was made up of. Could the Spaniards trust the Brits with their business? They decided they could. The next call we got was to ask if we could recommend a Spanish speaker to translate the sales agreement from Spanish to English.

For the Spanish, and indeed most of the world, what matters is to do business with people they like and trust. That means taking the time to get to know them. By taking the visitors to meet the chairman at his home (hospitality and connections), showing them round the area (roots and local commitment), and offering entertainment (an opportunity to develop personal as well as business exchanges), the British team catered for the need to build trust and good relationships with their Spanish guests.

It's a rule of thumb in Spain: if you're working with a Spanish company and they don't invite you to lunch at 2pm, it may be a signal that things aren't going well.

But where do our expectations come from and why are they so important in our attitude to business?

Where do our expectations come from?

Think for a moment about what you expect from any relationship. What will satisfy you? What would make you feel that your expectations haven't been met? At root, these expectations are determined by our core values: what we really believe is important. It's how we judge the behaviour and attitude of others. Do they share our values?

Values come from a number of sources, all of which are inter-linked.

- Parents and upbringing

  Very often we share or reject our parents' values. But the way we were brought up will, to a large extent, determine what we expect of ourselves and of others.

- Social environment

  Where we grew up will also have an effect. City or countryside, working, middle- or upper-class background, all influence what we expect and the way we behave.

- School

  This is a major influence on us, both through the values taught explicitly and implicitly by the school itself, and by the school atmosphere and how we fit into it.

- Business

  Most people we talk to recognise the influence of a particular firm or industry they have been involved with, which they admire, and whose values they have absorbed.

- Regional values

  People from regional backgrounds greatly value the locality that they come from and may consciously or unconsciously reflect local attitudes. So it's important to recognise and value the regional background of your client or colleague. Enquiring about it and showing interest in its character and achievements is an important part of building trust.

- National values

With all these other influences jostling for possession of our personalities, is there room for national values? Yes. Historical background is a key influence on us, even if we may not have a detailed knowledge of the facts of our local history. It determines how we see ourselves, and how we see other countries and particularly rivals. When President George Bush uttered that phrase "War on Terror" after the Al Qaeda attacks on the World Trade Centre in New York and the Pentagon in Washington in 2001, he used the word 'crusade', and the Arab world took note. Ah, yes – history repeating itself.

British people who know China well are sometimes surprised that the Chinese still remember the opium wars of the end of the 19th century. Why? It was when the British introduced opium from India to South China, provoking a local rebellion. When the French have a disagreement with the British, it isn't long before the expression 'la perfide Albion' surfaces, and that goes back to 19th-century tensions between the two countries. So history influences who we trust and mistrust, and who we like and don't like, yet we may not even be aware of it.

So does religion. The main world religions – Buddhism, Christianity, Islam, Judaism, Hinduism, Agnosticism and their related sects – have been at war at various times for centuries. These conflicts have influenced us in various ways, and we have repressed emotions about religious symbolism and behaviour. Some people find crucifixes repugnant; others dislike yarmulkes (Jewish skullcaps). Some don't understand why people mutter over strings of beads. Oh, for heaven's sake! Why, as happens in some Islamic societies, do they have to close the shops in order to pray? How does that help business?

A vice-president of a leading US bank had a meeting with the Thai Minister of Finance. The meeting went well, and the American relaxed. He was quite a big man, and he stretched and crossed his legs and rested his right ankle on his left knee. Then the Thai minister got up, politely excused himself for a moment and left the room. And he never came back!

What went wrong? The VP hadn't done his homework. He hadn't found out that in his visitor's culture, the head is the most sacred part of the body and the foot is the dirtiest. To show the soles of your feet to your interlocutor in the Far East and the Middle East is an insult. That's why in 2003 we saw TV newsreel footage of Iraqis beating Saddam Hussein's image on posters with their shoes. It also explains why an Iraqi journalist threw a shoe at President G W Bush in a press conference in Baghdad.

The belief about the relative sacrednesss of the head and the feet also affects advertising campaigns. The poster for the movie *Hollywood Buddha* 2008 showed a person sitting on the head of the Buddha, and provoked riots among monks in Thailand. When a leading sneaker manufacturer launched its products in Thailand, someone had the bright idea of lining up the footwear alongside monks' sandals outside a Buddhist temple. They didn't notice that the monks' sandals pointed outwards away from the temple, and placed the sneakers pointing towards the temple entrance to show the logo on the back of the shoes. They also failed to notice the large statue of the Buddha just to the right of the temple: the creative director probably thought that it would add local colour to the shot.

By now you've probably guessed the result – the poster was withdrawn a week after its release. Communities that are not particularly religiously observant often fail to respect the sensitivities of communities that are. The lesson is, do your cultural due diligence. This is not the last time you'll hear this message in this book.

The media can often perpetuate negative cultural images. There is a rivalry between the UK and Germany that dates from the unification of Germany under Otto von Bismarck in 1871. Britain defeated Germany in the First and Second World Wars (1914-18 and 1939-45), with the support of the Americans, the Russians and the nations of the British Empire (some say because of it), but thereafter, the only occasion when Britain beat Germany in the Wold Cup was in 1966 when the English football team under Bobby Moore was victorious.

Have the British been able to forget that moment? In the build-up to the 2002 World Cup the British popular press was full of headlines relating to 1966, and when the German team lost to England by five goals to one in a World Cup qualifier, the British popular press were delirious.

If you think this is irrelevant to business, here's an example of why it's not. A German automobile manufacturer gave its British arm the task of producing a new customer rental programme for car leasing Europe-wide. The British division did what the British often do in such circumstances, and gave the job to a company that they had worked with successfully in the past.

The Germans found out and withdrew the contract, claiming that the tendering process hadn't been observed. The Germans then put the programme out to tender, and found a German company that could do the job at a lower price and a higher specification than the British. Our task in this process was to bring the two sides together.

You can imagine the atmosphere. The Germans were charm itself, while the Brits were cold and distant and pretended that nothing was wrong, while, obviously, everything was wrong. The passive-aggressive standoff continued until finally one of the British broke the ice. 'Five-one!' he shouted across the room. This punctured the tension. The British could point to a victory; honour was restored and discussions were able to continue.

The popular media can play an unfortunate role in perpetuating this kind of image. When Germany hosted the 2002 FIFA World Cup, the downmarket British newspaper headlines were full of Second World War epithets. The Germans were 'Huns' and 'Jerries', and souvenir shops were full of merchandise bearing the slogan 'Five-one'! The incidents even provoked a mild protest from the German Ambassador to the UK. For the record, after the World Cup everybody commented on the courtesy and good organisation of the German authorities. But why should we have expected anything different?

So who is your national media demonising now? And are they right to do so? Another case for cultural due diligence.

Here's a final example from Brazil. Like the Spanish, the Brazilians like to get to know you. A leading French telecoms company outsources some of its projects to Brazil, but communicates with Brazil in English during telephone conferencing. The relevant managers on either side of the Atlantic have never met and almost certainly never will, and are communicating on the phone in an alien language. English. Empathy is difficult to achieve and misunderstandings are common.

Finally, the senior French manager found the solution: 'telepresence' or videoconferencing. He put his team on television and so did the Brazilians. He also did something else. He arranged that the last ten minutes of the call should be concerned with small talk, about football, inevitably. All the French executives that we talked to agreed – just one 'telepresence' meeting improved motivation and cooperation on both sides.

Why? The session had put faces to names and voices. The two sides had built a relationship, even without meeting face to face.

Cultural fears

If you think that the world has enough problems with our perceptions of cultural values, now think about cultural fears. These often depend on history. For example, would you believe that Russians have a fear of being surrounded? Poles can also feel suspicious of foreigners, since their 'flat land' has been invaded by so many nations so often over the centuries.

Indians, and other members of the former British, French or Portuguese empires, are very sensitive to anything that might be understood as being patronising or 'colonial'. Countries in proximity to powerful nations often feel resentful if not called by their proper names: Canadians resent being called Americans. If you're not sure of the correct term, referring to them as North Americans is acceptable. The Scots, the Welsh and the Irish of Northern Ireland are Welsh, Scottish and Irish, not British, and certainly not English. Brazilians speak Portuguese but are in no way beholden to Portugal: they consider themselves separate and more powerful. Sensitivity in these areas is vital.

Keep your eyes and ears open. If at any time you sense a resistance to how you are addressing people, stop and, if necessary, ask. Your sensitivity will be appreciated.

How you address people and even how you face people may be culturally determined. So be sensitive not just in business, but also in everyday life and etiquette.

As for business, so for etiquette

Barry works a lot in Paris right now. One day he was walking down a narrow street as an older woman was coming towards him. He moved to the left to let her pass but she advanced, still on the left, looking quite angry. 'What's wrong with her?' Barry wondered. Then he realised. This was France, where they drive and walk on the right. By standing on the left he was blocking her path.

The incident is trivial: the difficulty was just a conflict of expectations. But he was in her country, and presumably it was his responsibility to understand and adapt.

Here's another example, this time, Mike's. In Egypt almost no one calls him Mr Nicks. To the locals he is Mr Michael or Mr Mike. Why can't the Egyptians, and many others in the Middle East, get it right? Call him 'Mike' or 'Mr Nicks' but not both. His family name is Nicks, not Mike. But that's just the point: 'Nicks' is his family name, his father's name, not his name. His name is 'Michael' or 'Mike'. Hence, Mr Michael or Mr Mike. Mike thought the people he was dealing with should know better. After all, they understood English. But in their country they do things differently. His job is to recognise and adapt to them, so that's what he did.

In business, etiquette issues also play a part. They rarely ruin a business relationship, but they can create a poor first impression. In China and even more in Japan, business cards matter. They are an indication of your position and status in your company. They will carry the company name, the department, the job title and perhaps these details in the mother tongue on the front, and in English or other languages on the back. The protocol is universal.

When you meet, proffer your business card with both hands, script facing towards the recipient, and bow slightly from the neck. The recipient will take your business card with both hands and study it. He or she may make some appreciative comment such as 'Ah, business development director'.

He or she will then reverse the process. Accept their business card with a slight bow and with both hands, study it, and comment on it politely. Place the business card you have received on the table or in your business card holder.

Do not on any account stuff the business card you have received into a pocket. Above all, do not write on it. Why not? For most Westerners, a business card is a means of contact, and they might be scattered across the table like a poker player dealing a hand. But for Asians a business card is a symbol. It represents them and their company. The business cards you receive are a record of your links with the company concerned.

Don't just shove them in a drawer. It'll only fill up and you'll have to throw them away. Scan them into your computer or file them – then you can write something next to them if you want. And one last thing: if you haven't got a business card, apologise profusely and, the first chance you get, email your details to the contact.

One critic said that the movie *Outsourced* is perfect for MBA students. The film describes the experiences of a young American executive sent to run a contact centre near Jaipur in India. He goes from bewilderment and slight despair to learning to appreciate and love the richness and variety of experience that is India. In one memorable sequence he has tea with his hostess. She looks in horror as he picks up his tea with his left hand. 'What?' he says, surprised at her expression. She says nothing but her husband gets up and graphically describes what the left hand is used for and why you don't use it to handle food and drink. If you're at a party in India , never take food with your left hand. Use the right hand or, if it's heavy, both hands. If you use just your left hand, don't be surprised if no one else touches it afterwards.

If you don't meet the local customs in etiquette, people may not like it, and it might damage the business relationship.

Tool 1: RADAR Expectations

We said in the introduction that the key to understanding culture is knowing what to look for. We also said that one of the keys to building international trust and confidence is meeting expectations. So what are those expectations likely to be? Where do we need to look? What are the key expectations drivers?

The RADAR expectations profile contains the five expectations killers. They are:

- Attitudes to relationships
- Attitudes to company
- Attitudes to contact
- Attitudes to risk
- Attitudes to performance

Expectations form the basis of good relations across cultures. Meeting other people's expectations is the essence of rapport. Failing to meet them is a major business killer.

Attitudes to relationships

We've talked a lot about this. The whole world likes to do business with people they know, like, and trust. However, some nationalities prefer to build that trust through doing successful business together. Other nationalities prefer to build the relationship and then do the business. The start-up may take longer but the business relationship may last longer.

As a Korean businessman, resident in Switzerland, put it, 'Get the relationship right and the business will follow as day follows night.'

For task-driven markets, the building of relationships before any income results is simply a waste of time. Every trip abroad, every hospitality expense, every airfare and hotel bill is a drain on resources, and revenue projections may seem like pie in the sky. Especially with today's security restrictions and limited travel budgets, schmoozing prospective clients is even less acceptable than it was.

The economics of outsourcing processes to countries such as India, the Philippines, China or Eastern Europe used to be simple: it cut costs by a third in Eastern Europe and two thirds in Asia. However, nurturing the relationship with regular trips overseas to manage the process and troubleshoot problems pushed costs back up.

At one point, a leading telecommunications company was sending people out to its call centres once a month for a week or two at a time. Part of this was due to administration, but part of it was involved in building and maintaining the relationship. No wonder that with increasing customer complaints, companies began repatriating outsourced services to western Europe.

One Indian company we worked with complained that they didn't feel part of the parent company family. When we reported back to the HR Director in Europe, she expressed surprise that there was a family to feel part of. On investigation, we advised on a number of strategies the parent company could use to make its overseas contact centres feel more central to the operation. One was the 'telepresence' kick-off meeting we mentioned earlier. Another was photos of the Indian team members on the company Intranet, together with mini-biographies with information about background, families and interests. Another feature, also on the Intranet, was information about the locality where the parent company was based, with news of local events and points of interest. In addition, the European group took a team photo and sent it down the line to their Indian colleagues and received a similar photo back.

The MD of the European team was astonished on a visit to India to find the European team photo framed and prominently positioned behind the Indian general manager's desk. He realised that such seemingly unimportant gestures are at the root of good relationship building. He also realised how few European and American companies do it.

In what sociologists like to call the Northwest cluster of countries (broadly, Germany, Austria, Switzerland, the Nordic and Benelux countries, UK and Ireland, USA, Canada, Australia and New Zealand), relationships are built through successful business operations. The Germans will often try a new company out with a small project that's scarcely worth the money. If the initial deal proves successful, they'll carry on. Countries that operate like that are known as task- or deal-based.

Task-based countries find it difficult to commit to long-term relationship building without a compensating revenue flow. Equally, relationship-based countries feel the same qualms about producing short-term revenue without knowing and having the time to build trust with the supplier or client before-hand. The relationship between 'relationship investment' and turnover is a tricky one, but in a global economy more and more corporations are having to address it.

Relationship-oriented or task-oriented?

We all like to have good relations with people we do business with. But some of us prefer to build the good relations through the business, while others see the relationship as the essential basis for doing the business. This is absolutely crucial to understand. Most of the world does business through relationships. It's not what you know, it's who you know.

If I am in the US, the UK or Northern Europe, a tender process may be successful. If I am in the Middle East, Southern Europe, Latin America or the Far East, building a successful relationship with my prospective client first is vital. The problem is that building that relationship can cost management time and money with no immediate return. It demands remembering birthdays and celebrations, providing presents and hospitality, and making visits.

Leading companies setting up new operations in India are on a plane from Europe not twice a year but once a month. Business colleagues in the Far East travel once a quarter. Fly to Hong Kong and from there travel to key markets in Taiwan, Korea, Singapore, Malaysia and Thailand. In these parts of the world, a six-monthly visit would be the absolute minimum. Why? Because the personal contact is seen to be essential. The message is, to get to know the client, get on a plane.

Right-level relationships

Not only that, but the relationship must be established at the right level. A leading telecoms company in Europe was sourcing handsets from Shanghai. The operations manager spoke Mandarin and was married to a Chinese. The president of the handset company – the supplier, mind you – refused to see him. Why? The operations manager wasn't senior enough, and eventually needed his director to accompany him. Imagine the finance manager's face when he saw the expense claim: two business-class fares, two rooms at a top Shanghai hotel so as not to lose face, and hospitality expenses, not to mention the management time wasted.

Why was all this necessary? It wasn't just about establishing a good personal relationship. It was about establishing a personal relationship at the right level.

Right-respect relationships

Relationships are not just about personal contact. They are also about showing the right degree of personal respect. In Latin countries this is shown through courtesy and politeness, friendliness and a degree of formality with senior people. In the East it is shown through not allowing anyone to lose face – personal dignity. In a conference call with Indonesia, the French convenor of the meeting went round the virtual table, asking participants what they thought of a proposal. The Indonesians found the Frenchman's behaviour insulting. 'How dare they ask us questions like that with no time for considered reflection and group consideration!', they said. A much more respectful approach would have been to signal, some minutes before, his intention to seek opinions and then at the right moment invite participants if they would like to comment.

Attitudes to company

Things are changing but in many countries loyalty to your company is still a prerequisite. People are expected to join a company or an organization and stay there, maybe until retirement. By the age of thirty, or even younger, most managers will have settled down in one job and will gradually rise higher as they get promoted or will expand their responsibilities with age and experience.

The main example of this is, or was, Japan's principle of lifetime employment where you joined a company from university as a 'sarariman' (a salaried employee, usually male) and worked through to retirement. This has changed as during Japan's economic difficulties there has been a move, especially in smaller companies, to short-term contracts, which has changed the 'loyalty factor' to a degree.

However, the attitude is still different from many British or US companies, for example, where failure to change your job and look for the next opportunity is often construed as lack of ambition.

Even in a country like Germany, loyalty to the company (and its loyalty to you as an employee) is still considered important. An employee of Siemens, for example, may settle into his or her job at around thirty and stay with the company for their working life, expanding their responsibilities as they do so.

So one of the things I, as a visitor, will want to know is this - to what extent is company employment seen as long-term with a stress on internal development and loyalty to the organization? To what extent do staff I am dealing with see themselves as 'company people'? At the other extreme, to what extent are people concerned about their individual career first? Is there likely to be high mobility of labour and managers?

'Career first' attitudes can affect whether your team stays together or disintegrates. For example, the degree of labour mobility can be an issue in working with VDT's (virtual distributed teams). Especially in emerging markets, managers can change companies for relatively low increases in pay and conditions. The result is the team leader you have put in place in, for example, India, may be gone within a very short time due to competition in the labour market.

The great value of 'company first' employees is loyalty but the downside of loyalty might be, in some cases, lack of competence. 'Company first' mentality might also lead to a reluctance to seek new organizational solutions that might be more successful on international joint ventures and merger and acquisitions.

We came across interesting situations with some Asian countries where the development of a management style which was open to international involvement was actively discouraged. Managers were routinely recycled back home so that they did not lose touch with their own company and national cultural values. Clearly, staying in touch with your own culture is no bad thing but there is a danger of international managers failing to seize market opportunities because of a narrow-minded view of their company's self-interest.

It is important for any international manager to monitor the degree to which a 'company first' or 'career first' mentality operates among team members and to be prepared to act where the success of a joint venture or international project might be compromised.

Close contact or distant contact

In a close contact culture, as is most of the world, telephone and face-to-face contact is the preferred way of working. Email and distant working is a poor second. For the relative few countries that prefer more distant contact by email the failure to get on the phone or to travel for a face-to-face meeting is perceived as lack of interest and lack of commitment. As a result, demotivation, missed deadlines or deadlines ignored and inferior quality all occur simply because the partner in the country concerned thinks that because you haven't maintained personal contact, you don't care. So why bother? Better to focus on the projects of those who do.

If you are working with a 'distant contact' culture it is important to find out what the deadlines are, to get a clear specification of the expected job outcomes and process and to only contact when there is an issue that needs resolution. Above all, deliver on or before time or, if there is a delay, make sure that you have pre-advised so that other stakeholders can re-organise and work around you.

Attitudes towards risk

'I can't get anything done,' a manager complained to us. 'I see an opportunity and I want to take advantage of it, but my boss insists on playing it by the book. She has no initiative!' It's true, some managers are more adventurous than others – but so are some business cultures. A manager might be constrained by all kinds of factors – local legal limitations, cost and resource considerations or simply a culture that likes to move very carefully.

Germany's like that. Their reputation rests not on the dynamic seizing of opportunities, but on careful analysis and preparation, followed by efficient organisation and execution. In other words, lots of research, lots of planning and lots of evidence. Japan is similar in this respect. The Japanese take ages to reach decisions, but when they do they move very fast. So check out before you go into any negotiation: are lightning decisions the order of the day, or careful painstaking research and considera-tion? Be prepared to adapt and plan your timescale accordingly.

If a company or culture is risk embracing, it will calculate risks but it will be prepared to take them. In this environment, as long as you can demonstrate that you have a clear objective, a business plan, and risk analysis and that you are reasonably confident of success then you can go ahead and present your ideas.

If a company or culture is risk averse then you need more. You need evidence to demonstrate that your idea has been applied and proven successful in a different country or environment, and that you have confidence it will add to performance and profitability in your operation. Failure to do this will lead to lack of confidence, suspicion and refusal to invest.

The RADAR expectations

Here is our first tool. What are the expectations of the business relationship that will create trust across borders and build all important rapport? As part of your cultural due diligence in planning any new international business relationship, make sure you find out your partner's expectations. When you meet them ask how they feel about the issues we have described.

To help you, we can summarise them like this:

Attitudes to people	Relationship	Task
Attitudes to company	Company first	Career first
Attitudes to contact	Close contact	Distant contact
Attitudes to risk	Risk embracing	Risk averse

The STAR code

Wake up and smell the coffee!

The problem with other business cultures is that they are different from ours, and that makes us uncomfortable. After all, money's at stake here. And when we feel uncomfortable what do we do? We run away and retreat into our shells, and take refuge in our own methods and, yes, prejudices.

Others have a different approach. They go in with all guns blazing: 'It's my way or the highway!'

Psychologists call it 'fight or flight'. Sometimes it works, and sometimes it doesn't. What it doesn't do is enhance understanding – but here's a tool that does. We call it the STAR code because it's in the shape of a five-pointed star.

Here's what you do when you're in a crisis:

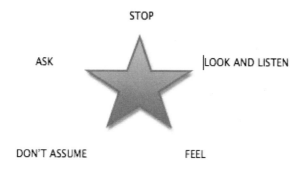

STOP

ASK |LOOK AND LISTEN

DON'T ASSUME   FEEL

STOP!

Slow down. Do nothing.

LOOK AND LISTEN

Observe the people. What are they doing, how are they dressed? How do they address each other? What does it tell you about their attitudes and the way they work?

FEEL

What's the atmosphere like? Friendly, hostile or just indifferent? Who is likely to be your most sympathetic person to talk to?

DON'T ASSUME

This is really important. If you assume, you'll risk jumping back into your own prejudices.

ASK

Be prepared to ask politely why people are behaving in a particular way. Ask what people think. Choose your most sympathetic contact to pose your questions. They may have been in the same situation as you in another country. In many countries, polite questions are not intrusive: they're taken as showing interest.

Using the STAR code intelligently will lower your blood pressure and help you to get answers in confusing situations. Try it.

Five things to remember

1. All cultures have cultural expectations and fears. Meet these expectations and avoid the fears.

2. Culture affects etiquette: etiquette gaffes may not be fatal, but can create unfortunate first impressions.

3. Do your cultural due diligence. Find out as much as you can before you start negotiations.

4. Use the RADAR expectations profile to focus on key potential issues.

RELATIONSHIPS	Relationship first, or business through the relationship?
TIME	Time-tight and time-loose cultures
HIERARCHY	Respect cultures
RISK	Risk-embracing and risk-averse cultures
TEAM	Individual and team decision-making

5. Use the STAR code to guide your behaviour when you are unsure.

Chapter 3
Why international communication goes wrong – and how to get it right

In 2003 the media reported that US and British military battalions were occupying Iraq with not a single Arabic speaker among them. Then the occupying forces disbanded the Iraqi police and military, leaving almost no one capable of communicating with the locals or helping to organise them. The Americans and the British ignored or didn't notice key differences between the different sects of Islam. In particular, they appeared to give no recognition to the fact that although Saddam Hussein and his family were Sunni Muslims (descendants of the Companions of the Prophet), most of the country's population were Shi'a Muslims (descendants of the Relatives of the Prophet). Then the occupiers were surprised when civil unrest engulfed the country.

Afghanistan is a patchwork of rival fiefdoms ruled over by strong military leaders, often termed 'warlords' by the media. The northern Tajik peoples who run the capital Kabul are not the same as the Pashtuns in Kandahar in the south. It is an environment where blood is thicker than water. If water is information then blood is relationships, formed over centuries. Not to put it too finely, the 'occupiers' or 'peacekeepers' (use what term you will) were talking to the wrong people.

In northern Mali in 2012 in the Sahel region of West Africa, the 'terrorists' were members of groups including Al Qaeda, local insurgents, Tuareg separatists and others. By lumping them together, the overseas soldiers sent to fight them and bring peace back to that beautiful country created one huge opposition.

All these operations broke two fundamental rules:

- Know who you're fighting
- Know who you're talking to

One size doesn't fit all. As any good international salesman will tell you, 'You need to know who is talking to whom.' You need to understand the communication networks.

This chapter is about four areas of communication:

- Networks – who talks to whom, and who doesn't
- Flow – how networks communicate
- Styles – how they deliver their message
- English – how it's used in an international environment

Communication networks

As in war, so in business. A private banking group in the US was shocked to learn that in its Thai branch, important client information was being withheld between local hires working on the same account.

'What the hell?' a director exploded. 'Are these people working for the company or not?'

No, as a matter of fact. They were members of different clans which had withheld information from one another for generations. Were they going to change their ways just because they were working for an international bank? Blood is thicker than water!

'If something's going wrong I want to be the first to know. Good or bad, I need to know, so I can deal with it.' That was the Australian manager of a luxury goods firm in Poland. He was dynamic, open, friendly, and committed to great products and great customer service. However, over time he began to realise he wasn't getting information from his older sales managers responsible for eastern Poland. After a couple of nasty surprises, he called us in. What was going on? 'Don't they trust me?' he asked.

'They don't trust anybody,' we replied. 'For 60 years they lived under a regime where bad news could cost you your job, your liberty and even yours or your family's life.' The employees had a culture of *not* sharing information except within their close network. And that network happened to be always at the bottom of the information food chain. The Australian manager had been raised in a culture of relative openness, where information is escalated upwards and can be dealt with. They lived in a culture where escalating information was dangerous.

Was there a way out? There was, and in Poland it is a practice called *Sto lat*. It means 100 years. *Sto lat* is the song Poles sing when one of their family or colleagues has a name day. Your name day is the day when your name coincides with the day dedicated to a saint in the Roman Catholic church. So on St Patrick's Day, Pawel brings in cakes and sparkling wine and, at some point in the day, his colleagues down tools for 20 minutes to share a drink and a bite and sing *Sto lat*. And they chat. Then they go back to work.

The Australian manager went downstairs from his office and joined in. As he did so he chatted – and he joined in the ground-level information exchange. He had no more 'nasty surprises'.

It's obvious why this is important. When working internationally, don't assume that communication networks are necessarily the same as in head office. Well-established, non-formal organisations may divert the stream of information. What can you do? *Don't assume.*

Instead:

- Find out where people are from and how they relate to each other, not just personally but ethnically and maybe politically. This will help you understand where communication network problems might arise.

- Join in office social occasions when you can. This will provide an environment where colleagues share information they would not normally offer in a team meeting.

- Do whatever you can to create a climate where sharing information is seen as normal. If you do it yourself, others will follow.

If you're working at your company's headquarters, far from your team:

- Cultivate a local, maybe one who has worked at HQ and understands the central information culture.

- Keep in regular friendly contact. He or she can help you identify communication logjams and in some cases help resolve them.

The Star code tool will help you here. But we don't pretend it's easy. Even in a country like Japan, a long-established modern industrial society, people still make a distinction between Japanese and *gaijin* managers, and a Japanese manager who is seen to be too at ease with Western styles of communication may be quietly ostracised by colleagues.

In Korea the 'unperson' (waeguk-in) is a recognised and very uncomfortable position to be in. If you are dubbed an unperson for any reason, people will be unfailingly polite but you will be routinely excluded from all but the most routine information. This is not uncommon for Western managers who are seen to have done something to lose face or cause a colleague or manager to lose face.

However, even where an open communication network exists, there are still the practical problems of communicating internationally. The communication networks may be open but the communication flows may be closed.

Communication flows

One team is employed by a market-leading company in telecommunications – videoconferencing, communication data, equipment and installation. Another team is based in the Paris office of one of the big four international financial service firms. The team members are mainly French, North African and a smaller number of French-speaking West Africans and Indians, and they all have the same problem - communication.

In the Students' Union of the University of East Anglia in England, a student scrawled a piece of graffiti on the wall about his professor, Vice-Chancellor Professor Malcolm Bradbury, a noted novelist and international academic. 'God is everywhere,' the graffiti read. 'Professor Bradbury is everywhere but here.'

We live in a business world of increasing electronic communication and decreasing personal communication. In some ways this is increasing communication flows exponentially. But in other ways it is causing a big problem.

'Everywhere but here' is the big problem. Our colleagues in leading international companies in Paris are reporting to managers in Delhi, Mexico City, Singapore, New York, Atlanta and London. But they never see their managers. They report in weekly conference calls (usually by phone but occasionally by video) to people they have never met, of different nationalities, in countries they have never visited and know little or nothing about. Worse still, in many cases, these 'virtual' managers are responsible for their yearly appraisals and therefore their bonuses.

It is a miracle of common sense and goodwill that the system works as well as it does. But no one pretends it is ideal.

So why not get together once in a while? That's where the second layer of problems kicks in – budget and security. You probably haven't noticed as you queue to get on another overcrowded plane, but in many companies you don't travel, because of budget restrictions. Shoe bomber and hijacking scares also mean that no one important gets on a plane, if they can help it.

What do we do instead? We IM (instant message), we text, we conference call, we video conference (occasionally), we email (even that is going out of style, apparently) and we phone (although accent problems often get in the way). We just don't get to see people face to face.

How does this affect our communication flows? A UK company had secured a new project, and its fulfilment unit was its Brazilian supply team based in Rio. The project manager didn't run a 'kick-off' meeting as a conference call as usual. He booked a 'telepresence' studio so the two teams could see each other.

There were a few problems. The Rio office had a camera that only showed the whole team, so anyone leaning back was out of shot, especially at the edge of the group. When anyone opened their mouth to say something, they had to gesture so the British could identify the speaker. Brazilians enjoy colourful clothes so they had to be careful that striped dresses and shirts didn't strobe on screen. Oh, and they had to learn not to pick their teeth, do their nails or get on with emails when someone else was speaking – both distracting and demotivating.

The London studio was state of the art, with voice-activated camera zoom lenses. Even so, the project manager was careful to check the desk. Was it clear of empty coffee cups and untidy papers or half-eaten sandwiches? He also walked up to the camera and checked the wall behind the speakers. Any compromising information on view? What image was the head office going to present on-screen?

He remembered the online video sales conference where someone forgot to remove the graph on the wall showing sales figures plummeting downward. And the video photo-opportunity providing publicity for the British Duke of Cambridge, Prince William, in his role as air sea rescue officer at a naval base. There he was at work with a list pinned to the wall in front of him of the phone numbers and extensions of all the Buckingham Palace staff – in full view of the camera.

What were the results of the video 'kick-off'? Uniformly positive. People reported much better relationships and much easier communication between the head office and the local Brazilian office. So much so that the project manager instituted a virtual breakfast before each conference call. This was a ten-minute general chat between participants so that personal information could be exchanged and questions answered before the business of the day. As the sessions involved Brazilians, he noticed that the virtual breakfast was as much about soccer as anything else.

A US company based its European operations in the UK. To save money, instead of having regional reps to deal with accounts payable (bills) and accounts receivable (invoices), the operation was based on six people and two supervisors. The team was a mixture of Brits and internationals, and their responsibilities were to chase unpaid invoices or deal with queries regarding bills payable.

We were responsible for training the team to deal with their international responsibilities. It soon became clear that the Northern Europeans were much happier with email contact. And that Southern Europeans were happy with both email and voice contact. Many of the British team members didn't get replies to their initial emails. If they didn't, they simply sent another email. They preferred 'distant' communication.

On the other hand, the Southern Europeans would happily call to check if the email had been received or to follow up a non-response. Sometimes they would even phone the correspondent to warn them to expect an email. They preferred 'close' communication.

It's important to know when the phone is as efficient or even preferable to email. The answer lies in our expectation drivers in Chapter 2. Remember the difference between relationship-driven and task-driven cultures. Relationship-driven cultures tend to prefer 'close' communication by phone. Task-driven cultures tend to prefer 'distant' communication. Think why your emails are not getting results. Maybe you need to get on the phone more.

It's clear. Electronic communication is replacing face-to-face communication and this trend will increase as technology develops. We need to look for ways to personalise electronic communication, such as virtual breakfasts and video kick-offs. Even email is changing and we'll look at that in a few pages. But never forget, if budget and security considerations allow, getting together personally once or twice a year face to face is the way to ease communication flows.

Communication styles

Japan is famous for being the most indirect country on earth. Saving face is absolutely vital and therefore you never say anything that might be critical or risk causing offence. The exception is when managers go into 'teaching mode' when they can be very abrupt and shout. The indirect way of giving instructions and information assumes that the recipient knows how to read between the lines. This is fine if you are Japanese, but for foreigners it isn't.

This was Svetlana's problem. She was a manager in the Moscow office of a major Japanese international corporation. If she didn't understand the instructions of a Japanese manager, what should she do? Should she say, 'Sorry, I didn't understand. Could you explain it again, please?' No.

To ask that would suggest that the manager wasn't clear, and that would cause him to lose face. To say she hadn't understood would cause *her* to lose face. To make it work she had to take responsibility for the communication. She said, 'I'm sorry, you

were perfectly clear (he wasn't) but could I check I have understood? You want me to wait until you give permission to send
this email to my client?' 'Hai,'replied the manager, 'please
arrange.'

As Svetlana said, 'I ended up hating myself for doing that and
hating the Japanese system for making me do it.'

All that was happening was that the Japanese manager was following the time-honoured convention of making suggestions,
not giving precise instructions. This is one of the six key communication differences that exist between international markets, and it is vital to know them and to be prepared to recognise them and respond appropriately.

To do this you need the RADAR Communication Styles tool,
another vital weapon in our international armoury. We present
the styles in six paradigms like this:

Tool 2: RADAR Communication Styles

1 **DIRECT** I say what I mean. Truth matters.	**2** **INDIRECT** I adapt what I say to the situation. Avoiding confrontation matters.
3 **PRECISION** I explain things in detail. Avoidance of misunderstanding is crucial.	**4** **SUGGESTION** I infer what I want. I make suggestions. You have to read between the lines.
5 **WHAT/WHY** I say what I want then, if necessary, I explain why.	**6** **WHY/WHAT** You cannot possibly understand what I want unless I explain first WHY I want it. Context and background are all important.
7 **FORMAL** I like respect when you talk to me. Use surnames, titles, and avoid too much colloquial language.	**8** **INFORMAL** I like informality, first names, friendly language. I think people who are formal may not want to know me.
9 **NEUTRAL** I keep my feelings to myself. I don't smile too much, I prefer not to touch or be touched.	**10** **EMOTIONAL** I believe showing emotion is part of communication. I like to express my feelings.
11 **INTERRUPT** I speak fast. I interrupt people. I am tolerant of interruptions.	**12** **WAIT YOUR TURN** I use a slow and measured speed. I wait my turn to speak. I also dislike being interrupted.

This is an easy tool to use, and very useful in understanding other people's communication styles. It also helps you know how to respond.

How to use the RADAR Communication Styles

1. Recognise that you have a *personal* communication style. Look at your style and note the areas where you feel most comfortable. For example Barry's personal style is 2,5,8,10 (he spent a long time in Africa), and 11.

2. Map your style against the nationality you are dealing with. This gives you a platform for examining your inter-locutor's personal style.

3. Recognise that every style carries a perception. This perception is frequently negative. For example, direct communicators often think indirect communicators are vague or, worse, liars. Indirect communicators often find direct communicators rude and dogmatic.

4. Evolve a strategy to deal with the type that is different from you. For example, if you are a direct communicator, say where you are coming from. Tell your listeners you are direct and that you say what you think. If you are dealing with an indirect communicator be prepared to ask more questions, but do it politely and avoid the inquisitorial style. We give you more advice in the next section.

How to deal with each type

Direct communicators dealing with indirect communicators

Say you're direct. Tell them you say what you think. Ask more questions but try and use a 'Tell me' style rather than a 'What did you?' or 'Why did you?' style.

Indirect communicators dealing with direct communicators

Don't get upset. Respond to questions as directly and as honestly as you can. See the question-asking approach as an attempt to understand the detail of whatever you are talking about.

Precision communicators dealing with suggestion communicators

Precision communicators often think suggestion communicators are confused and unclear. Explain that you are a detail merchant, and tell them you need explanations in detail. Tell them you will stop them to ask questions if you are not clear.

Suggestion communicators dealing with precision communicators

Suggestion communicators like to focus on broad issues and get frustrated when they are interrupted on points of detail. They are 'broad-brush merchants'. If you're this type, be aware of 'detail merchants'. Don't get upset when they interrupt to ask questions in the middle of your explanation.

What/why communicators dealing with why/what communicators

What/why communicators expect to say what they want and then why they want it, if necessary. They are frustrated when why/what communicators explain things without saying what the point is. If you can be patient and wait while why/what communicators talk, it will pay off. You will be perceived as showing interest. It will help build the relationship. If you need to interrupt, do so politely and say that what the other person is saying is interesting and you'd like to hear more – but later.

Why/what communicators dealing with what/why communicators

Don't get upset: recognise the differences in style and priority. If you can, focus on the 'what' but if you can't, explain what you are doing. Use a phrase like, ' I'll tell you what you need to know, but I have to give you a bit of background first.'

Formal communicators dealing with informal communicators

You perceive the informal communicator as lacking respect. In fact, it is just a style. You can remain formal but be friendly. With luck your informal interlocutor will be sensitive enough to recognise your style and adapt.

Informal communicators dealing with formal communicators

You perceive the formal communicators as distant and cold, but in fact all they want is respect. Demonstrate respect by adopting a degree of formality. In due course, you will find the atmosphere becomes more relaxed of its own accord.

Neutral communicators dealing with emotional communicators

You perceive emotional communicators as loose cannons, unreliable and potentially out of control. But accept that people who express themselves emotionally are simply 'letting off steam'. Remain calm and be friendly, but you don't have to be emotional yourself.

Emotional communicators dealing with neutral communicators

You perceive neutral communicators as stiff, calculating, hiding their cards. You need to calm down – use a calm voice, calm gestures and avoid touching. That will create trust.

Fast communicators dealing with slow communicators

You perceive slow communicators as boring and having nothing interesting to say. Calm down. Concentrate. Listen and don't interrupt.

Slow communicators dealing with fast communicators

You perceive fast communicators as inconsiderate, because they don't appear to listen to you. But recognise that many languages have no internal stress within a sentence: the stress comes at the end. As a result the language can sound very fast. When people of these language groups speak in English they adopt the same style. It's linguistic interference not rudeness. In Latin countries, particularly, speakers are often more impulsive, so they interrupt. It feels rude but in fact it is just a style of speech. Your response. Wait. Listen and make your point again. If people persist in interrupting, just say, 'Let me finish!'

Every time we meet a foreigner we don't know or visit a new country, we use this tool to predict the style. Then we measure it against the person we are dealing with. It is both an extremely useful tool for assessing communication styles and a good way of reducing emotional pressure when someone doesn't address you in the way you'd like. This is especially important when people are using English as a lingua franca, as we'll see now.

Does language matter?

Richard Lewis is a polymath. He speaks 10 languages and was the founder of one of the world's biggest language school chains, Linguarama. After an initial career in Japan and Finland where he taught, among others, Princess Michiko of Japan and wrote speeches for the now Emperor Akhihito and taught the former Finnish Prime Minister, Johannes Virolainen, he launched Linguarama and became one of the UK's earliest advocates for the learning and teaching of English for communication.

He later sold Linguarama to found a new organisation, Richard Lewis Communications, focusing on training executives to understand other cultures. He is the author of the famous Lewis model for understanding world business cultures, developed in his ground-breaking book, 'When Cultures Collide'. For more than 50 years he has been a leader in both English language and cultural communication. How does he see the relationship?

'Language and culture are synonymous,' he says, 'but you need to know both.' Understanding the language of the country you are in is important, but it takes time. And few people have the time or talent to master 10 languages! However, when you're dealing with a culture, understanding something about how it works will help you build good business relations with its people. This will help you in the good times but also support you in the bad. If you're spending a long time in a country, even when you don't know the language, a knowledge of key cultural customs and behaviours will help you in the early stages. Understanding ways of greeting and leave-taking and basic etiquette are important in creating the right impression.

But how do you communicate if you don't know the language? By using English, of course. The second half of the 20th century and the opening of the 21st century has been dominated by the astonishing rise of English as an international medium of communication. Starting after the Second World War in 1945, and driven by American power on the back of the British Empire of the previous century, English has become the world's lingua franca and is likely to remain so for a considerable time to come.

English is now one of the key languages of international institutions, such as the UN. It is the principal language of international air traffic control, of ship-to-shore communication and countless other official international communication environments. Although China boasts the largest number of Internet users in the world, 98% of the world's international communication on the Internet is carried out in English.

The fact is, if you want to work in a multinational company or in the international field, you have to learn English. English is now a 'lifestyle' subject in many education systems around the world, alongside their own national languages, history and geography. Most significantly of all, China, the world's most populous country (1.3 billion people), is turning out over half a million graduates a year – in English, and sends hundreds of thousands of students overseas to learn the language.

For native English speakers, such as the British, Americans, Australians, New Zealanders and Canadians, the advantages are obvious, the disadvantages less so. Linguists like to distinguish between native speakers and non-native speakers of a language. Native speakers of English speak English as their mother tongue, while non-native speakers learn it as a second or foreign language. This has two implications – one linguistic, one cultural.

It is a known fact that non-native speakers of English can understand each other in English quite well, but often can't understand native English speakers – and often prefer to avoid doing business with them as a result. Native speakers need to adapt their style internationally, and we'll show you how to do this. However, there is also a cultural implication.

Never assume that non-native speakers are like you just because they speak English. They use the English language as an international vehicle of communication, but they maintain their own cultures. Therefore, even if you are communicating in English, you need to understand something about the cultural style of your colleagues and clients. But given the richness and complexity of cultures, how do you know where to look?

Using English

Jean-Paul Nerrière is French. He was an international vice-president of IBM and travelled the world on company business. He reckoned you could have any conversation in English with a vocabulary of 1500 words. He called his new essential vocabulary Globish, and you can google it at www.globish.com.

Ignore the rumours. English isn't going away any time soon. Quite rightly, more and more schools are offering classes in Mandarin (the Chinese written language and increasingly the leading Chinese spoken dialect). However, China itself is producing hundreds of thousands of graduates a year in English. Economically, China may be about to become the leading power but it will take over the world in English. Initially, at least.

For most people in the world, the problem of English can be summed up in two words: native speakers. Native speakers in the UK, Ireland, the USA, Canada, Australia, New Zealand, India, Africa, the West Indies and other English-speaking nations also have a problem: non-native speakers can't understand them – their accents, their idioms and their humour. It's become so bad that UK Department of Industry statistics reveal that lack of ability in foreign languages is a major drag on British exporting. Many non-native speaking countries simply prefer to do business with other non-native speaking countries. At least they can understand them.

What can native speakers of English do? The RADAR Use of English, will help. It will also help non-native speakers understand each other.

Tool 3: The RADAR Use of English – six rules

There are six key rules for the efficient and clear use of English. Both native and non-native speakers should observe them to clarify spoken communication face to face or on conference calls.

The six rules of clear spoken English:

RULE 1	A-R-T-I-C-U-L-A-T-E.
RULE 2	PAUSE
RULE 3	NO JOKES
RULE 4	EXPLAIN IDIOMS
RULE 5	SPELL OUT ACRONYMS
RULE 6	KISS (Keep it short and simple) • One thought per sentence • Each sentence 15-25 words

RULE 1: A-R-T-I-C-U-L-A-T-E

Experts agree: speech sounds clearer if you open your mouth.

RULE 2: PAUSE

If you go too fast, you may not sound clear. Slow down a bit, but not so much that you sound patronising. Pause for a beat before names, places, dates, numbers and events. That infinitesimal pause allows the listener's brain to absorb the message. Practise in the bathroom. Recite your name, job title, company and location. Practise saying your address and introducing your family, for example, 'This is my wife (pause) Pat, and these are our children (pause) Sheila and (pause) Billy.'

RULE 3: NO JOKES

Really? Don't they make the atmosphere more relaxed? Well, not always. People often don't understand them, can feel insulted by them and sometimes they take them seriously. Best to avoid jokes unless you are sure of your audience.

Also, there is a time and place for everything. Some countries consider jokes in meetings to be unprofessional behaviour. The Germans are like that, but the British quite like jokes – they feel a touch of humour makes things a little less serious and more relaxed. The rule is, don't joke unless you know it's safe to do so.

RULE 4: EXPLAIN IDIOMS

Even the Germans and the Dutch, generally considered among the most fluent English speakers in Europe, admit they have to guess. You can't stop using idioms –it's in your DNA if you are a native speaker. But you *can* monitor your speech. When you spot an idiom or a colloquial phrase, explain it, but this time in simpler words. Otherwise it's back to the drawing board, er – time to start again and rethink.

RULE 5: SPELL OUT ACRONYMS

Thomas, a French international manager, tells a good story. As a young manager his boss gave him responsibility for sales in Belgium. 'Remember, Thomas,' the boss said, 'this is one of your KPI's.' Thomas asked, 'Excuse me, sir, (the French can be quite formal), but what's a KPI?' The boss replied, 'I've no idea, but it's very important.'

And, just in case, KPI stands for key performance indicator.

RULE 6: KISS

KISS stands for 'Keep it short and simple'. This involves a few simple rules.

- One thought per sentence.

- Each sentence no longer than 15-25 words.

  So avoid hesitating, restarting, and changing your mind in mid sentence.

- Avoid using words like 'and', 'but', 'in spite of', etc.

- Check what you have written and ask yourself, 'Can this be split into two sentences?' If it can, do it.

- Check your wordage. Can you split a 35-word sentence into two? Yes, you can.

Don't say, 'I haven't got time for all this.' Remember, time spent on clarity means time saved on understanding and execution by the recipient.

Email communication

We said we'd look at emails. If we apply these rules to emails, what do we get?

RULE 1	KISS – use one thought per sentence
RULE 2	Write short sentences
RULE 3	Start each new topic with a new paragraph
RULE 4	Put a line space between each paragraph and the sign-on (Dear Barry) and the sign-off (Regards, Mike)

Do this and your emails will be easier to read and understand and will get better and quicker responses.

Read the following two emails. They both contain the same information. Which one is easier to read and to absorb?

1

Hi Barry,

Thanks for your email with draft Chapter 2. I like the way it is constructed and the points to remember at the end are very useful. However, I think it might be a good idea if you were able to give more examples, especially of situations where you feel people have failed to understand the expectations of their clients and as result the deal has fallen through or serious misunderstandings have arisen. Could you come back to me as soon as possible on this? Regards Mike.

2

Hi Barry,

Thanks for your email with draft Chapter 2.

I like the way it is constructed. The 'points to remember' at the end are especially useful.

However, I think it would be a good idea to give more examples. You could choose situations where people have failed to meet client expectations.

The situations would need to focus on deal failures or serious misunderstandings

Could you come back to me as soon as possible on this?

Regards,

Mike

Emails – the new brutal

Finally, a quick look at writing style. There is a trend to begin and end emails with the name only. There is also a trend to avoid any personal goodwill.

A typical email might read:

Barry

Send me your version of Chapter 4 asap. Mike.

ASAP stands for 'as soon as possible'. Neither of us writes like that. A more typical style is:

Hi Barry

Could you send me your version of Chapter 4 asap? Chapters 1-3 are looking good.

Regards

Mike.

This time we have a more personal greeting and a personal comment. It feels much more friendly and I'll feel more positive about replying to it. Many internationals find the 'new brutal' demotivating. They prefer the 'old courteous' with a greeting, a sign-off and a short personal message. Before you compose or respond, look at the last email you received from the person you are writing to. What style are they using? 'Old courteous' or 'new brutal'? Should you use the same style?

Finally, a word of warning. Not everyone takes the polite style of address seriously. We have been told if we use a very polite style of writing in Eastern Europe and parts of Asia the email will immediately be considered non-priority and put on the back-burner for response. In this case the advice is simple. Avoid phrases like, 'Would you mind..?' or 'Could you possibly...?' and give simple clear but polite instructions followed by appreciation.

Here's an example:

'Dear John,

Please send the 2nd quarter sales figures by 5pm UK time tonight.

Thank you, I appreciate your work.

Yours,

Ted

In other words: Instruction first, appreciation second. You have been advised.

Five things to remember

1. Check the communication network and communication flows of your team.

2. Join in social events to find out what team members really think.

3. Use the RADAR Communication to compare styles and adapt.

4. Use the Use of English rules to ensure spoken English and emails are clear.

5. Check your correspondent's communication style before you decide how to respond.

Chapter 4
How to make an international presentation

Presentations are how we make our mark on groups and audiences we want to influence. So why do we get it so wrong so often?

A man who doesn't get it wrong is Archbishop Emeritus, Desmond Tutu from South Africa. He is an amazing public speaker. Diminutive but with enormous presence, his speeches (sermons?) sail through the air across the audience, swooping and gliding with no obvious landing point. You go along with it, hopefully, enjoying the ride but wondering vaguely if there is anything behind it.

And then suddenly, he dives. He says something so sharp and practical and matter of fact that you are brought up short. That's what he did in London at a conference we attended. A member of the audience asked him about the 'weapons of mass destruction' accusation that had supposedly instigated the US/British attack on Iraq to overthrow its dictator Saddam Hussein in 2003. Subsequently, it was discovered that no such weapons existed and that the 'dodgy dossier' that proved they did was a sham.

As he answered the question, Archbishop Tutu glided round the subject as he always does, his voice rising and falling, until suddenly he said: 'I think they should apologise. I think they should apologise for misleading the British people, I think they should apologise for misleading the world.' The words are not a verbatim quotation, but the message was clear.

Now here's the complete opposite. The Chinese dignitary was introduced by the host. To polite applause he walked across the platform to the podium, put his papers on the rostrum and began to read. His voice was flat and controlled. There was no emotion and no stress. He did not look at his audience. He just stood and read. At the end we sat and applauded once again, politely.

We were none the wiser about what he had said and probably neither was he. We had all just engaged in a ritual – a presentation by a local dignitary. The conventions were observed, the ritual completed. He retired and so did we – to tea or coffee.

We live in a world of presentations. We present at meetings, at conventions, in lecture halls, in 'webinars' and in sales meetings with new clients. It is amazing that with so much presenting going on, so many people do it so badly. This chapter helps you to improve your skills by understanding the demands of making an international presentation. There are hundreds of books on how to present, and we're not going to repeat them. Our focus is: what will help you to get the result you want when you're pitching to an overseas client or presenting to an overseas audience? First, let's look at what you need to find out if you are presenting to an overseas audience in English.

We had to make a sales presentation to a group of managers of a Japanese multinational. The CEO and managing director was there, as well as his general manager, and on the British side were the HR group director, the general manager and the section leader. The problem here was one of addressing the expectations of formality and respect to an audience of two different cultures.

The British side was relatively relaxed. First-name terms and a slightly jokey atmosphere. Let's not take ourselves too seriously. The Japanese on the other hand were much more conscious of protocol. The boss was clearly the boss. All the others paid him due deference. Only the designated responsible person spoke at any one time and subordinates stayed silent throughout. The British ranged widely across the agenda, touching on each point. The Japanese preferred to focus on a few points and examine them in detail.

What we did was to adopt a relatively egalitarian but polite approach towards the British side, while observing deep respect and courtesy to the Japanese. The approach worked but it felt strange at times.

A friend of ours, at one time the youngest commercial manager in the BBC, had a useful mantra: 'A message is not delivered until it's received,' he used to say.

So the issue is not just, what do you want to say? It's also, how does your audience want to hear it? Consider these variables.

- The audience: Who are they, what kind of jobs do they do? What kind of education might they have had? Anything you can find out is useful.

- Expectations: What do they need? Is it information, entertainment or do they need to buy a product or service, or change what they do in other ways?

- Style: What are their expectations of the way you should present? If you decide to do something different, perhaps following your own unique style, will they be pleased? Shocked? Dismissive?

- Jokes: In Chapter 3 we advised 'no jokes', but is this always relevant? The right comment at the right moment or perhaps just an amused response to something that happens in the room can add enormously to a presentation. But you can't predict it, just respond with charm and good humour.

- Duration: What's their attention span? How long are they prepared to listen?

- Follow-up: What happens at the end? Do they applaud? Do they ask questions? What's the protocol?

- Visual aids: What kind of presentation aids do you need? PowerPoint? If so, how do you lay it out?

Different national audiences are conditioned to expect different things. Some focus on the content: they want to learn something new. New information, new ideas, new skills. Therefore they listen primarily to the words you use. Germany is like that. They like hard information, statistics, reports of successful implementation. And they like to make up their own minds. Hard sells don't work for the Germans. Or for any Northern European country. Describe features and describe benefits, but don't attempt a hard sell.

The US and India are quite similar in some ways. They're both happy with the 'What's in it for me?' presentation. However, India likes to focus on eloquence and education. On the other hand, the US and Canada prefer it to be short, sharp and sweet with a touch of humour.

Latin audiences are interesting. They want evidence of education and they want to know what you're like. Therefore, some Latin presenters spend a long time extolling their educational accomplishments and background before getting into the topic under discussion.

José Antonio in Madrid was like that – organised and efficient, but he took 20 minutes to get into the subject. The rest of us sat around trying to stop our fingers drumming on the table in impatience. Who did he think he was trying to impress?

Well, the client, as a matter of fact. He was a Spanish banker, and he was impressed. We got the deal we wanted – José Antonio knew exactly how to present to get the right result. Latins aren't so interested in information. They know where to find that. They want to know what kind of person you are and the best way to do that in a meeting is to listen to you talk and assess how you describe yourself.

We were in Russia, lecturing to a Russian audience. Barry is good at audience interaction, inviting questions, asking questions of the audience and proposing short internal discussions in informal 'buzz' groups. On this occasion in Moscow we were short of time and explained that we'd 'cut to the chase'.

You could almost hear the sigh of relief. The Russians had come to listen to experts, not to chat to each other! They like to feel the person they are listening to has mastered their subject and can discuss it authoritatively. They also enjoy a personal touch and an appreciation of Russian expertise and experience.

If you're presenting in Russia and anywhere in Eastern and Central Europe, do your homework on the home-grown experts and refer to them. Showing recognition and appreciation of the work of leading researchers or experts from the regions concerned is important for getting audiences on your side. However, be alert for the danger signals. Mention a hero of yours and if you see pursed lips and averted gazes among the audience, don't insist. Your hero may not be as popular locally as he or she is internationally.

Formality and respect are the hallmarks of presentation in China and East Asia. Show respect to the chair and honoured guests. Don't gesticulate or get overexcited.

Over-expressiveness might translate as unreliability and lack of self-control. And slow down – people often don't understand as well as you think.

So let's summarise. The chart below outlines the presentation expectations of some of our key markets:

UK	FRANCE	GERMANY	SOUTHERN EUROPE	CENTRAL and EASTERN EUROPE
Friendly, soft sell, humour	Logical, soft sell, expressive	no jokes	Emotion, take facts for granted, appreciate education, want to know what you are like	Information, distrust hard sell, recognise local heroes/experts
INDIA	CHINA	RUSSIA	BRAZIL	
Emotion and eloquence, benefits: what's in it for me/for India? Hard sell	Sincerity, modesty, restraint, benefits: offer know-how, create trust	seeks information, open and honest approach	Emotion and style, enthusiasm, reference to Brazil	

How do you organise your argument? Do you identify problems or offer solutions?

Barry was presenting to a Japanese company. He outlined the problems he was going to address and then tackled the solutions. The feedback forms after the presentation were ambivalent. 'We would have preferred a more limited coverage of items and a deep analysis of the problems,' wrote one delegate. What did he mean? The Japanese, like the Germans, prefer to focus on understanding the problem in depth. They like intensive coverage of the issues and sometimes only want a brief solution at the end. This is sometimes known as 'extensive background context'.

Barry's approach was derived much more from the US model – give a brief review of the problem areas followed by extensive coverage and analysis of the various solutions. This is known as 'limited background context'. Where the two groups are in the same session, extensive and limited background context can be difficult to combine. Whereas Americans and the British tend to start from a point and then explain how they got there, many other nationalities prefer to present the background and logically proceed to a conclusion. Especially in Asia, it is useful to explain your methodology and say how you intend to approach the topic so that your audience knows how to adapt.

Attention spans

Have you noticed? Attention spans are getting shorter. If you can say it in half an hour, why do you need 45 minutes? And since we're on the subject of time, can you do it in 20 minutes? The famous Pecha Kucha presentation style involves the 20/20 approach. That's 20 PowerPoint slides, with 20 seconds spent on each. Do the maths – that's a total of about six minutes!

Pecha Kucha is a Japanese term, dreamed up by architects for product presentations and now a popular party trick at conferences. Experts tell you that all anybody remembers in a presentation is the first and the last three minutes. So in a 30-minute presentation, what happens to the other 24 minutes?

This is basically an American approach – time is short and time is money. But not even Americans always observe this. How do different parts of the world see attention spans? Assuming you are worth listening to, how long are people prepared to listen?

Hugo Chavez, the deceased Venezuelan president, used to go on for up to four hours, both live and on his radio show. In doing this he was imitating his Cuban role model, Fidel Castro, who, in his heyday, was another four- or five-hour man. Maybe only a few leaders can get away with this. The rest of us can't afford to be so self-indulgent. Depending on the occasion, the average talk might be 60 minutes with a question and answer session included at the end. But conference presentations are increasingly limited to 30 and 45 minutes, and many even specify 20 minutes. If you're presenting a product or process at a works meeting or on a conference call, five minutes might be ample and ten your absolute maximum. Even then, half your audience probably have their mobiles out or are checking emails as you talk.

One thing you must do – tell people how long you will present for. The brain programmes itself to listen. If people know you are planning to speak for ten minutes, they'll listen for ten minutes. Then time's up! Turn off! Unless you're exceptionally interesting, of course – but better not take the risk.

Typical attention spans:

UK	FRANCE	GERMANY	SOUTHERN EUROPE	CENTRAL and EASTERN EUROPE
45 minutes to one hour, including Q and A	One hour	One hour plus questions	One hour	One hour
INDIA	**CHINA/JAPAN**	**RUSSIA**	**BRAZIL**	**US/CANADA**
30-45 minutes	One hour or more, depending on topic	One hour	One hour	30-45 minutes plus Q and A

Shall we start?

The other problem is starting time. On time or late? Nordic, Germanic and English- speaking countries have a more or less precise sense of time. Things start when the programme says they will. Others are much more relaxed. Our advice is to always get there in good time. You can set everything up – especially if you are using any kind of equipment, and you can say hello to any early birds. This will help you feel more at home with your audience and get a better sense of what they want to know.

How to get your message across – the Three S structure

How do you get your message across clearly and quickly? Well, you could do worse than emulate Steve Jobs. The late founder and president of Apple was a superb presenter. Another

American presentations expert, Carmine Gallo, studied his methods and made a video presentation of Jobs' approach.

Gallo recommended three key things:

1. Create a headline. State it at the beginning, repeat it and end with it. The headline, just one sentence, is your message.

2. Give them an outline. Tell them what they're going to hear. Give them a road map. We would add, tell them how long they're going to listen for.

3. Have a memorable moment. This is your key point, your key example, your demonstration, your piece of evidence. Build up to it and then give it all you've got. Make sure it reinforces your message. When Jobs introduced the MacBook Air in 2008 at the MacWorld Conference, he pulled it out of a brown, manila inter-office envelope and balanced it on one hand to show how light it was. That was memorable.

Let's stay with presentation for a minute. One of the problems faced by international presenters is making themselves understood. Audiences listen but miss words or whole paragraphs and simply don't know where the presenter is on the presentation. This happens much more often than we like to think. What can we do to help?

We took a tip from the great Second World War British Prime Minister, Sir Winston Churchill. He was a famous parliamentary orator, who was asked by a young MP (Member of Parliament) for tips on making his first speech in the House of Commons.

'Simple, dear boy,' we imagine he said. 'Tell them what you're going to say. Tell them you're saying it. Tell them you've said it.'

We've taken these three pieces of advice and turned them into a system that we call the Three S presentation structure. The Three S's stand for Signpost, Signal and Summarise. We teach it to people all over the world. Here's what you do:

Signpost

Your signpost is a road map – it tells your audience where you are going to go. It has four components:

1. Topic title

2. Presentation duration

3. Summary of your key points

4. When you will accept questions –either during or at the end of the presentation.

Signal

You signal to say you've finished one point and are beginning the next. You have no idea how important signalling is: I've sat among audiences who were convinced the speaker was on his third point when in fact he hadn't finished his first. Time to get the mobile out and check messages.

Here's one really important point. At the end of each point, summarise what you've said in a single sentence or phrase. It's called a transition. It's a way of concluding your point and moving on to the next. Here's an example:

'Use a short phrase to summarise your point.

That's my first point.

Now let's move on to my second point.'

This is good signalling.

Summarise

Remember our first and last three minutes? This is your chance to remind your listeners what they've heard. Once again the advice contains three components:

1. Summarise: explain your key points in one sentence each.

2. Conclusion: say why the topic matters, or reinforce it if you have said it already.

3. Close: finish and invite questions.

The Three S structure is so simple. Everybody knows it. However, it's amazing how few people apply it. If you do it, we guarantee that you will get a much better response from your audience.

Has he finished yet?

The speaker made his remarks, spoke with a rising intonation and looked at the audience like a fish thrown by a wave onto the shore and not quite sure what it was doing there: wide-eyed, unblinking and fins flapping.

How often do you see that? The audience doesn't know what to do – should they keep silent, wait or applaud or leave? A simple 'Thank you' or 'Thank you very much' with a falling intonation does the trick. It's the international signal to the audience to give you the appreciation you so richly deserve. But hang on. It's not applause you're hearing, it's the drumming of knuckles on the table. What's going on?

Relax. You're in Germany. The German way of showing appreciation in an office or small group meeting is to drum on the table. Find out if there are any unusual ways of expressing appreciation among your audiences so you don't get caught out.

A colleague from Kazakhstan remembers an occasion when he was speaking to a group of British exporters. After one remark, a member of the audience said 'Hear, hear' (a British expression meaning, 'I agree with what you said'). Totally confused, the Kazakh official leaned over to us and asked, 'What's the matter? Can't they hear me?'

Q and A

Richard Branson, the British entrepreneur and chair of the Virgin Group, was talking to students at a prestigious university in Japan. At the end, in his relaxed way, he asked, 'Any questions?' Dead silence. Nothing.

In Japan, and to some extent in China, if I asked you a question it means I haven't understood or that you haven't been clear. In that case we both lose face, me because I'm a dummy and you because you can't make yourself clear. Better to shut up and remain silent.

Branson had the answer though. 'OK, the first person to ask a question gets a free first-class return ticket to Los Angeles,' he said. Hands shot up!

We don't all have airline tickets to give away, but there are tactics you can use to elicit questions.

First, don't expect any. You may get some, but you may not. Listening in appreciative silence is an Asian virtue.

Secondly, don't leave. Say you will be available in the room or nearby if anyone has any questions. Then stick around for ten to fifteen minutes. You'll find lots of people will ask you questions. They just don't like to do it in public.

Mind you, you sometimes get more questions than you need. Sheila gave a presentation to her German head office in Munich. Afterwards, she was bombarded with questions. 'God,' she said to us later, 'They hated me. They asked so many aggressive questions!'

'Relax,' we said. 'The more questions they asked you the more it shows how interested they were.' Germans tend to ask lots of detailed questions. The British will ask fewer.

We can't hear you!

We were in Dubrovnik: large international audience, great presentation. At the end, there was a question from someone at the front. At least, we think it was a question, but we were sitting at the back and couldn't hear it.

There are lots of reasons to repeat a question. Check that you've understood it correctly, give yourself time to think, and reformulate it in a way you can answer. And, yes, make sure that everyone in the audience has heard it. It's a basic courtesy. So when somebody asks a question don't rush in with an answer. Repeat it first so the audience can all get the benefit of both the answer and the question.

Here's another tip: when you have answered the question, check that the questioner is happy with the answer. A simple, 'Does that answer your question?' does the trick.

Visuals

You'd think that PowerPoint would be a fairly uncontroversial way of supporting a presentation. Not a bit of it. If you asked a PowerPoint trainer how to construct your presentation, he or she would probably give you the following advice:

USING POWERPOINT

• Use black and white rather than colour. It is easier to read.

• Keep your text to 7x7. Seven lines maximum per screen and each line of text no longer than seven words.

• Put your screen titles in a size of not less than 32pt.

• Put your text at ideally 28pt but not less than 20pt.

• Use illustrations where possible. A picture is worth a thousand words.

Good advice. However, the Chinese, Japanese and Koreans criticise Westerners for wasting space. They prefer to fill the screen with information and data and then to pick out what they want. Research has shown that when Westerners look at an image, such as a PowerPoint screen, they focus on one central piece of text or image and work out from here. So you need to highlight your information.

East Asians tend to do the opposite. They take in the whole screen and then go to different points for the detail. Now, if you are a Westerner, you know why in Beijing, Seoul or Tokyo you are confronted with these impossibly complicated spreadsheets or charts that some poor manager has slaved all night to produce. And if you are an Asian, why Westerners appear to be wasting space when they think they are saving time and improving concentration.

At least the Westerners and the Asians are united on one thing. Black and white is best. And then they watch a presentation done by a Spaniard. Latin expressiveness with bright yellows, oranges, reds and greens lights up the screen. Unfortunately, in the daylight glare of the conference room, all the beautiful colours merge into one another and you can't read anything.

And then there's this. A Middle Eastern professor was making a presentation at an academic conference. Used to talking to students, he was more lively. There was more emotion in his voice and more stress in his sentences. To help everyone follow, he had prepared a PowerPoint presentation. And there was the problem.

He had projected his entire speech in 12pt on the screen. There was no way anyone in the audience could see it. If by chance anyone had been close enough to read it, the print was so dense it was impossible to take in. He'd forgotten the basic rule – if the audience can't see it, don't show it.

Internationally speaking, a philosophy of black and white, 7*7 and 32pt and 28pt is best. Oh, and research shows that upper and lower case is easier to read than just UPPER CASE or just lower case.

Do we need visuals?

Latins often distrust PowerPoint presentations. They know that presentations and statistics can lie. What they're interested in is the character of the presenter. Consider leaving the PowerPoint aside and just concentrate on letting your personality communicate with the audience. The two aren't mutually exclusive of course, but just consider doing it.

What can go wrong? Rules of the road

Finally, a few rules to help you adapt when you are presenting to a group you don't know.

A slip of the tongue

We all do it from time to time, but we don't all cause international incidents when it happens. We're talking about gaffes, such as the one committed by the German SDP politician Peter Steinbrueck. When he heard the result of the Italian general election in February 2013, he said that he was appalled that 'two clowns had won'. He was referring to the success of the comedian Beppe Grillo and the former Prime Minister, Silvio Berlusconi.

As a result the President of Italy, Giorgio Napolitano, cancelled an official dinner with Steinbrueck and fellow German politicians criticised him for his 'unserious' approach. Be careful that your personal remarks don't cause you problems.

Mind your language

It's not just gaffes that cause offence. Try not to swear, if you are inclined to use strong language, and be careful about the idioms you use. People may misunderstand or misinterpret them.

Be careful of so-called false friends if you're speaking in a foreign language. Mike is a fluent Spanish speaker, but when Barry was presenting in Spain on one occasion, he warned about the dangers of making international presentations. 'Es dangeroso' he said, neatly transposing the English word 'dangerous' into what he thought was the Spanish word, 'dangeroso'. Except it's not Spanish. 'Dangerous' in Spanish is *peligroso*. No wonder the audience was confused.

Georgina gave a presentation about her highly successful English/Spanish teaching operation in Spanish to a group of local dignitaries. Describing a situation where she had felt embarrassed, Georgina said '*Soy embarassada*'. To her surprise half the audience sat tight-lipped and the rest clapped vigorously. Only afterwards she discovered she'd revealed she was not embarrassed but pregnant. *Embarassada* means pregnant in Spanish.

Body language is a part of your overall language. As we'll see in Chapter 7, gestures in your country may not be perceived the same way in others. Two fingers stuck up, the thumbs-up sign and the A-OK finger and thumb gestures have very different meanings depending on where you are. And even eye contact can be a challenge. In one presentation our Japanese audience collectively appeared to have gone to sleep. Luckily, we knew they were in deep concentration, and sure enough they remembered everything we said.

Self-control

An emotional approach may appeal to Latins but it doesn't go down well with Asians. It is important never to show impatience, anger or frustration to the latter. Lose your temper and you lose credibility.

Check the audience style

Make sure you adopt the right level of formality or informality for your audience. Check their expectations: do they want facts and figures, assurance of your qualifications and experience, or an oratorical flourish? The big danger for native speakers of English is that they are often too relaxed and informal. The danger for non-native speakers is that they may be the opposite.

Check the audience. Listeners or participants?

Don't assume your audience want to participate in Q and A sessions, quizzes or group and pair work. They may just be there to listen to you.

The lesson from all these points? With international audiences, don't just focus on your content. Do your cultural due diligence as well.

Five things to remember

1. The seven things you need to know about an international audience (who they are, their expectations, and the style, humour, duration, follow-up and visual aids that you should employ.

2. The Steve Jobs approach – (headline, outline, memorable moment).

3. The 3 S structure (signpost, signal and summarise).

4. How to deal with Q and A (questions and answers).

5. How to use powerpoint and visuals (black and white, 7x7, 32pt headings and 28pt text). If they can't see it, don't show it.

Chapter 5
How to run international meetings

Barry arrived early for his meeting in Rio de Janeiro. He went to reception, announced his arrival and sat down to wait – and wait. After about 20 minutes the phone rang. The receptionist picked it up. Barry knew just enough Brazilian Portuguese to understand the gist of the conversation.

'Is Barry Tomalin there yet?' 'Yes, he's sitting in reception.' 'Right, I'll leave now.'

Time delays are part of meetings all over the world. People arrive late, postpone meetings, and start late and finish late. The idea of starting and finishing on time is not universally held.

Key issues that international managers have to face in arranging and participating in meetings are:

- Set-up
- Timing
- Types of meetings
- Aims of meetings
- Who runs meetings
- Attitudes to agenda
- Meetings protocol – where to sit, when to speak
- Dealing with interruptions
- Meetings outcomes

'I like meetings round a desk or a table in an office,' says Adam. 'I like the formality and the feeling we can get things done.' That's funny: in many countries the office is the place where you don't get things done. Meetings take place in hotel lobbies, in restaurants, and in social rather than business environments. Offices are used to announce decisions, ratify agreements and allocate responsibilities, but not for getting things done. So it's important, if you're working with people of different cultures, to establish where meetings take place and where the actual work is done. It may not be in the office.

Timing

'Shall we start?' Rob asked. There were six people in the meeting, but Sergei hadn't arrived.

'No way,' said his Russian colleagues. 'Sergei's running the meeting.' Sergei was the boss and in Russia you don't start the meeting without the boss.

Hierarchy is one reason why meetings start late – waiting for the most important person. Another is power – keeping people waiting because you know you can.

Punctuality is relative

Meetings may start late but they can also end late. In France it is important to finish the business at hand so meetings go on until they have finished. Americans, on the other hand, may leave a meeting on or even before the scheduled finish time because they have another meeting to get to. In 'time- loose' countries it is important not to schedule too many meetings in the day, because they may start or finish late. One meeting in the morning, one in the afternoon and one in the evening would be a safe schedule.

Types of meetings

Many countries rigidly define the type of meeting and determine the appropriate behaviour that accompanies each.

- Information meetings. These are for giving company or project information. You may ask clarification questions but discussion of the issues may not be encouraged.

- Allocation of responsibilities. This is for explaining who does what in a project. Questions of clarification are welcome. Others aren't.

- Regular meetings. These are for updating of projects and routine work. Some discussion of issues is appropriate here.

- General meetings. These are for policy planning. General discussion and exchanges of views and opinions are encouraged.

In Britain, the US and Australia all meetings have elements of all of the above, but in more stratified countries such as France and Germany the types of meetings and the appropriate behaviour may be more strictly enforced.

We were running a seminar in Helsinki and set up an informal meeting and debate. Two Germans had reservations. 'We need to know the point of the discussion, the problem we are intended to resolve, the intended outcome, the process that will lead to resolution, who will be involved and what they will be doing.' Logical but intimidating!

It's not enough to understand the type of meeting you will be attending. It's also important to know how people expect the meeting to run – and who runs it.

Who runs the meeting?

Meetings in the UK, the US and Australia are often run by quite junior people. They are usually the operational managers with most experience of the question under discussion. Departmental meetings will normally be run by the head of the relevant department, but could be chaired by someone else if the head is not available. The point is that the content and outcome of the meeting are important, not who runs it. This is not the case worldwide.

In many countries meetings are an opportunity for the exercise of power and responsibility, so the senior person present runs the meeting, by definition. This is regardless of expertise, experience and even competence. Respect for authority and hierarchy is all.

Attitude to agendas

Further on in this chapter we emphasise the importance of agendas, especially as a way of helping non-native speakers of English to participate in meetings. However, the attitude to agendas varies greatly. A great many meetings have no agenda – just a topic for discussion.

Even if there is a detailed agenda, why do we keep to it? The Swiss take a linear attitude to agendas. Change the order or link something to something else and the chair will ask you to observe the agenda. 'If there is time at the end,' they say, 'we will include your point.'

Across the borders in France, Spain and Italy, the attitude to agendas is far more relaxed. Any point needs to be discussed from all angles – it becomes a 360-degree conversation which links all the items in the agenda.

Who sits where?

We were in a meeting. The bloke in the middle seemed completely disinterested and half asleep. The young guy on the end looked at us unblinking, eyes wide open, interested. So we addressed our remarks to him. However, this was a Japanese meeting. The guy by the door was the junior man on the team. We'd spent the whole presentation addressing the least important member of the team – the non-decision-maker. Meanwhile the decision-maker mused on peacefully in deep concentration.

In Europe, where you sit is not terribly important, but in Asia it is vital. The senior person will sit furthest from the door, with the best view out of the window, and the junior people will sit near the door. The ancient theory decrees that if the assassins should break in, the juniors by the door would be first to die. This would give the senior person time to draw his sword and fight off the assassins or escape. Either way, seating is important. Observe the ritual when you are abroad and honour it with your Asian visitors when you are at home.

Who speaks, who keeps quiet?

The same thing applies to speaking. In an Asian meeting the junior members – even someone who might be quite mature in years and experience – speak only when asked. In Western meetings, if you have something to say, you say it, regardless of hierarchy. OK, sometimes you take your life in your hands when you do so, but everybody respects in principle your right to do so.

Barry was working with a group of Asian accountants in a leading international accountancy firm. The three Asians were seated opposite him and he asked them questions – directed to the one in the middle in front of him. An embarrassed silence ensued until one of the Asians started signalling with his eyes. 'You've got the wrong guy,' his eyes said. ' The senior accountant is on the right.' Barry got the message. He addressed a question to the accountant on his right, and got a response. Lesson: identify the leader before you start.

Dealing with interruptions

How do you deal with interruptions in a hierarchical meeting? In the movie *Rising Sun*, a cross-cultural thriller that is set in Los Angeles and involves Japanese and American culture clashes, Sean Connery plays the part of an LAPD detective who knows Japan well and has the respect of the Japanese. In one scene he and his cohort share a meal in a Japanese restaurant with a Japanese CEO. At one point in the discussion, an American junior manager speaks up. He is frozen out by his Japanese boss and has to apologise for interrupting. Later on, however, he confides something to his colleague, on the same level, and Sean Connery asks a question. That is the American's chance to speak, but only when he has been addressed by a senior.

Most Westerners have no idea of the Asian protocol of interruption, and their questioning may be seen as individualistic and very impolite.

Meetings outcomes

Even when you have overcome all these organisational and protocol problems, the question of the outcome of any meeting may be by no means clear. In Western countries, the outcome is expected to be a commitment to a series of action points implemented by the managers present and designed to deliver a result. The decision may be reviewed in a later meeting and modified or changed, but the action-point procedure is seen as the way forward. This is the pattern followed in the US, the UK and Germany.

This approach is not shared in more hierarchical societies. In Italy the function of a meeting is to gauge the mood of the participants and to canvas opinion on various courses of action. Decisions will be taken outside the meeting by the senior managers.

In Asia, a meeting outcome can be very different again. In Japan, the aim may be to keep everyone in the loop, but decisions are made outside the meeting. In China and India, too, decisions will not be taken in the meeting itself.

The lessons are obvious. Never assume that your way of doing things is shared by the people you are working with overseas.

Before you go into a meeting, especially an important one, check what it is expected to achieve. If there is no chance to ascertain this – and there often isn't – be prepared to be the strong silent person. Watch and observe – you will be seen as a strong leader, and you will have the opportunity to learn the best way to proceed.

Translators and interpreters

We have worked so far on the assumption that meetings will take place in the speaker's mother tongue or in English, but what if you have to use translators and interpreters? That poses a whole new set of problems.

A British company had organised a meeting with a Turkish client in Ankara, the capital of Turkey. An interpreter was needed and the client offered to provide one, although the company would pay for her time. The interpreter, Deniz, was charming and spoke excellent English (she had spent time in London). The meetings went well but the MD of the British company began to feel suspicious.

'Why,' he wondered afterwards, 'was she not translating everything that was said? They seemed to be saying a lot more than she was translating. She also entered into long conversations with them in Turkish.'

They were staying at the Sheraton in Ankara and some of the meetings were held on the comfortable sofas in the hotel lounge. On the third morning, the MD came downstairs to breakfast and found his interpreter having breakfast with the client. 'At that moment,' he said, 'I was seriously worried. I felt that she was working for them rather than for us, even though we were paying her.'

What could the British MD do? He could sack the interpreter, but that would be an unforgivable snub to the client's pride, and could ruin the negotiation.

He was not even sure that his suspicions were justified – the negotiations were progressing well and Deniz seemed very professional. Maybe he was being oversensitive. In the end he did nothing, but the suspicion remained in his mind that maybe he wasn't getting all the information he needed.

What could he have done differently? The Briton shouldn't have accepted the client's offer of an interpreter. He would have done better to contact the commercial attaché at the British Embassy in Ankara: they would probably have a list of recommended interpreters and translators on their books. That way he would have been sure that his interpreter was professional and independent.

Barry was lecturing in Russia. His audience included both English and Russian speakers so he needed a translator. Luckily, Anna, his sponsor in Russia, was on hand to do the honours. A fluent English speaker, she was the perfect choice. Even so they both agreed to do certain things.

1. Barry gave her a printout of his speech to go over and also a printout of his PowerPoint presentation.

2. Anna familiarised herself with the speech and also arranged a translation of the PowerPoint slides into Russian.

3. Barry and Anna went over the speech and identified any technical or unusual words and phrases that needed

checking. In one or two cases they substituted them for simpler words.

4. On the day, Barry made sure he spoke in short sentences and then stood back to allow Anna to translate.

5. At the end of the presentation there was a Q and A session. Barry repeated the questions in English and Anna translated into Russian. Barry answered in English and Anna then translated into Russian. Everything that was said in English was translated into Russian and vice versa.

Simultaneous translation

Mr Chen, a Chinese businessman, was having his first meeting with a director of an American company in Shanghai. The session would set the tone for the relationship. Although Mr Chen understood some English, he used an interpreter and so did the American, who hired a translator on the recommendation of the local US consulate.

The US director followed the steps that Anna and Barry had taken in the presentation in Russia. She went over the broad outlines of her proposal with the interpreter, and made sure that any potentially difficult technical words were understood.

In the meeting, the Chinese and the American sat almost next to each other with the two interpreters like ghosts just behind them, whispering into their ears.

The Chinese looked down as he listened and then spoke to the American, looking at her as he did so. And that's where the American made her big mistake. When she was talking she looked at the interpreter who would translate. When she was listening she would look at the interpreter who was talking to her, not at her Chinese counterpart. The Chinese was insulted.

Never do that. When you are listening, look at the other person, not at the interpreter. In this instance the gaffe wasn't a deal breaker, but it didn't make a great impression.

Virtual meetings

It's a sign of the times – recession, shrinking costs and increasing security. Executives don't travel; they talk on the phone. You can go and see major clients, but you often have to talk to colleagues, suppliers and managers on the phone in different countries. You may never meet them, yet in some companies, as we saw earlier, the managers you never confront in person are responsible for your appraisal and awarding your end-of-year bonus.

For many managers overseas, these conversations have to take place in English wherever there is a non-native speaker of the national tongue on the phone. This adds additional stress to an already stressful situation. But as a manager there are a number of things you can do to make life easier.

1. Convocation. Give people as much advance notice as you can, provide contact numbers and other key data, and circulate a reminder in good time.

2. Topic. Give the meeting a clear focus. It may be a specific project, a regular weekly conference call or a general exchange of ideas, but the aim must be clear.

3. Agenda. Make a list of key points you want to discuss, even if it isn't exhaustive. Circulate this in good time before the meeting.

Jean-Francois is a departmental manager in Paris who participates in weekly conference calls. He is French, the call is in English, and he understands about 60% of the discussion. The convocation and the agenda land on his desktop. He reads the convocation and scans the agenda, and sees an item he wants to contribute to. He calls Jim, the conference convenor.

'Hello, Jim, I've just got the agenda for Friday. I'd like to contribute on item five. Can you call on me when we get to it?'

So far so good. Jean-Francois has gained some uninterrupted space to make a short presentation. Maybe on the day Jim will forget, but if Jean-Francois reminds him, Jim will remember what he promised.

On the day of the call, Jim remembers to check who has what equipment. His desktop console tells him who is online, their name, location and job title. Sometimes even their photo is on the screen, and he can also see who is mute (microphone turned off) and who is speaking.

Jim needs to check that everyone has the same equipment. This is not always the case: some offices may just have the phone, and it may not be possible to mute the microphone. Others may be working at home and not have access to the office facilities. Conference call convenors swear that they can hear children, cats and dogs and even goats in the background of some calls.

Jim checks where everyone is and what equipment they are using. He makes no assumptions that people in Egypt, India, Mexico, Brazil, the USA and Singapore have access to the same sophisticated system he is using.

On the call itself there are a number of distractions.

1. Background noise

Heavy traffic, office conversations and, for home workers, domestic noises-off. There's not a lot you can do about this, except perhaps ask the participant to close a door or a window or move to a quieter location.

2. Clicking jewellery and computer keyboards

People often don't realise that the things they do while listening can cause distractions. Heavy jewellery rattling on the wrists or knocking against the table, the clicking on and off of a ballpoint pen, or tapping on the computer keyboard as you do your emails can all interrupt a meeting. Either turn your microphone to mute or stop.

3. Heavy breathing

Barry was on a call. Suddenly he was aware of the heaving breath of another participant. What was going on? The participant was on his mobile phone and walking along a busy road. He had a cold and the sound of his breathing was distracting from the call. Eventually, he had to get off the line.

A colleague of ours in France has a robust response to heavy breathing. He says, 'Is Darth Vader on the line? Kindly mute yourself.' (Darth Vader was the heavy-breathing villain in the Star Wars movies.)

4. Dead air time

Jim is on the phone, but is suddenly aware that there is no response from his colleagues in Mumbai (India) and Guanzhou (China). The air seems dead.

'Is anyone there?' he asks. 'Yes, we're here,' replies his Indian counterpart.

Unlike most of his European or US colleagues, Indians and East Asians prefer to listen and not interrupt. Therefore it is important for Jim to ask their opinions. But asking an open question is not enough: hierarchy is at play. Executives on the Indian and Chinese teams may not speak unless asked to by their team leader. To be sure of a response, Jim needs to identify the senior person on the call and address his questions first to him or her. The team leader will then nominate the executive who should respond.

Advice on video conference calls

Chantal is setting up a new project in Paris, but part of her team is based in Brazil. She knows that the Brazilians value face-to-face contact for relationship building, and so she decides to run the project kick-off meeting as a video conference. She's run these sessions before as voice-only conferences and noticed how it took many extra personal calls to build any kind of cooperative relationship.

The meeting goes well and she notices that relationships are established much quicker and are much warmer as a result of the video conference. However, she is also aware of a number of precautions she needs to take to ensure video success. It's all about creating the right impression in vision.

1. Check the dress code

This can be a problem. Are the participants' clothes too casual or too formal? Are they too bright or too dull? Is there a danger that striped tops, shirts or ties will strobe on screen?

2. Check the wall behind the group

Make sure no compromising material is attached to the walls. One company famously managed to display a sales graph showing falling sales, another a Pirelli calendar. Check the background: does it represent your company image appropriately?

3. Check the table

Is it tidy? Papers tidily arranged? No empty coffee cups or half-eaten sandwiches? No confidential material on display?

4. Is everyone in vision?

There are ten people round a table, so can the camera catch everyone? If someone is on the edge or leans back they may be out of shot. Remind everyone to lean forward so that they can be seen.

5. Who's talking?

Some video conferencing studios have voice-activated cameras that automatically zoom in on the speaker, but most don't. Therefore Vijay and Jamila in Delhi may find it difficult to spot who is speaking in the group in London. A simple gesture to show you are speaking resolves that problem.

6. Don't pick your nose!

You probably don't pick your nose but you understand the problem. When someone else is speaking you may decide to concentrate on your nails, your emails, your papers or look around, smiling and even mouthing comments to other people. The only problem is, everyone who is watching can see you. Don't fidget, and focus on the speaker. Remember, you are in vision.

How to manage a meeting

Mehdi, an Egyptian, is running a conference call. He knows there will be a number of American, British and Australian colleagues on the line, and he worries that because his English is a bit slow and hesitant, his colleagues will dominate the conversation. What can he do to manage the conversation effectively? Here are some suggestions.

1. Take control from the beginning

This doesn't have to be dictatorial. Thank people for joining the call and go round the virtual table to ask people to identify themselves. Even if names are displayed on your console it's still helpful to hear the people and identify the voices and the accents.

2. Get someone else to take the minutes

Most convenors of conference calls take the minutes themselves, but chairing and handling the minutes is really hard so ask someone else to write the minutes. Arrange this before the meeting – you don't want to waste time asking people to do it in the meeting itself.

3. Have an agenda and follow it

You need a structure to follow and to appeal to when people digress. Agendas give you confidence and add to your authority.

4. Introduce each point and explain who will address it

Make sure you introduce each agenda point, then invite someone on the team to introduce the topic.

5. Elicit contributions

Control the discussion of each point by asking who wants to participate.

6. Sum up and decide what to minute

Thank people for their contributions and summarise the points to minute.

7. End the meeting

Sum up the key conclusions, check if there is any other business (AOB) and fix the date of the next meeting.

8. Stick to the point

If someone talks too much or goes off topic, ask them to sum up or stick to the agenda. Saying you are running out of time is also useful.

9. Dealing with disagreement

If someone disagrees or gets argumentative, suggest discussing it 'outside the meeting'.

There is no question that conference calls, whether by telephone or video, are the future of meetings. Where they take place in English it is really important for native speakers to be sensitive to the difficulties that non-native speakers may experience. It is also vital for non-native speakers to develop knowledge of how to better run and take part in conference calls.

Five things to remember

1. If you are the co-ordinator familiarise yourself with the key differences from your own style.

2. Employ your own translator. Don't let the 'other side' do it for you. Meet and brief translators and interpreters before the meeting.

3. Use best practice guidelines for phone and video conference calls.

4. Follow the steps to manage an international meeting.

5. If you are a participant, plan your intervention by checking the agenda and arranging with the meeting convenor.

Chapter 6
How to negotiate internationally

'Let us never negotiate out of fear but let us never fear to negotiate.' That was President John F Kennedy's exhortation in his
inaugural address to the USA in 1961 during the Cold War.
Negotiation can be scary. In international environments it can
be even scarier. Why? You don't know what the rules of
engagement are, you don't know what the etiquette is and you
don't know how to persuade people to agree. Even in English
you don't know if they mean the same thing as you do, even
though you are using the same words.

In the 1962 nuclear testing negotiation between the USA and
the USSR, the Americans proposed an inspection programme
to check if nuclear weapons agreements were being observed.
They proposed ten inspections and the Russians refused, insist-
ing on three. As Roger Fisher and William Ury in their book
'*Getting to Yes*' point out, no one ever asked if that meant ten
inspections of each site, ten inspections all together, or maybe
three for key sites. As a result, no room was left for discussion
and accommodation. The two sides remained apart and no
inspections protocol was agreed.

Fisher was Professor of Law at Harvard University and a world-
recognised negotiator. He developed the Harvard
System of Negotiation, seven principles which guide most if not
all negotiators in the world today. They are:

- Know what you want to achieve

- Know your walk-away point

- Know what concessions you can make

- Know your BATNA (Best Alternative To A Negotiated Agreement) if the negotiation breaks down

- Prepare a range of options for negotiation

- Look beyond the other negotiator's position to identify their real interests

- Be hard on the problem but soft on the person

The pitfalls of negotiation across cultures

This sounds like common sense. But in fact a number of factors can ruin your negotiation if you haven't taken them into account. The key to negotiation is preparation, but not just knowing what you want and what the other person wants. It also means doing due diligence on the other side's cultural attitudes and understanding how those can influence the negotiation. We have identified a number of pitfalls that negotiators fall into.

1. Hierarchy. Have you taken hierarchy and seniority of the negotiating team into account?

2. Authority. Does your team have the power to negotiate, or do they have to refer back to head office for decisions?

3. Representation. Who should be present at an international negotiation?

4. Persuasion. Who do you have to convince? The boss, the board or each team member?

5. Translators and interpreters. What is the role of translators and interpreters in negotiations?

6. Status. What does where you sit in a negotiation say about you?

7. Procedure. Is the negotiation procedure different to what you are familiar with?

8. Concessions. What is the role of concessions? When should you introduce them and under what circumstances?

9. Walk-away points. Your 'no-go' areas, where you stop the negotiation.

10. Finalisation. How do you finalise a contract and is a final contract final?

1. Hierarchy – match status to status

In many markets it is vital to match leader status to leader status, both in political and commercial negotiations. If you fail to do so, your negotiation may not get off the ground. If you cannot achieve that because you are a small supplier negotiating with a big client, you may want to explore the value of introducing a high profile position to your team – someone from the embassy or an individual highly respected in the industry or country you are dealing with. Many firms in China and the Middle East work through agents, who both know the ins and outs of negotiation procedures and are well connected. Before you hire such an agent, do what you can to check out the value of the connection. Don't take it on trust. The lesson? Find an agent with proven connections that you can check.

2. Make sure your supplier can deliver

A Brazilian business development director talked breezily of his connections in various areas of government and industry. Over two or three meetings we mapped out proposals for an agreement between his organisation and ours. Then came the board meeting and the managing director's decision: 'We don't want outsiders as part of this project. We're doing it all in house.' Our done-deal was undone. Our well-connected middleman turned out to have his limitations. The lesson? Make sure the person you negotiate with can deliver.

3. Are you high enough up the food chain?

Talking to the wrong person in an organisation can waste days and months in management time. The great mistake of people in delegated management systems, where individuals have their own responsibilities, budgets and clear escalation procedures to top management, is to assume that the manager at their level in the other country has the same powers.

Martin negotiated a supply deal with a large Indian client. They spent months on it leading up to a big sales meeting. After the sales meeting, nothing happened. That's when Martin realised that his Indian colleague didn't have the same access that he had. The Indian colleague had never even raised the issue of collaboration with his senior managers because he was far too junior to do so.

Martin's lesson? Next time, he would reach up into the organisation to as high a level as he could in order to get a result. That official would then order Martin's original contact to cooperate. Martin's original contact had only been responsible for implementation, not policy, and had no authority to negotiate.

4. Stick with your contact

Once you've got a good contact, respect it. Jane is a go-getting media executive, who was setting up a deal with a chain of potential partners in Germany. There was a big meeting in Bonn where all the representatives would be gathered and her contact would present the proposal. To help things along, so she thought, she emailed details of the proposal before the meeting to all the representatives. Result: the project was withdrawn from the meeting agenda and she never heard from her contact again.

Jane's lesson? In Germany you don't go above your line manager or managerial contact.

5. Authority

Tony is a scientific advisor and his company makes specialist parts for satellite technology – just what his negotiating partners in Russia needed. That's why their opening question at the meeting surprised him. 'Before we start, can you assure us that you have the authority to negotiate this agreement?' Of course not. He was a science advisor, an expert in specifications and in assembly. Neither he nor his company had realised that this wasn't a presales meeting but a commercial negotiation. After the usual courtesies, the meeting was over. No progress.

Tony's lesson? Particularly in Central and Eastern Europe, make sure there is always someone present with the authority to negotiate and take decisions. Things can move much faster than you expect. If that is impossible, beef up your person's representative power as much as you can and make sure they have a hot line to head office in case anything needs approving or discussing. Make sure that the hot line is open and someone responsible is on hand to take the call.

Outcome? In this case, delayed but successful. The Russians needed the technology. The British firm re-approached the Russians with the right level of negotiating authority and got the sale.

Lesson? Check the aim of the meeting and make sure you have the right level of decision-making power present.

6. Representation–who should be present?

An American corporation flew over to Cairo to negotiate the final stages of a deal. As part of the group, they included their legal advisers from a well-known company of international solicitors. As the US director introduced his team, he noticed that the president of the Egyptian company looked quite ill at ease. At the break, the president took the American aside.

'What's the matter?' the Egyptian asked. 'Don't you trust us?' 'Of course we trust you,' replied the American. 'Why do you think we've brought all our team over?'

'Then, why the lawyers?' asked the Egyptian.

In the Middle East, lawyers are responsible for the paperwork and ensuring legal compliance after the deal has been agreed. In the US, lawyers are responsible for making sure the deal is right and getting the best result for their clients: they are integral to the deal-making process. The problem in this example was a simple mismatch of expectations about who should attend the meeting.

Outcome? The misunderstanding was sorted out and the deal went ahead as planned. However, the lesson is, check who will be at the meeting from each side and what their role will be. Make sure that any possible misunderstandings about who should attend are sorted out before the meeting takes place.

7. Should juniors be present?

The directors of a major British corporation assembled in India to sign a contract. As often in Asia, but also in other continents, astrology plays a part in deciding the auspicious date, time and place to sign an agreement. In fact, work had been going on for six months before the contract signature. As they looked around the assembly, the directors from the UK noticed a man they didn't recognise among the group. It turned out he was a local site manager. 'Why was he there?' they wondered.

It turned out the site manager was the person who had introduced to the Indian group the possibility of collaboration with the British corporation. This is not unusual, but usually, having done his job of introduction, the junior manager bows out and lets the big boys get on with the important stuff. In Asia, the person who starts the deal remains an honoured part of the process.

Outcome? No problem. The British directors were a pretty practical bunch and an extra body wasn't a problem. Later, they appreciated what the invitation of the site manager said about the Indian commitment to the process.

8. Persuasion

At one level this goes back to point two – stick with your contact. However, it is not always obvious in a meeting who holds the power in a negotiation. So who do you pitch at – the boss, the team as a whole or each individual? It varies from country to country.

9. United front

First, let us state very clearly that the other negotiating side will probe for disunity. They will try to find weaknesses in your team. A British company negotiating in Moscow was disconcerted to learn that the other side knew exactly what the profit margin on their product was and was intent on negotiating hard to lower the price. Apparently, a manager on the British team, unhappy with the size of the mark-up, had let his concerns slip during conversation with one of the Russian team. On another occasion, an Israeli team member let slip that an IT programme security test had shown weaknesses and was causing delays in product release. This gave the Russians a bargaining weapon to drive down the price.

Outcome? These revelations offer weapons to the other side to force concessions or even break off the deal. Make sure that there is a 'Grand Central Station' for all information disclosure, usually the negotiating team leader. Also make sure that any disagreement in your team about strategy and tactics is handled internally. This means being prepared to listen to and settle disagreements before the negotiations meeting and while the team is on site.

10. Boss, team or individual? Who needs convincing?

In top-down markets, the person who needs convincing is the boss. If the boss is convinced, he or she will take the lead in persuading the others in the team. Your job is to understand the key issues facing his or her organisation and making a convincing case that you have the answers.

11. Finding a champion

In team-consulting markets, you have to decide who needs convincing. Is it the boss or the top influencer in the team? Can you rely on the manager concerned to carry your proposal forward with the team, as would probably be the case in Germany?

Often, it is important to find a champion, an influential member of the management team. This person can do three things. One, they can plead your case in the team. Two, they can advise you on best next steps, and three, they can keep you up to date on progress. In Japan, where team consulting and decision-making is both the norm and time-consuming, a champion, if you have one, is a must.

12. Lobbying individuals

Some management teams need convincing individually. A BBC boss in the UK never went into a meeting without calling each participant and canvassing their support. He took the trouble to find out what their interests were and what their objections might be and made sure that when he presented his proposal, as many of the participants as possible were already on side. The UK and the US are both lobbying markets. Poland too is a market where it is advisable to brief each board member individually before the meeting.

13. Personal agendas

Some management teams present a united front, but actually each participant can have his or her own agenda. China can be like that. You are lined up across a table from the Chinese team: the hierarchy is established and the protocols are under way, but each member has a different point of view or a pet concern that may or may not support your proposal. How can you find out what it is?

14. How to spot the personal agenda

First, listen carefully to what each person is saying. The language will be coded. There will be no hint of disagreement. But as you listen you can read between the lines and you will learn to spot areas of individual interest or concern. What can you do about it? Nothing in the meeting itself, but possibly during the banquet or evening dinner afterwards. Talk to the person you think may have a special concern, but don't mention your suspicions. Keep the conversation general, but you may find that this is the moment where you will learn that the chairperson's view is not the only one held around the table.

15. Your policy

Your policy? Find out how decisions are arrived at and be prepared to lobby individuals you believe might support your project. The downtime between meetings or before the meeting is the opportunity to do this. Make sure your own team presents a united front in meetings by making sure that their individual doubts and concerns are taken into account.

Using interpreters

Why use interpreters?

Many meetings need interpreters. Even when people understand the language quite well they like to use interpreters.

Sometimes this is to increase confidence and make sure nothing is missed. Sometimes it is to allow them to listen to things that you are saying that are not translated. A sales manager gave us a piece of good advice. 'If you think they understand you but aren't telling, tell a funny story,' she said. 'If they laugh, bingo! They understand.'

Don't translate that

We've listened to Japanese meetings where the Japanese negotiating team leader tells the interpreter, 'Don't translate that.' The policy of translating is supposed to be transparent. You translate what the person says to you and what you say back. Sometimes the interpreter has to paraphrase. That's acceptable. But 'Don't translate that' may be the equivalent to withholding or suppressing information.

Don't explain too much

We were in Turkey for a meeting with an important government official. The government department identified an interpreter. He joined us the evening before and we took him through the project and made sure he was familiar with the process we were describing and any specialist terminology we might use. The interpreter seemed like a good guy, knowledgeable and enthusiastic. The meeting went well and a couple of weeks later we heard – nothing. In fact, we heard nothing for six months. Then we learned that the project we had proposed had gone ahead but as a local venture with our interpreter! It could have happened anywhere.

Whose interpreter are you?

A French conglomerate was negotiating in Shanghai. The Shanghai corporation kindly provided the interpreter, but at French expense. The French found it difficult to brief the Chinese interpreter – she wasn't always available, and in the meetings she was very deferential to the Chinese colleagues. The French assumed this was just appropriate cultural politeness. Until one evening. Halfway through the negotiation they were having supper at the hotel and saw the interpreter at another table. She was with members of the Chinese negotiating team. A pleasant dinner with friends and colleagues, or what? From that point on, the French team were careful not to discuss any confidential information in her presence.

Take your own interpreter

The lesson is obvious – if you can, take your own interpreter as part of the negotiating team. If you can't, contact your embassy and ask them to recommend someone. Be very careful about accepting an interpreter hired by the other negotiator.

Status

Seating

We were in Frankfurt, involved in negotiations with a Chinese company. It wasn't going well. That evening we were invited to a dinner party organised by our Chinese hosts. In China, you don't decide where to sit – the host tells you. The further away from the host you are, the less important you are seen to be. This particular evening we were politely seated towards the end of the table – a sure sign that something we had done had displeased the Chinese.

Speaking

A Chinese proverb says, 'He who knows does not speak. He who speaks does not know.' In Japan the person who speaks may not be the boss. The boss's job is to set the strategy and then to sit silently and observe. His subordinate is the one who presents. This contrasts oddly with the Western tradition of the team leader leading the presentation in a negotiation. The important thing is to establish as soon as you can who is the boss on the other team and address your remarks to him or her. This is not always easy, but an experienced negotiator gave us a tip: 'When you're in a meeting, they will usually serve tea. See who gets served first on the other side. That's the boss.'

Intervening

In Western negotiations if you have something to say, it's normal to say it. But in Asian negotiations you don't speak unless you are invited. This means, in a negotiation, that if you want to ask a question of the finance officer, you actually ask the negotiation leader and they will nominate the appropriate person to answer. You may then question the finance officer directly, but the interchange is usually initiated by the team leader on the other side.

The table

In the West, status tends to be ignored. Round tables are preferred as they create a non-confrontational atmosphere and functional equality is the norm. At the very least, on a rectangular table it is considered better to sit at the end or on a corner than to be ranged opposite the other negotiation team in a straight line. However, you may have no choice in where you sit and the important thing is not to feel disadvantaged or confronted by it. It is just protocol.

Procedure

In the West, negotiations tend to have a fairly common proced-ure. Professor Gavin Kennedy of the University of Strathclyde in Glasgow, Scotland, identifies a clear progression of five stages:

1. Prepare
2. Debate
3. Propose
4. Bargain
5. Agree

Prepare: where each side explains what they want to achieve.

Debate: you discuss the pros and cons of each position.

Propose: make a proposal to the other side. This may be a suggestion for negotiation procedure, or a suggestion for agreement.

Bargain: you argue the advantages and disadvantages of the proposal.

Agreement: you agree on the deal and proceed to contract.

The cultural problem

The model is fine except for one key cultural factor. The model itself is linear, and proceeds from 'Prepare' to 'Agree' in a straight line. But countries don't always work that way. Secondly, when they do go back and forth between stages it is often difficult to tell from the language they use what stage they are actually at. This is particularly a problem for countries in the Middle East or Asia, where indirect communication and coded language may be the norm. Reading between the lines to know whether the other party is bargaining or has gone back to 'Prepare' is often a problem.

Concepcion is an international business development manager but she started her career as a language teacher. As her name suggests, she is a Spanish speaker – in this case from Argentina. She got so frustrated working out what people meant and what stage of the negotiation they were at, that she compiled a glossary of expressions. She prepared a spreadsheet with a column for each of the five stages and when she heard a phrase, she tried to fit it into one of the categories. Now she says she can tell immediately where an English-speaking negotiator stands by the phrases he or she is using.

Body language

However, it's not just spoken language that misleads, but also body language. The famous southern Indian head roll from side to side doesn't signal agreement: it says, 'I'm paying attention'. The Greek and Bulgarian emphatic movement of the head in a single up and down movement doesn't signify agreement: it means no. Many nationalities don't believe in smiling just to be friendly, so a serious expression here can indicate concentration and attention, not disagreement.

Don't assume apparent agreement means real agreement

When people use indirect means of communication it can cause immense problems. When an Indian for example tells you, 'No issues, no issues' (= no problem), double check that he or she is not just being polite. There may actually be no issues. On the other hand there may be considerable problems that he or she feels it is inappropriate or inconvenient to raise at this time. The rule is be grateful for the first but be prepared for the second.

The order of events

Americans like to get their 'Prepare' phase over early. They sit down at the negotiating table, having done their homework, and state their position and put their proposals on the table immediately. They then get annoyed when they discover that other nationalities do it differently. The French, for example, listen to the 'Prepare'. Then they go to 'Debate', and question and discuss the proposals at length. Then they go back to 'Prepare' and state their position. At that point they may put their own proposals on the table.

Prepare the procedure

The lesson is obvious – never assume the other side will negotiate in the same way as you do. By all means use the five stages as a baseline, but explore how different nationalities might react.

Concessions

The occasion was the Moscow international broadcasting station in English, *Russia Today*. The programme was a cultural debate ably led by the anchor person, Marina Dzashi. On the programme was a Russian businessman, a professor from Moscow State University Business School, a representative of the Russo-British Chamber of Commerce and one of us. The debate was the role of concessions in business negotiation. The stimulus was an article in a business magazine by a Russian businessman saying that concessions had no place in his business vocabulary and were 'a sign of weakness'. His job was to force concessions out of others, not offer them himself.

Not all Russians feel that way, as the broadcast showed. However, the programme also showed how attitudes to concessions vary between cultures.

Preparing concessions

Any sensible negotiator will look at what points are essential to the success of the negotiation and what points are negotiable. These are the concessions.

When to use concessions

Negotiators use concessions in different ways. Some negotiators offer concessions early as 'deal sweeteners'. In Russia, experienced negotiators advise that concessions should only be offered in return for concessions conceded by the other side. In India, your first proposal might be received with shock and expressions of impossibility. This is a bargaining tactic. State your proposal again, exactly as it was the first time with no concessions. It is a way of showing you are serious about the business. In some countries, senior business partners may be brought in at a late stage in the negotiation to seal the deal. In this case, it is important to have one or two concessions up your sleeve to offer at this stage. Don't concede all your concessions too soon.

Positions vs interests

Fisher and Ury in *Getting to Yes* emphasise the importance of going beyond positions (what people say they want) and focusing on interests (what people really want). This, they believe, is the only true basis for concessions. How do you do this in an international negotiation? The answer is to show interest and explore. The time to do this is in the downtime periods in between the round-the-table negotiations. Show interest in the company, their market and find out what's important to them – economically but also socially. This may reveal to you why they are interested in negotiating with you. It will also give you a clue as to what may be appropriate concessions. As Fisher and Ury say, go beyond the position and get to the real interests.

Salami tactics

It's a bit obvious to expect Italians to use salami tactics, but they do. Salami tactics is a bargaining tool used to reduce price 'slice by slice' by examining every aspect of the deal in detail and making proposals to cut costs. Antonio was a charming and generous host and an ace salami negotiator. He tested every aspect of our proposal and succeeded in obtaining concessions to thin our profit margins until we were barely above cost plus. Lunch was good though!

Fair-price and low-price markets

Germany and the Nordic countries have a concept of 'fair price'. They know what a product is worth and are prepared to pay the price. The area for negotiation is in the profit margin and the service quality. A Danish negotiator might calculate the price of the product or service and place a modest mark-up to cover service quality and profit margin. This means their margin for negotiation may be quite limited. They often criticise British and American negotiators who place too high a margin on their products, but anticipate making large concessions during the negotiation. Americans and Indians often operate a low-price market strategy. Their basic package is reasonably economical, but their add-ons come at a much higher price.

The lesson: different markets have different ways of dealing with prices, margins and above all, concessions. Research the market style. You may not come across it on every deal but forewarned is forearmed.

Walk-aways

When do you walk away from a deal? When the price is too high? Our old friends quality, price and time of delivery all come into play, but in some countries 'face' and personal dignity can play a part.

You hurt my pride

In Russia we were negotiating a deal. The negotiation was long and detailed and the atmosphere quite tense. At a particular point, the Russian negotiator quite simply stopped the negotiation and left the meeting and didn't come back. He was clearly offended. Someone had said something that upset him personally and he simply walked away.

Hard on the problem, soft on the person

This aspect of walk-aways illustrates Fisher and Ury's dictum, 'Be hard on the problem, soft on the person.' Culturally, it is not always obvious where to draw the line between hard negotiating and personal antagonism or insult.

Finalisation

The spirit not the letter is what matters. The negotiation is over. The points are agreed. The contract is signed. It's all over, isn't it? No. Different markets have different views of contracts. In the US and in the Anglo world in general, a contract is a contract. When it is signed, people do not expect to change it. However, in Asia, a contract is the beginning of a relationship. If circumstances change or new conditions arise, they expect to be able to renegotiate. One American negotiator complained that her Chinese counterpart had come up with new proposals 'before the ink on the signatures was dry'!

The point is that as long as the sprit of the agreement is unchanged, the details are always subject to renegotiation. Asians often don't understand Western reluctance to review contractual details in the light of changing circumstances.

The Italian job

One Italian company had the right attitude. They were part of a three-way deal between themselves, the UK and Taiwan. The UK arm had made a mistake in the contract and needed to draft an appendix to rectify it. The Italian flexibility was admirable. 'As long as I have a contract, I'm happy,' said the director. 'Get a new contract agreed with Taiwan and we'll tear up the old one.' Problem solved. Not sure it would have been so easy in the US.

Lesson: many countries see the signed contract as the start of a relationship, not just the condition of a deal. Therefore they may propose amendments. Don't be closed to this process on principle. Treat each amendment proposed on its merits. It may turn out to your advantage.

Conclusion

In global business, different markets approach negotiation and contracts from different points of view and in different ways. When preparing your position prior to negotiation, make a point of checking the possible cultural issues that might be raised. Brief your team as part of your negotiation strategy and be ready to deal with differences if they arise.

Five things to remember

1. Negotiators from different countries approach a negotiation from different points of view. One size *doesn't* fit all.

2. Remember Fisher and Ury's Harvard System of Negotiation (in Chapter 6) as a basic framework, especially 'interests not positions' and 'hard on the problem, soft on the person'.

3. Research the key pitfalls to avoid in international negotiation.

4. Learn the five stages of negotiation.

5. Remember the international differences in ways of viewing and making concessions.

Chapter 7
What not to do and what not to say

They say that an unguarded remark by the French President Jacques Chirac in Estonia might have cost Paris the chance to stage the Olympic Games in 2012. On a trip to Tallinn in early 2005, Chirac mentioned to a colleague that it would be ridiculous if London were entrusted with the games. How could anyone trust a country with such bad food, he allegedly said? Indeed, the only country with worse food in Europe, he added, was Finland!

Apparently the remark was picked up by two Finns who happened to be members of the International Olympic Committee which selects the Olympic city. Hey presto! London beat Paris by four votes!

The story, like all the best stories, is apocryphal but it makes the point. Never criticise another culture. Have you ever put your foot in it? Ever said or done something so stupid you are embarrassed to think about it even now? Of course you have – we all have. So this chapter looks at key areas where things can go wrong, and indicates areas where a little cultural due diligence can be useful.

In business there are three areas which tend to cause trouble:

- Greeting and leave-taking
- Gift-giving
- Hospitality

But that's only part of it. As we said earlier in the book, mistakes in etiquette won't kill a deal, but it's worth trying to avoid them.

Formality and informality

How you greet people is mainly a question of formality or informality. In some ways, the world's business cultures are getting more informal. This is partly a result of US influence and also partly the fact that informality is faster. It saves time.

Nevertheless there are a number of things you need to pay attention to.

In Germany, make sure you retain a degree of formality. Don't go to first names until you are invited. Among more senior executives the academic title of doctor (if an individual has a university doctorate) may be appropriate. In German meetings we have heard German managers address American and British colleagues by their first names, but immediately switch to surnames with German colleagues.

In France, although first names may be accepted with foreigners, the French themselves like a bit of formality and therefore the use of *Monsieur* and *Madame* are important. A double standard often operates in Italy. The surname and title may be used in the office but the first name may be used at home. In China and Japan, the business card is always presented, usually with a slight bow and with both hands. The card is studied and placed on the table or in a card holder. It is never put in a pocket and no one writes on it. That would show disrespect to you and to your company. The Americans and British tend to distribute cards as a means of follow-up contact. The cards have no intrinsic value in themselves, which is why they are distributed around the table like poker cards or left for people to pick up if they wish.

Another feature that people agonise over is whether to kiss, bow or shake hands on greeting. Handshaking on meeting and departure is common worldwide, although the Americans and British may just wave. The French and Germans, however, feel that physical contact provides a good positive start to any day. Where men in particular have to be careful is in offering to shake hands with women in the Middle East or on the Indian subcontinent. In the Muslim world, women should have no physical contact with men outside their family. In India some women, and men, are more used to the *namaste* greeting than to shaking hands. *Namaste* is the raising of both hands joined in prayer to the forehead, accompanied by a slight bow of the head.

The best thing to do if you're not sure (and most of the time you aren't) is to wait and see what the woman does. If you are a Western woman, the same touch taboo obviously does not apply, although in some cases the people you meet may be unfamiliar with Western handshakes. Getting the greeting right is a matter of etiquette. If you don't know, ask.

You can do the same with names. Never assume that the person you are talking to has the same degree of informality as you. Barry spent an evening calling a senior African diplomat by his first name and was surprised when the diplomat in question showed no interest in anything but the most perfunctory contact. Barry had shown disrespect, and hadn't noticed he was doing so.

But the reason why he had used the first name is also interesting. He had assumed a professional similarity which allowed a degree of familiarity, but clearly the other side did not agree.

The lesson is always to ask, 'How should I address you?' in order to check what the person you are dealing with expects. If they say, 'Just call me Tony,' then you know you can proceed with confidence.

Gift-giving

Barry once received the same present from a Japanese client that he had given to the Japanese the year before on a previous visit. How come? The Japanese had never opened it. Why not? You don't open gifts in front of the giver, because to do so might risk offending them or causing you to lose face if it's not liked. So it goes into a cupboard with all the other gifts. No insult intended. Just the way it is.

Gift-giving is a minefield: what to give, how much to spend, and how to present it varies across communities. In Japan, the wrapping is as important as the gift, so get your present gift-wrapped in the hotel boutique. In China, red is lucky so try to use red wrapping paper.

What you give can also cause problems. When United Airlines opened their flights from Hong Kong to Osaka they gave every business-class passenger a white carnation. It took a while for the airline to realise why the business-class trade didn't pick up until they discovered the problem. White equals bad luck in Japan: it's the colour of funerals. When United substituted it for a red carnation, business improved.

In China, Japan and Korea the unlucky number is four. So if your correspondent is a keen golfer, a pack of four golf balls is not a good idea.

Two or six is better, or better still eight, which is a lucky number. In Singapore you have to be very careful about giving gifts above a certain value, because corruption laws are strictly upheld. Even flowers can be a problem. Different countries have differing conventions about the number of blooms which are appropriate for gift-giving. Japan and Germany prefer odd numbers, but China and Britain prefer even numbers. No one needs reminding that red roses are the flowers of love and are inappropriate in most business environments.

However, you may need to check that the flowers you want to give are not the flowers associated with funerals.

If you're travelling and want to buy gifts for your clients and business partners, then the airport duty free is not a bad bet. Maria is Bulgarian, resident in the UK, but travels frequently to Russia and Central Europe, areas where presents are expected in business. She reckons to spend about £60 a trip in duty free. What on?

British food and drink are popular, such as shortbread, single-malt whisky and even jams and marmalade. Souvenirs are also popular, especially toys for the children. Confectionery is a popular gift, but don't make the mistake a colleague of ours made in Oman – he chose liqueur chocolates. But Oman is a Muslim emirate and alcohol is forbidden or disapproved of.

Hospitality

The third area of etiquette you have to watch out for is hospitality. First of all, who gives it, what do they give, and who pays? There is a rule of thumb in all countries outside Northern Europe, the US, Canada, Australia and New Zealand that if you are in my country, I pay. If I am in your country, you pay. Going Dutch (everyone paying for themselves) is not what most people do.

What scares people most, according to reports, is the Chinese banquet. This is a two-hour ritual consisting of a large number of different courses. If invited you must never refuse – it would be an insult. It may also be your only chance to get to know your negotiators on the other side personally. So, no matter how you feel, go. The food will be delicious and the drink will flow. Part of the Chinese aim may be to get you drunk. Some people say that's the way they believe they can find out what you are really like. So expect frequent toasts of gambei and frequent refilling of glasses.

A former deputy British ambassador to China gave us a piece of invaluable advice. From time to time, he said, your host will take his chopsticks and place a morsel of food on your plate. 'Try this,' he will say. 'It's a little local delicacy.' Your job is to eat it. It will taste delicious.

'But never,' says the former deputy ambassador, 'ask what it is. If they tell you, you may never be able to swallow it.' Fried sea slugs, anyone?

Now you're ready to leave. Do you make your excuses and get up and go? No, you wait. In due course the host will get up, thank everyone for coming and that's the time to rush to the cloakroom for your coat.

Now you're in Saudi Arabia, where you've been invited to dinner. How will the evening run? Half an hour's chat, one hour at the table to eat and maybe an hour sitting down over coffee? Not so in Saudi, where the custom is to spend an hour and a half in conversation until the meal is served, when the diners fall on it like wolves. Full and happy, you might expect to enjoy coffee and more chat, but you could well find that your fellow guests have gone. Never assume that your own culture's meal and entertainment conventions are shared by others. Do your homework. That's what our cultural briefings are all about.

Remember the advice we gave about taking food with your fingers. Right hand good, left hand bad.

Who pays?

Once a month in Paris, Barry dines with Hamid, an Egyptian client. Every time Barry offers to pay, but Hamid declines. 'I am resident in France,' he says. 'You are a visitor. So you are my guest. When I come to London, you can pay for me.' The Ritz it is, then. However, Julian, another friend, is also a Paris resident but Julian is English by birth and upbringing so when they eat out they always split the bill. Every New Year, Barry's family goes abroad together with his sister-in-law and brother-in-law. When they eat out they always split the bill. The point is that different social groups have different hospitality conventions. In Barry's family they 'go Dutch' (each family pays for itself). With English colleagues, he takes it in turns to pay and with Hamid, Hamid pays in France and Barry will reciprocate when Hamid comes to London.

Most of the world operates on the 'host pays' principle. It is only in the so-called Northwest cluster (UK, Germany,

Netherlands, Scandinavia, US, Canada, Australia and New Zealand) that 'going Dutch' is honoured. However, the principle of reciprocation of hospitality is important. First, if I accept your hospitality as a client or business partner, am I putting myself in your debt? Secondly, if I wish to reciprocate your hospitality, how can I do so? It is important to reciprocate hospitality if you can, but in a foreign city it is not always easy to arrange. How do I know where to go? How do I know what to do? Here are a couple of suggestions.

If you are staying at a good hotel, check out the hotel's best restaurant. Is it the kind of place that non-residents frequent? If you host a dinner at your hotel you are to some extent *chez vous*. In India and China particularly, five-star hotel restaurants are very popular. Alternatively, ask your host to recommend a venue. That way you can be sure it will be somewhere he or she likes and feels comfortable in. A third option is to ask the concierge for a recommendation. He or she will make the reservation and make sure you get special guest treatment, which will impress your host.

While we are on hospitality, don't forget diet. We invited three Indian colleagues to dine in a five-star hotel in Mumbai. One was Hindu, one Muslim and one Jain (a Hindu sect devoted to nature). Luckily, the hotel knew that the Muslim wouldn't touch pork, the Hindu would avoid beef and the Jain was vegetarian (maybe even vegan). The hotel was able to cope, but could a restaurant in London or Paris handle those demands?

As far as alcohol goes, many Muslims don't mind if you drink in their presence, but if they are not drinking it is a courtesy to do the same. Thanks to Hamid, a devout Muslim, Barry became addicted to Orangina.

Entertaining at home

To be invited to someone's home is a rare privilege. But once again it has its pitfalls. What do you take? Wine? Flowers? Chocolates? Food? In Spain, France or Italy, don't take wine unless it is of very high quality, because it could imply that you don't trust your host's taste in wine. In Britain if you don't take wine, don't go. In Russia, don't take vodka: most people in Moscow or St Petersburg drink wine nowadays, if they drink alcohol at all.

Should you take flowers? Apart from the colour and number, do you wrap them or unwrap them before giving them to your host or hostess? In Germany it is customary to unwrap flowers before handing them over. Professor Dr Schmidt came to our university party to say farewell to the department secretary. It was a hot day, and he unwrapped the flowers before he arrived. By the time he handed them over, they looked as if he had stolen them from someone's front garden!

A word about superstition

You have probably noticed that we have started referring to superstition – irrational (in some people's eyes) beliefs that influence behaviour. Unlucky colours and unlucky numbers have already featured. The number four is unlucky in Japan and, in China, red is lucky for example. In Germany, flowers are unwrapped and offered inside or outside the house, but never over the threshold. In the UK, the US and other countries, 13 is unlucky and black cats are either lucky or unlucky, depending on where you are.

What most Westerners don't realise is the impact that superstition can have on business. Try getting an 'eight' telephone number or car registration in China: hard work. Try getting one with the number four: piece of cake! Is your company name an upper or a downer? You might want to rethink titles such as T4Training or Food4Thought. Mind you, I8u, ('I hate you') may not help much either.

Chinese business cards will often be printed in red with gold embossed writing, for maximum luck.

If you're married, think about the time that you got married and when the reception took place, and compare it with the following example of a Punjabi wedding in Delhi that we were invited to. Hundreds of people enjoyed wonderful buffet food, and there was an arbour garlanded with flowers where the wedding ceremony would take place. But when? The celebration went on and on, with the happy couple sitting on a throne in chairs and guests going up and greeting them. They finally had the wedding ceremony at 3am, by which time everyone except the immediate family had gone home. Why so late? The presiding 'priest' had determined that that was the most auspicious astrological time for the ceremony.

Never underestimate the power of astrology in business, especially in Asia. Contracts are signed, and travel undertaken, on auspicious days. If the time isn't auspicious, the journey or the contract signing may be postponed. As with dates, so with buildings.

Feng shui in China is the science of geomancy, and it determines if a building is deemed lucky or not. A feng shui expert is employed to tour any new or official building, sense the energy flows and recommend ways to improve it.

For example, a large window may be a source of outflow for money. To prevent it, put a bar across the window or at least a plant in front of it to keep the money inside the organisation. That's what they did with the Jardine Matheson building in Hong Kong: the bar disfigured a beautiful round window, but supposedly protected the company from losing money.

If something happens that you don't understand, think whether luck and astrology could provide the reason. This may not be part of your everyday decision-making, at least in theWest, but it could be important elsewhere, especially in Asia.

What not to say

All the experts agree that there is one key to successful talking – listening! Listen to what the other person is saying and focus on what they are feeling. The process is called active listening and you can do courses on it. As Minna, a Moroccan executive said, 'People hear my thoughts but they don't hear my feelings.' 'Hearing feelings' is what active listening is about. The problem is that it takes time. Do I really want to listen to a long explanation or story that is not relevant to my needs? What's the pay-off?

The payoff is that you are showing interest, and that is half the battle of meeting expectations in a relationship-oriented market. People need to feel you understand them, and that you appreciate their position and their problems. Active listening is the surest way of demonstrating to your business partners that you do. Don't see listening as a waste of time. See it as an investment in the business relationship.

Ice-breakers and ice-makers

Are you like us? There's one thing we are all interested in when we go abroad – scandal. What we want to know is what the locals think about – who, what, where, why and how. Unfortunately, those are precisely the topics that cause embarrassment and pain and which may leave a nasty taste in the mouth of your colleagues and business partners if you insist on talking about them.

You may remember some years ago how Dominique Strauss Kahn, former head of the International Monetary Fund and pretender to the French presidency, was undone by an alleged sex scandal in New York. As a result he had to withdraw from the IMF and also from his presidential ambitions. As with all such scandals it became a major international talking point, and arriving in Paris it was natural to mention it. But not to people who, as it turned out, knew Strauss Kahn personally. Be careful. Be diplomatic.

Germans can't understand why the British still like to talk about the Second World War and Germany's role in it. They find it embarrassing and irritating, especially since most of them weren't even born when it happened. The Chinese are embarrassed by the three T's – Tibet, Taiwan (Greater China) and Tiananmen Square (the harsh putting down of a student demonstration in Beijing in 1989). Indians are embarrassed by constant talk about poverty in their country (they don't know what to do about it either). Russians know what is wrong with Russia, but they will fiercely defend their country if outsiders criticise it.

The topics you *can* talk about are ice-breakers – general business, sport, weather, national achievements and national sights of interest. The ones you need to be careful of are ice-makers –

subjects which will freeze the conversation and chill the relationship.

A common subject of conversation is the family: 'How many children have you got? How old are they? What are they doing?' But this is not appropriate in China, where Premier Deng Xiaoping introduced the one-child policy in 1979 to limit population growth (China has the largest population in the world, with approximately 1.3 billion people). Families with more than one child could be fined and even jailed, and the results were, as you might expect, good and bad. There was population control but the result was also a generation of spoiled 'little emperors', a lack of girl children and a great deal of parental pain and anguish. Nowadays, with China's growing prosperity, the rules have relaxed somewhat, but young men in the provinces are still finding a lack of women to marry. So think twice before you ask your Chinese colleague, 'And how many children do you have?' The answer will be just one, but behind that answer may be immense pain and anguish.

In the Middle East a different problem may arise. In the Muslim world, women are required to lead private lives. It is considered impolite and an expression of inappropriate interest to ask after someone's wife if you are a man. This may be the case even if you have met the man with his wife in London or New York. In Riyadh (Saudi Arabia) or Doha (Qatar), a man's wife may not be an appropriate topic of polite enquiry by a man, although a woman will have no problems.

Cultural fault lines

It is clearly useful to know where to look for topic areas that might be sensitive in another culture. A first step is to identify the areas of sensitivity in your own culture. To borrow a phrase from John Cleese's immortal comedy series, *Fawlty Towers,* what are the 'Don't mention the war' zones in your culture? If you can identify those, it will give you some ideas of possible areas of sensitivity in other cultures.

In geology, fault lines are the weaknesses in tectonic plates that form the Earth's crust and whose movements cause earthquakes and tsunamis. We have used the term cultural fault lines to describe areas of sensitivity that cause tension between communities. Broadly, we can divide these into six categories:

1. Linguistic

The writer George Bernard Shaw described Britain and America as separated by a common language. However, language differences can cause immense social tensions. The use of French in Belgium is one example. Belgium comprises two communities – the French-speaking Walloons and the Dutch - or Flemish - speaking Flemings. The two communities experience considerable tensions and although Belgium is officially a bilingual nation, Flemings respond badly to people who only speak French and vice versa. For two years, the two communities were unable to form a government – and this in a nation at the centre of the European Union.

2. National

The UK is made up of four nationalities plus members of immigrant communities. The largest are the English (who tend to call themselves British, except during national football and rugby matches). But beware of assuming that Scots, Welsh and Northern Irish are all happy to be called British – and certainly never call them English. They are defiantly nationalist, culturally if not politically, and outsiders need to be aware of this.

Check – are you calling Canadians Americans rather than North Americans? Make sure you get your political identities right. If unsure, ask, don't assume.

3. Religious

In 2013 as the world lifted its embargoes on Myanmar (Burma) in recognition of its moves towards democracy, news was released of Buddhists fighting Muslims and even a Buddhist monk taking part in the violence. Buddhists tend to be considered non-violent, and this made the news even more shocking. In Northern Ireland, Protestants and Roman Catholics are still suspicious of each other after years of violent conflict. In Palestine relations between the Jews of Israel and the Palestinians of Gaza are tense. Even in Islam itself, the centuries-old rift between Sunni and Shi'a sects continues, and in China the religious Falun Gong is an outlawed sect. Studying which region espouses which religion or which sect is essential to avoiding pitfalls.

4. Discrimination

Despite a generation of equality there is still discrimination between races in many countries, and this can cause immense sensitivity. You still need to be especially sensitive to racial differences in countries with a colonial background or in the USA.

Sexual discrimination, and especially discrimination on grounds of sexual orientation, is a live issue in many countries and is maybe not something to be discussed until you know the people you are dealing with well. It's also important to be aware that standards of talking to people, badinage between the sexes, for example, may differ between countries. What is acceptable in your country may not be acceptable in mine. It may be necessary to bite your tongue until you know the people well enough to point out the difference. Remember that social and political questions such as legislation on gay marriage are intensely live issues. Be careful about sharing your views until you know the context is right.

5. Rich and poor

In Italy the area south of Rome down to Naples is labelled the Mezzogiorno (half day) state. Why? Traditionally, it is the poorest region of Italy, the part that needed the most state help and which spawned the Mafia. By contrast, certain elements in the more prosperous north have expressed a wish to secede.

In class-conscious Britain, the older industrial north considers itself poorer than the rich south, where services and light engineering support the economy. A traditional rivalry exists between the two. In Germany, the richest state in the European Union, the former eastern states still feel themselves to be at a disadvantage compared to the richer west, a quarter of a century after German reunification. So if I am dealing with a particular market, I will want to be sensitive to the perceived wealth differences between different regions.

6. Historical

Finally, history. It is too easy to praise a country you like and to ignore its rivalry with the country of the people you are selling to. It's equally easy to criticise a country you don't like and then realise it's your client's greatest ally. Brazil is Portuguese speaking but is now the dominant partner between the two countries and the leading Portuguese-speaking nation. Brazilians don't react well when you stress their historical and colonial links with Portugal.

How do you find out this essential historical information? Read a brief history of the country or go to the overview and expectations sections of the country briefings in this book. Economic indicators are a guide to performance, but historical indicators are a reliable guide to cultural expectations and opinions. The best international managers are often good students of history as well as students of management and balance sheets.

Summary – what not to say

Politics, money, religion, race and sex are subjects to be treated with care. Your sensitivity and tact will reap its rewards.

Five things to remember

1. Pay attention to local conventions regarding greetings and leave-taking, gift-giving and hospitality.

2. In the case of hospitality, be aware of the conventions regarding who pays for what. Try and find ways of reciprocating when you can.

3. Note that in some countries superstition may play a part in decision-making, even in business.

4. Be careful about broaching sensitive topics with people you don't know. Take time if you can to read a history of

the country you are visiting. It will alert you to some of the areas of sensitivity.

5. Be especially sensitive regarding possible cultural fault lines. If in doubt, ask.

Chapter 8
Working in international teams

What is a team? A group of people working together or playing together to get something done. The key word is together. It's hard enough to get a team playing together when they are all from the same place. What is it like when they are from different countries? This chapter looks at three types of international team:

- The multinational team in-country
- The multinational team spread across countries
- The VDT (virtual distributed team)

All have similarities. They all have foreigners from different cultural backgrounds working together, but how they work together can be very different. We need to look at five key variables.

1. What are the team selection criteria?
2. Who leads the team?
3. What are the team working methods?
4. How are team decisions made?
5. How does the team produce results?

'Team think' or 'me think'?

Obviously 'team think' or 'me think' varies according to your background, education and professional experience. There will also be situations where you think 'team first' and others where you think 'me first'. However, if you work internationally you need to be aware that some parts of the world identify 'team think' as a virtue and others consider that 'me think' is the right approach.

Consider Japan as an example. For a Japanese worker a key word is *wa*. *Wa* means harmony. It means being at one with nature and with others. Above all, it means, for those who are inside the group but not outside it, resolving issues by a process of collective agreement. A Japanese team takes decisions together. Everyone is consulted. Everyone contributes. The process of consultation is important. It is called *nemawashi*, literally, 'binding the roots of the rice to make it stronger'. Everyone then signs off on the agreed result. That is called *ringi-sho*. The Japanese believe that it takes longer to agree, but once everyone is on the same page you move forward faster. Even if the decision is influenced and communicated by a senior manager, the internal communication process is important.

Team players or family players?

A philosophical and business principle also becomes a principle in daily working life. A Japanese team will often go out together at the end of the working day to a coffee shop or bar, or to a karaoke session. In Japan it feels like company or team first, family second.

In the UK or US, by contrast, it is the other way round – family first and team second. The principle of consultation is still important but the individual chooses to belong to the team. He or she may be totally committed to the team but it is a personal choice, and not part of the company or country ethos.

This is why many Japanese executives, among themselves, criticise their British and US colleagues as 'bad team players'. They are not automatically available to the team. The important word is automatically. One way to partially resolve the situation is to consciously make yourself available to go out with the team, say once a week. In a very short time, you will find the criticism withdrawn, and you'll win the accolade of being considered a good team player. In all kinds of ways, a Japanese worker will put the team needs ahead of his or her own, while the British or US worker will work for the team as long as it fulfils his or her own needs and aspirations.

Fusion projects – the inclusive team

Jeanne Brett, of the Kellogg School of Management at Northwestern University in the USA, explains that most multicultural teams are dominated by one or two nationalities She tells the story of an American military officer assigned to lead a team that had to exhume mass graves after the Bosnian war. The team consisted of American, Russian, German and Turkish officers under UN command. At the start of the project, the Americans acted as if they knew it all, the Germans and Russians didn't get on, and no one paid attention to the Turks. As a result the project ground to a standstill.

To revive the situation, the leader divided the work into subtasks and put a four-person group in charge of each one. The four-person group each consisted of an American, a German, a Russian and a Turk. The American leader discovered that communication became much easier in the sub-groups. He also discovered that the Turks knew more about exhumation than many of the others, because they had worked to dig out earthquake victims in Turkey. He also found that because there was trust in the small groups, cooperation and communication was better in the large group meetings.

Jeanne Brett calls such a way of working a fusion team. She says that people involved in fusion teams often develop more novel and practical solutions than in teams dominated by one or two sub-groups. She also notices that someone in the team usually has a sense of possible cultural differences and how to harmonise them. If in doubt, she says, over-communicate, don't under-communicate. She also points out that fusion in the wrong environment can turn into confusion. It's important to remember, she says, that a fusion solution that works for one team won't work for all groups at all times. Learn to adapt and be flexible for best results.

Forming, storming, norming and performing

All teams go through a process of forming (getting together), storming (finding out how to work together), norming (establishing procedures for smooth communication) and performing (getting the job done). If the team doesn't norm, how can it perform? One problem in multinational teams is often the group's working language, which is often English. This usually puts the native speakers at an advantage over the non-native speakers – particularly when team members complain about each other's accents. An Indian team leader saw this as a 'storming' problem right from the start. Here's how he set about 'norming' it.

The team leader and other members of the group had quite a strong accent, so at his first meeting the team leader established a norm for communication. 'You can hear, I have an accent,' he said, 'but we have to communicate. So whatever our problems we will communicate until we understand. And if you have any problems, never hesitate to say so. We'll keep going until we understand each other. OK?' Establishing the norm by talking about his own possible communication difficulties, he put everyone else at their ease. Identify the potential communication problems and set the norm as early as possible.

You say tomato and I say tomato

One of the key aspects of 'norming' is making sure the team all understand the same thing by the same words. Experienced team leaders will always give the same advice: check that everyone has a common understanding of concepts such as milestones, specifications, budgets and deadlines. These are pretty concrete terms with clear explanations. However, there are also qualitative words, a good example being initiative.

In the Northwest cluster, initiative is a virtue. It can mean being the first to initiate something, break a logjam or find a new solution. However, in more consciously team-minded communities, initiative can consist of advice.

Initiative can be seen as synonymous with dominance, aggressiveness and even imperialism. Taking initiative in Northwest cluster countries may mean introducing a new idea, but adopting the initiative in an Asian environment may mean improving an existing idea or achieving a new consensus through discussion. Failure to recognise and clarify the difference between quantitative and qualitative terms at the beginning of a project can lead to team misunderstanding.

A Dutch team leader in an international project repeatedly took the initiative, proposing ideas and taking first steps. She always said, quite correctly, that her initiatives were subject to agreement by the team. But her team colleagues didn't see this as initiative: they saw it as dominance. In their view she should have consulted first, then put the idea forward as a joint initiative. Only then would they have felt more confident as a team. In some cases they even called her approach immature. For her, she was doing what comes naturally. The Dutch, after all, make decisions in committee. But she adopted the Western process of 'raise issue, propose, discuss.' For her colleagues it was more important to raise the issue, discuss it, and then allow a proposal to arise out of the discussion. That process made them feel more secure and together as a team.

In the end, the team leader, frustrated by the lack of agreement with the initiatives, withdrew from the group and the funding she led collapsed. Ultimately, the problem was not initiative but one of style. If she had understood what taking initiative meant for the group and how they should be handled, she would have achieved much better results and perhaps the project might have been saved.

The lesson is, at the first team meeting, discuss and agree the terms you use, and encourage a climate of checking and clearing definitions. The growth in understanding and confidence will improve international team productivity, even if the process takes a little longer in the early stages. Allow for it in your planning.

Individualism vs collectivism

Anyone working in international teams has to recognise that these two attitudes are deeply rooted in different communities. In the UK and the US my ability to think out of the box, push myself forward, display innovative thinking and initiative gets me a better position in my company, more cash, a better house and a bigger car. In Japan, my loyalty to the company comes first. I will get more money, buy my house and change my car for a new model, but I will do it through hard work and loyalty to my team.

In teams it is vital to understand the difference as one of process. It is all too easy to stamp an individualist as selfish and a team person as lacking in get- up-and-go. Appreciate where people are coming from and you will find they will move in your direction, as long as you are prepared to move in theirs.

Two of the world's oldest and most highly respected companies, one British and one Japanese, were collaborating on a major aeronautical engineering contract. Both were renowned for quality engineering and high standards. For the British, team-working, checking and counter-checking each component made their production process stately. The Japanese should have been the same but were, in fact, much faster on their feet. We discovered that their previous collaboration had been with a US engineering giant. As a result, they had learned to speed up their quality control processes and behaved in a much more individualistic fashion, whereas their British counterparts were following a much more collectivist procedure.

The lesson is, when you are working with an international team it is important to give time early on in the project to discuss attitudes to team-working, as well as an understanding of key principles and concepts. As we have demonstrated, these are not things we can take for granted.

Team integration and team alienation

A particular problem in teams is integrating new members. In our experience, there are two types of teams, permanent and temporary. Permanent teams stay together and work as part of a department or a project. They may lose members on the periphery or gain temporary attachees, but the core group stays together, and shares common values, working patterns and procedures. They also build considerable group and personal knowledge and loyalty to other team members. This is especially important in crisis teams concerned with lifesaving, crime prevention or military manoeuvres. How the new member fits in is often the plot of TV dramas.

We have to recognise, however, that in an international organisation, a tight permanent team is rare, especially in project management, where resource allocation, as it is called, may be on a temporary basis. People may be drafted onto a project for a number of man-days separated over the life of the project. Some of them may come from abroad.

The first thing we notice is how people from group-minded cultures can feel very alienated when they are part of a project run by international companies in the UK or US. One Persian engineer told us how she cried every night because she felt so lonely. 'I'm used to being in touch with my cousins every day in Tehran,' she said. 'Every Saturday we have lunch with my father in Tehran. In London I totally miss that and Skype and email, even running up a huge phone bill, can't replace the personal contact.'

However, we also discovered the opposite. In Colombia we were welcomed by our colleagues and absorbed into their families. We were invited to parties, barbecues, picnics, meals out and family outings. We were never alone. But after the initial euphoria, we realised that we needed more of our own personal space. As, allegedly, the film star Greta Garbo cried, 'I want to be alone!'

Loneliness is alienating. Company can be suffocating. What is important is to make sure your foreign team members feel included, that they have someone to talk to and that they are involved functionally and socially to the degree they want to be.

Forming a new team

The team was disgusted. Gianni had no qualifications, no experience to speak of, he was middle-aged and a senior manager, but not on the board of directors. What was he doing there? The answer was loyalty. He had known and worked with the team leader for years and could be relied on. He was, in short, a good guy to have around. Many teams have members like that. You can rely on them to get things done and support the team leader when things get rough. They are fixers.

However, not all teams are composed like that, and it is important to understand the national criteria which are often used in making up international teams. Imagine a project where each national participant must contribute a team member. How will each country make its selection? One country might choose a person with the right level of qualifications. Another might choose the most senior manager available, or the manager who has been longest with the company. Another might rely on a team member with the most practical experience of the area covered by the project. Another might select a fixer, a person who has no seniority, qualifications, or specialist expertise but is good at getting things done.

Now imagine the advantages and disadvantages of each team member.

The qualified person may have little or no experience: lots of theory but little practice. On the plus side, he or she will be able to add theoretical weight to the discussion.

The senior person may not know much about the project area but will have influence where it counts with project stakeholders and budget holders.

The longest-serving member may also have influence with stakeholders. The team member with practical experience will be good at hands-on practical aspects but less patient with stakeholders and budget controllers. The fixer may be a generalist, but skilled at finding solutions to enable the team to complete the project on time, on budget and to specification.

When 'storming' conflicts arise, they often occur between different levels of seniority and different levels of specialisation – specialists versus generalists, if you like. As a member of an international team, what do you need to do?

Here are the four essential things to remember:

1. Recognise

Recognise the different reasons why team members have been selected.

2. Study

Study the position of each team member in their own department or organisation. Talk to them outside team meetings. This will give you an opportunity to find out discreetly why they are on the project and what is their area of expertise and potential contribution.

3. Value

Next, focus on the added value they bring to the table. It is all too easy to focus on their perceived weaknesses – focus on their potential contribution instead.

4. Space

Remember different team members may make their greatest contributions at different stages of a project. It is important early on to recognise this and be prepared to give space to people to make their unique contributions. It's also important not to push team members to contribute before they feel ready to do so.

Who's running the team?

Here is another problem. Who takes over as team leader? Is it the senior person present, the longest-serving member, the one with a doctorate, the practical specialist with field experience or the guy who is good at running meetings and getting results?

An Anglo-Italian project replaced the senior Italian team leader with a young but highly qualified Cambridge university graduate, identified as a rising star in the company. Most of the project meetings took place in Italy, but the British team began to notice a problem. Italian team members were 'not available', team meeting rooms were not booked until it was too late, agendas were drawn up but not distributed and minutes were not circulated. The Italian team members were polite and courteous, but there was no cooperation and no work. When the British managers asked for explanations, they were told the young Cambridge graduate had not given enough notice, not provided enough detail or communicated clearly enough with his Italian counterparts. None of this was true.

Finally, the British managers were left with no alternative. They made the Italian senior manager redundant with a large payoff and appointed a junior Italian manager to the vacant team position. They had lost time, money and a useful and experienced management resource.

What had gone wrong, and how could the situation have been saved? First, it was important to recognise that the British management's action had caused enormous loss of face for the Italian. This had dissolved any sense of team loyalty and led to passive sabotage of the project on the Italian side. However, the British management could have maintained the Italian as nominal team leader and appointed the young British manager as his deputy. This would be entirely reasonable in a joint team. The deputy could then use his expertise to the full with the Italian team leader acting as mentor and guide. In this way, the experience of both managers might have been used successfully to optimise team results.

The lesson is this. In deciding team leadership, seniority and experience and qualifications often come into conflict. It is important not just to choose the most effective team leader, but also to ensure relations within the team show respect for senior members, for example, as advisers or senior consultants. This is especially important in India and the Far East, where issues of saving and losing face, or personal dignity, are especially important.

Team process

How do teams work together? In particular, what is the relationship between working on your own and working through team meetings? An example involving German and US teams is interesting here. The Germans were enormously frustrated. 'These Americans are always talking,' they complained to us. 'We just want to get on with our work, but they keep wanting to hold these long meetings. Why do they do it?'

The answer, we replied, was different working methods. The US likes to research and gather data and then to discuss with partners how best to achieve and implement results. The Germans like to discuss the issues and problems arising and then, when consensus is achieved, go off and do the job, each assigned to his or her own area of responsibility. It was simply a problem of process. For the US it was important to study first and speak afterwards. For the Germans it was important to discuss first and work afterwards. The problem is the differences in working practice made each side unavailable to the other when they were needed.

The lesson? At the beginning of any team, ask your colleagues how they prefer to work. Consider the team project as having three stages: plan, build and run. You need to know:

- When they need to discuss with their colleagues

- When they need to work on their own or in sub-groups

- How long before deadlines they need to receive project information and documents, or indeed, projects

It may be that they, and you, have never considered these as issues before. If not, this is a good time to start.

Now here is another problem. A British team leader needed work done to a deadline, and asked his Norwegian colleague, an IT specialist, when he could deliver. The Norwegian replied that he would be on vacation for six weeks and could only start work after that. The project leader was horrified – the delay would put the project back by a month. He had assumed, wrongly, that he would receive immediate availability. The lesson? Check for national and regional holidays and team members' vacation arrangements when you start.

The overall problem in international teams is resource availability. As we can see, you need to check for each team member:

- When they are available and for how long

- What their holidays are (both national, regional and personal)

- What their personal work style preferences are

Team decisions

Who takes decisions and how? The key issues in team decision-making are leadership and consultation, and risk-taking and risk-embracing team members. Let's take each in turn.

Leadership and consultation

There are three modes of team decision:

TOP DOWN	CONSULTATION	GROUP

As we saw in Chapter 6, in many countries the management system is top down: the decision is taken by the team leader. In many countries, top-down decisions are taken with or without consultation. If they are taken after consultation, the question is, with whom do they consult? Is it the stakeholders, who may be outside the project? Is it their own national colleagues, some of whom may be within the team and some outside it? Or is it with the team as a whole? The latter arrangement is rare.

At the other extreme we have group consultation, à la Japanese. The problem with group consultation vs group decision-making is that each nationality tends to fall back first of all on its own way of doing things, and only reconsiders when brought up short by complaints or non-cooperation from others in the team. It is important to ask how decisions are usually taken and communicated in team members' own countries, and not to take the decision- making process for granted. Failure to do this properly will mean that decisions are taken, team members will feel they haven't been consulted, and team morale will dive. Nothing demotivates team members more than the feeling that they are being left out of the decision-making loop and that their feelings and needs are not taken into account.

Risk-embracing or risk-averse

The other area of difficulty in team decision-making is the willingness to take a risk, or avoid risks at all costs. To some extent, this varies according to the type and complexity of the project. Teams who calculate risks but are prepared to take them are very different from those who insist on playing by the book. Once again, behaviour is partly conditioned by national preferences, and is known as the degree of uncertainty avoidance. High uncertainty-avoidance countries, such as Japan, will insist on far more checks and levels of sign-off, and will take longer to reach a decision. This may impact delivery and will certainly make it more difficult to resolve problems in an emergency. On the other hand, creating a no-surprises culture and proper long-term contingency planning may mean that last-minute problems are avoided.

Risk-embracing cultures (for example, Italy, Israel and India) are much more adept at responding rapidly to crises and dealing with them successfully. On the other side, they are much more impatient with drawn-out planning and lengthy consideration, and need quick results. The two sides often conflict.

How does the team produce results?

The key issue here is sensitivity to time and quality. For the Germans, everything needs to be complete at the agreed delivery time. For other nationalities, deadlines may be partially delayed or even ignored completely. Within limits, the US can handle delays but needs advance information. In international IT projects, teams may deliver months after deadline and actually factor the penalties for late delivery into their costings.

The one factor that mitigates delay in Germany is quality. If there is a need to improve or optimise quality in delivery of the final project, then a negotiated delay in delivery may be acceptable without prejudice to the supply team.

What is the solution?

The key to dealing with all these potential problems is to set clear ground rules at the start. When the team has been formed, use the 'storming' stage to investigate preferences regarding ways of working. Make sure you have a clear view of each participating nationality's default style and then examine it in relation to personal and group preferences. At the 'norming' stage, set down clear ground rules with agreed deadlines, working methods and resource availability, and make sure they are accepted by all. Also take the time to ensure that all key terminology and concepts are agreed. This will make the team process smoother and hopefully more effective.

Remote teams and virtual distributed teams

However, there are two factors we still need to take into account: team members operating in different countries, and virtual distributed teams.

Thomas is a senior executive in a German-based international company, who was asked to sort out the US affiliate located in Florida. The problem was that the American division was doing local deals on behalf of the company which were making money and hitting targets, but were not meeting international corporate goals. Thomas's job was to go out to Florida for six months and improve the sales and marketing process.

'How will you do it?' we asked him. 'I will be firm but fair and I will train them,' he replied. As the Americans say, 'No dice!' The American affiliates had no interest in international corporate targets. Thomas could only get them to raise their game by appealing to personal aspirations. Was it a new car they wanted, a yacht to go fishing on the Florida Keys or a new house? To his credit, Thomas accepted our advice, and within a year the American team were top of the sales board. The lesson? If you are dealing with people remotely, recognise that it is difficult to get them to respond to corporate targets. If you can align corporate targets to personal aspirations you will be much more successful. At a distance, motivation needs to be more personal.

Dealing with a leading solicitor's office in London, we were surprised to discover that the manager was based in London but her PA was in Vancouver and her HR training and development manager in Sydney. Phoning them was so clear that it felt like each was in the next room, but in fact they were on different continents.

This kind of remote working is the daily reality for many managers. Their team members may be based in London, Omaha, Mexico City, Delhi and Singapore. Their reporting line is to Frankfurt or Moscow, and their communication is via weekly conference calls supplemented by one-on-one phone calls when necessary. Restricted by travel budgets, management time and security considerations, the team never meets. No one thinks this is a great idea, but it is the new business reality.

In this environment, the problems we discussed about team cohesion and misunderstanding multiply fiftyfold. What advice can we give to team leaders and members to improve communication when they are communicating remotely? Use remote community resources to create a community.

Here are some of the techniques companies employ:

- Use one-to-one phone conversations and Skype and other media to build personal relationships with each member.

- Find out how people prefer to be addressed, what their working day is like, when is the best time to talk, and what communication medium they prefer.

- Create profiles on the company Intranet containing each team member's photo and personally written profile. Include family and personal interests, if team members are happy to do so.

- Set up an internal newsletter on the Intranet to exchange personal news and information. Encourage team members to contribute.

- Create a team mini-website to facilitate the exchange of information. The site could include a team debate. For example, what do we mean by 'initiative' or 'respect'? When, in your language, can we move from the formal *vous* equivalent to the informal *tu*? In this way, remote communication can be turned into an avenue of understanding between team members from different cultures instead of a barrier.

- Use the website to share learning from different work-groups in the team. This will build confidence and trust and recognise talent.

Conclusion

The key is to encourage remote team-working using remote communication tools. Your sincerity and persistence will increase trust and cooperation and help make even a remote international team work together successfully.

Five things to remember

1. Take time to find out the differences between team selection, leadership, management, and decision-making styles and attitudes towards timely delivery.

2. In a multicultural team, understand how different members operate and establish clear ground rules to coordinate action. Make sure there is a common understanding of key concepts, terminology and processes.

3. Learn how to create fusion teams that optimise each team members' strengths.

4. Understand different international attitudes to team leadership – control, facilitate, coordinate.

5. With remote teams, use remote communication resources to build relations and exchange information. Don't limit communication to the weekly or monthly conference call.

Chapter 9
International management styles

The way people manage varies across countries and across different types of organisations. By and large we would like to argue that if you work for a multinational in India it will be much the same as in the USA, but in some ways the experience varies. First, in all but a few cases, the culture of a multinational company reflects the culture of its founder, even where management is localised. Secondly, all companies to some degree reflect the culture and management style of the local environment. Adapt or withdraw seems to be the rule. So if you are managing internationally, how do you adapt your style?

Tool 4: RADAR Management Styles

Let's keep to our mantra. The first thing is to know where to look. Three variables help distinguish management styles. Here they are:

1. Time-tight or time-loose?
2. Top-down or delegation?
3. Working time and downtime

Each of these involves a number of different management styles. In this chapter we'll do three things. First, show how the three cultural management styles above influence business around the world. Secondly, measure your management style and show you how to compare it with others you deal with. Third, and finally, demonstrate how you can adapt your style to get better business results.

Attitudes to time

A British company had an Italian supplier and a Swedish client. The Swedes were calm and organised, reasonable and tolerant. They were also frustrated. The Italians were late. They never replied to emails. They seemed to prefer phoning to writing, so there was no paper trail of the project's progress, and above all they were consistently late on delivery. As the Swedish director said, 'They're lovely people to deal with, but why are they so unpunctual?'

Nothing, it seems, creates more problems than attitudes to time. They affect delivery and supply chain management, and every-day communication. In the USA, the UK or Germany, people expect you to acknowledge emails even if you haven't got the information they requested. In many other countries, people only reply when they have the information.

A well-known industrial psychologist, Edward T Hall, suggested that clashes between 'time-tight' and 'time-loose' managers are one of the biggest sources of cross-border frustration and irritation. Of course, 'time-tight' and 'time-loose' management applies to individuals in all countries as well. Take us for example. We're both British (time relatively tight). One of us works a lot for a German company and is pretty time-tight. The other is a bit time-loose. We're not telling you who. What it means is that one has to 'police' the other and in cross-border business relationships that can cause friction.

We have to understand that time-tight is not automatic. It is to some extent culture-specific.

Respect for age

In many countries in the Far East, but also in Russia and Eastern Europe, respect is paid to older people, as of right. This means that in a reception you might as a guest signal respect to the oldest person in the room first, regardless of their seniority in the hierarchy, although age and seniority often go together. Remembering points like this is an important part of international management skills.

Relationships are built in downtime

After a gruelling day's negotiation with the Chinese company in Chengdu with both sides lined up across the table like opposing regiments, the Chinese chief engineer ended the day with, 'See you at dinner, then.' The British engineer wanted nothing more than to get back to his hotel room and relax in front of the TV with a beer. Had he done so he would have caused his Chinese opposite number to lose face and probably ended the relationship there and then. The meal was the opportunity for the Chinese engineer to reveal his real feelings, and this would very likely show his British counterpart how best to proceed to ensure success. The moral? Never turn down an invitation. It is a prime opportunity to get to know people, let them get to know you and find out how to succeed.

Importance of etiquette

The UK and US and most of the Anglo world operates very informally compared to its Eastern and Southern counterparts.

How you dress, how you behave, how you talk and, above all, how you show respect are very important to creating the right image and making the right impression. It is an aspect that the West and the Anglo world increasingly ignore as irrelevant to the business process. Westerners tend not to put the same weight on business card rituals or seating positions as do their business counterparts in the East. Make no mistake, in the East and South etiquette is still important as an indicator of character and your appropriateness as a potential business partner. Research the key etiquette before you go. Our business style profiles will help you.

Gender inclusiveness

As a female executive you may already feel in a minority, but in some other countries it is even more of a problem. Women are either excluded from the business process or are very rare in senior management positions because of the continuing custom in some cultures of them leaving work after marriage or the birth of children. It is important to recognise, with men from these regions, that what appears as exclusive behaviour or even sexism is often just unfamiliarity with dealing with women in business. One female business executive gave us her three keys to success.

1. LEAD WITH YOUR BUSINESS CARD

Make sure your business card gives you the highest status possible by making clear your title and importance. The card is not just a contact facilitator – it's a statement of your position in your company.

2. BRIEF YOUR TEAM BEFORE THE MEETING

Make sure your team is aware of your position in the delegation. It is important that they treat you as a senior colleague and that this is seen by the other side. Extra care on their part is needed to show your importance.

3. DEFER AND REFER

Make sure that if questions that should be your responsibility to answer are referred to other members of the team, your team colleagues know to refer the questions on to you. None of this means you need to be harsh and strident. It is just taking proper precautions to make sure your position is recognised and respected.

Attitudes towards teams

Speaking of Japan, this is the ultimate team business culture. They have a process called *nemawashi*. Literally, it means 'binding the roots of the rice' to make it stronger. In practice, every member of the management team needs to be consulted and needs to sign off on any proposal, even if the ultimate decision is taken at the top. And there may be not just one committee in a Japanese company – there could be lots of them. 'It's like planes stacking above Frankfurt on a bad day,' one Australian manager working for a major Japanese corporation complained. 'There are committees above committees above committees. In some cases there are internal committees you've never even heard of!'

However, for the Japanese, the *nemawashi* system works. 'It means that when we start we are all on the same page and can move fast,' says one Japanese manager. 'Unlike the Americans,' he adds. 'They take quick decisions but then have to waste time selling it to the team.'

The lesson? Check the team culture and particularly its possible effects on the speed of decision-making.

Time-tight and time-loose

Time-tight means delivering on or before the time stated. Time-loose means being tolerant to various degrees of lateness. This can apply to all aspects of the business from product delivery and project release to payment schedules, and even to how quickly you respond to emails. Multinational corporations tend to run by the clock. How else can you coordinate activities across time zones? However, within countries or bilaterally between individual countries, other considerations come into play. The key is priority.

Priority time vs calendar time

One way of describing time-tight and time-loose societies is to label time-tight societies as ruled by the clock and the calendar. We can call this 'calendar time'. Time-loose societies are ruled by events and personal priorities. We can label this management style 'priority time'. Many nationalities prioritise their time by what's most important to them, not by the clock. Even worse, they feel that it is wrong to end one activity before it is finished just because you have to go somewhere else. This means you will be late for your next appointment – and the one after. It also means that if you are the next appointment, you will have to wait.

A British delegation waited in a North African Minister of Education's ante-room for six hours. Six hours! Maybe this was partly a power play by the minister, but presumably other matters took priority. Finally, they were shown in to see not the minister but his chief of staff. He looked them both in the eye. 'I like you. We will do this,' he said. And that was it. Back in the hotel, the delegation congratulated each other on sealing the deal. Unfortunately, two weeks later the minister and his staff changed and the deal never got signed.

An example of calendar time occurred in Germany. We asked a German manager based in Hamburg what would happen if we were late for a meeting. 'If you were late for our first meeting, I would put it down to cultural differences,' he said. 'If you were late for our second meeting, I would never speak to you again.'

How to deal with priority time

Once again, personal styles may differ but Latins, Middle Easterners, Africans, South Asians and much of Eastern and Central Europe and the Far East tend to work on priority time. They will multitask and allow a fair amount of flexibility between personal and business priorities. This may make them unreliable. They may not feel the need to keep you informed of delays and will get back to you only when they have something to offer or when other priorities allow. How do you haul yourself to the top of the food chain?

One answer is to make it personal. Emphasise how important to you it is personally. Stress the consequences of what will happen if you don't deliver on time. Be persistent: adopt the Indian expression, 'I'll be all over you like a blanket.' Above all, don't send emails – phone.

In some priority time-countries, emails are considered by definition to be non- priority. If something is urgent, phone. Don't use the office phone, try the mobile so you get through directly. Many successful executives phone to say, 'I'm sending you an email. Please make sure you read it.' Then they phone again:

'Did you get the email?' Finally, they phone again: 'What are you going to do about it?' In other words, they take time to personally emphasise the importance of their requirement. What's the problem? It takes up management time. But it's what you may have to do to get results.

Get a date in the diary

One thing we have found with priority-time societies is that a meeting entered into the appointment book will be honoured. Not necessarily at the time or even on the day agreed, but it will be honoured, even if it is rescheduled. So, if you need to contact someone officially, make sure they or their PA makes a date in the diary.

Short-notice appointments

One characteristic of priority-time societies is that it is often easy to get to see senior people at short notice if they are in the office. Always ring and see if people are available. If they are in the country there is a good chance they will make time to see you. It has been said that it is easier to get an appointment with the prime minister of some countries at three hours' notice than at three weeks' notice.

Dealing with delays and interruptions

One difficulty international managers face in dealing with priority-time societies is how to cope with delays and what to do when a meeting is interrupted. Delays are easier to cope with than they used to be. It used to be advisable to take a good book, preferably a long one: now you can take your laptop, tablet and mobile with you and catch up on emails and paperwork. Some executives we know simply retire to their hotel or office and ask the receptionist to call when the official they are there to see is free. Play this one carefully: it might be ~ considered insulting.

Interruptions are more difficult. Particularly in the Middle East, meetings may be interrupted by family and friends dropping in. If this happens, accept the fact and engage in the conversation, if appropriate. Then pick up on your own meeting when they have departed. Calendar-time managers tend to feel proprietorial about their meetings. It is 'me time'. But priority-time managers are much more relaxed about it. Best to go with the flow. You will earn brownie points for your tolerance and for fitting in.

Priority-time email etiquette

In priority-time societies it is important to do two things. First, preserve the greeting and sign-off courtesies in emails: 'Dear Mike' or 'Hi Mike' and 'Regards' are still important. The second is don't be too polite. Writing 'Could you do this?' or 'Would you mind doing this?' immediately condemns your email to the non-priority list. Better to give clear instructions and add your appreciation later. 'Please do this. I need it by 5pm London time today.' Then, if you wish, add: 'Thanks for all your hard work.'

Dealing with attitudes to time

We have already identified the difference between managers who do everything on order and like precise timetables (calendar time managers) and managers who prefer to focus on priority engagements and fit in everything around those (priority time managers). How do these managers need to change when confronted by a different attitude to time?

Calendar time managers travelling frequently to priority time countries learn to relax their timetables. What can be done in three days in Nordic countries will take three weeks in, say, South American countries. Why? Dealing with priority time means dealing with longer meetings, lunches and dinners, delays and interruptions. It is important to be flexible: an effect-ive calendar-time manager will plan two meetings a day with maybe a dinner appointment in the evening. This is not to say it is impossible to run a more intensive schedule.

Once again, depending on individuals, calendar-time cultures tend to prize doing things according to the clock. They respect time and punctuality. Emails are answered in strict order or in order of priority, but they are answered. Appointment times are respected and if they change, the change will be negotiated with you. If there is slippage on deadlines they will advise you in advance. The trains, as they say, will arrive and leave on time.

The Northwest cluster – the US and Canada, the UK, and the Benelux and Nordic countries – behaves like this, as do Australia and New Zealand. The most time- conscious culture is considered to be German – Germans, Austrians and Swiss. But so also are parts of Central Europe, such as Poland, Slovenia and the Czech Republic. Japan is noted for its punctuality, as are Singapore, Hong Kong and the big cities in China.

Dealing with delays and interruptions

How do you deal with calendar-time societies? You 'pull your socks up' as the British say. You ensure that you are strict about acknowledging the receipt of emails, setting deadlines for action and sticking to them. You are five minutes early for appointments and if there are delays or cancellations you always advise in good time. Many calendar-time executives say they don't mind delays if they know in time so that they can plan round them. What they can't stand is late notice or no information. Interruptions in meetings, if they occur, will be brief and to the point. They will normally be accompanied by apologies for breaking into another person's time slot.

Calendar-time email etiquette

Forms of address and sign-offs will often be more abrupt than in priority-time cultures. Don't get upset: it's just saving time. One email etiquette teacher recommends putting the degree of urgency in the subject box of each email. She suggests: Action Required (urgent), and Action Needed (important but not urgent). What is important is the time of response. Some people believe it is important to respond to Germany, Israel or the US within the working day, even if it is just a message to say 'Got your email – will respond'. Others believe it is important not to reply until you have the information, but not to leave it too late.

Tighten your timetable

If you are from a priority-time society and you are in a calendar-time society, be prepared to have more meetings and shorter ones. One hour to 90 minutes would be long. You might be entertained at lunch, but it is unusual for people to arrange evening or weekend entertainment unless you are good friends.

Attitudes to hierarchy

This is all about formality and respect. Take note: as we have already seen, respect for hierarchy matters in many countries.

Top-down and delegated leadership

Managers in what we have learned to call the Northwest cluster work increasingly in groups where each manager has a precise responsibility and budgets. They also have clear targets, either financial or qualitative, which are agreed at annual appraisals and reinforced by six-monthly reviews. This means that most managers know exactly what the limits of their responsibilities are and what they need to escalate to higher management. Managers are reasonably transparent about the process of leadership and decision-making although they may be less transparent about their motives.

Top-down leadership is just that. The decision is made by the top managers or director and the management team is responsible for implementation. The room for individual initiative at lower levels is much narrower, and taking initiative is discouraged if it 'bucks the system'. As a French senior private banker said to us, 'Messieurs, a company is not a democracy.'

In a delegated leadership system my job is to find out what the manager I am dealing with is responsible for, what his or her targets are and what they can sign off or need to escalate. Then I can deal with them and only them. In Germany, for example, if I go over the line manager's head to his or her boss I embarrass the boss and risk losing the support of the line manager I am dealing with.

In a top-down leadership system my job is to get as high as I can in the hierarchy and seek approval from the top man or woman who will pass instructions down the line. If I don't do that, I can waste a long time talking to the wrong person lower down.

Organigrams and influence

We've noticed that standard practice in many companies is to ask for the organigram of the company in order to know who is who and who does what. But in many other companies the organigram is not kept up to date and your first job on arrival will be to check that the organigram reflects the true position and personnel. But there is another problem.

Many managers think that the organigram hierarchy reflects a person's importance in the company – but often it doesn't. Influence is often very different from official position. We may think that the deputy president of a company is second in command to the president, but it could be that it is the supply chain manager who is the real number two. Why? Because the company is in a relationships-driven society, and the manager is a relative of, or went to school with, the president.

We were struck by the story of Massimo, aide-de-camp to a five-star general in the Italian army. Massimo's rank was fairly junior but his influence was enormous as he had the ear of the general. One day we asked how he had got his position. 'Simple,' he replied. 'The general and I were at staff college together. I knew he would rise in the ranks so I got close to him and followed his star.' Some managers call this practice favouritism or nepotism, but in relationship-driven markets it is seen completely differently. For them the most valued quality is loyalty. International managers need to realise that loyalty is often a key factor in promotion and may even trump merit. Find out when you can where the real influence lies and work with that. Don't assume the organigram will tell you the story. Too often it doesn't.

Delegation and consultation

Decisions may be taken at the top but may be preceded by an immense degree of consultation. In Chapter 8 we discussed the process of *nemawashi*, Japanese collective negotiation. But most countries also go through a process of formal or informal consultation. In Germany and France, consultation within the workplace is carried out with the Works Council and the Comité d'Entreprise. In the Netherlands, decisions are made only after intense and long discussions within the management committee. In Asia, trade council members and trusted cohorts are involved, although final decisions are taken at the top. Even in the UK, with delegated management and management by objectives, the principle of consultation is entrenched. You may not take notice of the results but you do have to be seen to consult.

Advice? Check the consultation procedure before you proceed. Don't proceed before you have done so. Remember that fools rush in where angels fear to tread!

Work time and downtime

An American publishing company was about to conclude a major publishing deal in France. The US publishing director proposed flying to Paris with his family for a short holiday and to finalise the details at the end of July. 'Ah, non, Monsieur,' replied the French managing director's assistant. 'The director is on holiday. He cannot be disturbed.' Americans don't take no for an answer, so the publishing director flew over, but found that his French colleague was indeed not available. He and his family were in the south of France. The pair never met and the deal was never signed. Had the US director been flexible and been prepared to fly down to Nice, the French director might have been prepared to break his holiday and have lunch, and discuss final details. But fly back to Paris? Never!

Different countries have different attitudes to downtime. Some countries, the Southern Europe ones in particular and some Nordic countries, make a definite distinction between working time and vacation. They keep their weekends free and don't even check their emails then. An airline controller in France got into trouble when his computer systems failed and planes were grounded internationally. The incident happened on a Saturday but the first he heard of it was on a Monday when he opened his computer and turned on his mobile phone – to find both flooded with angry calls and messages.

Lesson? Don't assume that people are available. Find out when they might not be.

In some countries, especially in Asia, downtime and work time are confused. If I have to take my children to school or go to the bank, I might not be available during a part of the day. If so, I will make up the time by working late but that may not be acceptable to very work-time conscious Germans.

Working in a German factory, we were conscious that at five minutes past five we were the last out of the building. We asked the Works Council representative why. His answer was revealing: 'If they leave late and have an accident on the way home, they can claim we were responsible because we kept them on too long.' Overtime is frowned on in Germany. If you stay late either you are inefficient and can't complete your work on time or your job description is wrong. Either way it is a criticism.

Have you ever tried to make appointments on a bank holiday? If you have, chances are you are a downtime worker with no sense of holidays and working hours. It's easy to do, especially internationally. If we are going to work in any countries, we check online not just for national holidays, but also local holidays. In India and other parts of Asia, Africa and Central and Eastern Europe, there may be religious or state local holidays we don't know of. Always check.

The last thing to check is how long holidays last. Don't make appointments in Russia in the first two weeks of January (Russian Christmas and New Year), in Western Europe in August (holiday time), in China for the week of the Chinese New Year (usually February) or, in the Islamic world, for Ramadan and the end of Ramadan. Always remember that failing to respect local working hours and holiday times can cost you time and money in wasted travel and appointments.

Know yourself, know others – the RADAR profile

For an international manager it is important to know your own style in order to compare it with the people you deal with. You may not have a detailed knowledge of the society you're confronting, but you definitely have some ideas. How can you make the comparison and see where you might have to adapt?

The answer is the RADAR profile and the RADAR system. It brings together the key cultural characteristics we have identified in this book. It enables you to chart your own cultural style, and to map your view of the market you are dealing with against your own style. Finally, it helps you identify the expectations, communication and managerial style gaps between you and the intended market and suggest where and how you need to adapt.

The RADAR profile contains nine paradigms divided by expectations, communication and management style. Each paradigm contains ten boxes. See following diagram:

Tool 5: The RADAR Profile

Expectations of business relationships

1. Relationship driven — Task driven

2. Risk embracing — Risk averse

3. Equality — Hierarchy

Communication

4. Direct — Indirect

5. Formal — Informal

6. Emotional — Neutral

Management

7. Teams — Individuals

8. Time tight — Time loose

9. Top down — Delegation

Decide on your style. Put a cross in the box to indicate your *personal* comfort zone. Then map your style against your key markets. Identify any differences that may cause tension.

Identify your style

Read down the nine paradigms and put a cross in the box which you feel most closely approximates your style. When you have finished, join up your crosses with a pencil. The result is a visual representation of your cultural style.

Identify the other's style

Now on the same sheet, identify the other person's style or the other market's default style. Put a cross in one box in each row to indicate your view of their style.

Then join up those crosses.

Compare the two lines

You now have a visual representation of your style and the other person's style. Where the lines are close together (for example, one to three squares) you can assume there are no major issues. However, if they are four or more apart there may be a problem.

For each gap ask yourself these three questions:

- Is the gap important? (If it isn't, ignore it)

- Do I need to change or does the other person need to change? (Usually the junior person in the relationship has to adapt, but not always.)

- How much?

That last question is vital. How much should you change? The good news is that you don't need to make a 100% change to get things right, even if they've started off on the wrong foot. The reason is the 80/20 rule. We're sure you've heard of it. The principle was coined by the 19th century Italian economist, Wilfredo Pareto, who claimed that 20% of a country's population created 80% of its wealth. In the 20th century it became the 80/20 rule – 20% of your customers provide 80% of your income. The same principle can be applied to cultural adaptation. A 20% change in behaviour achieves an 80% change in attitude. In other words, small incremental changes are what get results.

Tool 6: The RADAR System

The final issue is deciding what is the 20% of your attitudes or behaviour that you need to change. This is our final tool, the RADAR system. RADAR is an acronym. It stands for:

- **R** Recognise you have problem
- **A** Analyse it using the RADAR profile
- **D** Decide what 20% change you want to make
- **A** Act. Write it down and try it
- **R** Review it. Did it work? If it does, do more. If it doesn't, try something else

Inevitably, managing successfully in international environments is partly a matter of trial and error. However, if you can identify your style and compare it with others and then see what you need to do to adapt, you are well on your way to managing successfully in international waters.

Five things to remember

1. The three key variables that differentiate business management styles.

2. How to work with different time sensitivities. How to manage your timetable.

3. The different roles of a manager in international business. How the exercise of leadership and decision-making varies internationally.

4. How to use the RADAR profile to identify differences in management style.

5. How to use the RADAR system to improve working relationships.

Chapter 10
Going away and coming back

Kathleen has brought up four children in five countries, and has also held a senior position in a leading transnational media company. She knows a thing or two about relocating: for her it's both a challenge and an obstacle course. Reorganising the family, letting the house, arranging schools, organizing banks, doctors and social security, packing and just remembering what not to leave behind is just exhausting. Add to that the fact that she has to learn the parameters of her new job, attend briefings about the new country and discuss targets and procedures with her line manager and HR manager, and she has a full-time job just moving. Going away, or relocation as they call it, is a challenge. But so is coming back.

The process of coming home is known formally as repatriation. And both relocation and repatriation, as we shall see, have their own problems and their own remedies. But first, who relocates?

Relocation

In hindsight it was cruel, really. Eleanor was young and beautiful and an emerging poet and broadcaster. That was until she moved with her partner to Africa. Suddenly she became a trailing spouse, as they call it. A man or woman whose partner is in work, but they aren't.

Eleanor tried to fit in. She went to the library. She read enormously. She made a few friends, but the life she wanted had been taken away and there was not enough to replace it. Her husband was committed to making a success of his job and simply didn't see her point of view.

Her loneliness got so bad that she broke every plate in the house (government issue) and even overdosed and went to hospital. Finally, they went back to England on leave. But the energy that held them together was gone. She never returned. Richard went back to post and stayed on alone.

The problem in relocation is usually not the relocatee or the children. It's what they call, in that horrible phrase, the trailing spouse. Nowadays, when considering relocation, the opinion of the partner is as important to a company as the relocatee himself or herself. There are a number of things trailing spouses can do when accompanying their partner abroad. Many take a career break. They learn the language, history and culture of the country they are living in, often at the local university. They get involved in community work, sometimes through active expatriate societies. They travel and they discover. Some pursue alternative careers. They set up new businesses, often at a distance. They use the experience and expertise of their previous jobs, but for themselves.

One person we know set up a remote-working personal assistant's service, and supplied several companies with secretarial and other services. Another began working for the local museum. Before she relocated, she was at the British Museum in London. One young man learned the local language so well he set up a successful business as a translator and interpreter, even at one point being employed by the president's office. However, to do this requires confidence and a degree of toughness. This is not easy to do if you are feeling uprooted and out of your comfort zone, even in an environment such as France, Spain or Italy.

Hardship posts

What is it like in a hardship post? These are the relocation countries and cities where standards of living are considered to be lower than the average in metropolitan Europe or America. This might include Cairo or cities in Brazil or Indonesia. In fact, the standard of living may be very high but home (i.e. European or American) comforts may not be so easily available.

You could argue that a hardship post is defined by difference. Ordinary posts are different to a degree but they broadly conform to a European or American metropolitan lifestyle. Hardship posts don't. Baghdad's 'green zone' may be a haven for McDonalds, but it's still a hardship post. The heat and dust see to that.

Security

Security may also be an issue. The fact is that places that used to be considered secure posts no longer are. One such is in West Africa. Isabelle spent 20 years there, very happily, and brought up two children. One is now at college, the other is working. However, the political environment has changed. Government instability provoked a civil war and things are still potentially unstable. What was once an immensely stable environment is now risky. Isabelle's husband is still at post, but she is working in Paris.

Jim, a government officer, has been summarily evacuated not once but twice to avoid local disturbances. He's had to leave his house and possessions in the country of posting, and found himself high and dry in the UK with nothing to do. He has just endured summary evacuation, a traumatic experience itself. Now he has to endure weeks, maybe months, of not knowing what his future holds. Not only that, but in business terms he and his organisation suffer loss of productivity and revenue and, maybe for him, loss of income.

Julia is even more traumatised. She was in an office in Kabul when the Taliban attacked. Her desk was behind a concrete pillar. That's how she escaped death, although her two colleagues were killed in the blast. She raced out of the office towards the main building. The Taliban were on the roof and began shooting at her with machine guns. She escaped into the main building and the Taliban withdrew. Later when she went out she could see her footprints in the dust with traces of machine-gun fire parallel to them. Repatriated to Britain, she was in therapy for some time. She is now quite religious.

These examples are extreme forms of security, but even in less troubled countries you may have to constantly guard against theft. This may be much more common in a country with varying levels of wealth. In Latin America, Barry discussed going out to look at the Pacific Ocean, about five blocks down the road. 'OK, but take off your watch,' advised his host, 'and leave your bag here.' Sometimes the most innocuous- looking places can be risky.

Tom's tips

So what do you need to know before you go? Tom is the training manager of a large international fashion chain. This is his four-point checklist:

1. What do you need to know about the country and the people?

2. What do you need to do before you go?

3. What do you need to do after you get there?

4. What do you need to watch out for?

And we've added one:

5. How do you make friends with the locals?

1. What you need to know about the country and the people

You need to know a few basic facts, such as population, capital, currency and main centres. It's also important to know something about the country's different ethnic and religious groups. At least know they exist and what they are. Some knowledge of the geography and historical background is also valuable. What you are looking for is information which will help you understand and appreciate the background of the people you will meet and the land they live in.

We've provided examples of some key markets in the second part of this book but there are several more profiles on our website. Visit www.worldbusinesscultures.com to download them. You also need to know something about the people's business and social values and expectations, their preferred communication styles and their management styles. These we've explained in detail in earlier chapters and you can also see how these principles apply to specific countries in the profiles later on in the book and on our website. Read a history book if you have time.

None of this information will be wasted. You'll feel more secure when you arrive. You'll also be able to show an informed interest in the people you meet and deal with, which will be vital in building good business relationships. It may also help you to avoid putting your foot in it! And besides, it's interesting, in its own right.

2. What to do before you go

If you and your family are planning to move abroad for any length of time there is a lot to think about – both home and abroad. Let's take your home first. What do you need to plan?

- Your house: what will happen while you are away?

- Your children: education in the UK or abroad? If they are in primary school, is it worth pre-registering them for secondary school ready for when you get back?

- Your pets: what will happen to them? Can you take them with you? What are the quarantine restrictions?

- Your car: will you take it, leave it or sell it? If you leave it, how will you immobilise it or ensure it doesn't 'die' while you are away?

- Do you know the terms and conditions of your employment overseas?

- Do you know about any cost-of-living allowances, foreign-service allowances or any fringe benefits available?

- Have you checked pension rights and your tax situation?

- Have you arranged banking facilities?

- Have you checked visas, work permits and driving licences?

- Have you checked accommodation at your destination and, if initially you will be in a hotel, how long the company will subsidise you and what help they can give you in finding permanent accommodation?

- If your children are travelling with you, have you checked out the international school situation? (They will often train your children for the International Baccalaureate examinations.) Visit:

  en.Wikipedia.org/wiki/List_of_international_schools
  or google 'international schools' for more resources.

- Have you checked what you can take with you and how it will be transported? See the section on culture shock coping strategies for some things you may not have thought of.

- Have you and your partner discussed his or her role? Work, career break, study, homemaking? It's vital to discuss this before you go and if possible to check out the options before you leave.

3. What you need to do when you get there

- Register with the police: when you arrive you have a limited time to do this.

- Register with your embassy. This isn't compulsory but it is useful and it may get you an invitation to the Queen's birthday party!

- If you have accommodation, check what you need to do to buy or transport furniture, get phones connected, electricity, water and heating organised. Once again, your company or other expat colleagues may be able to help.

- Don't get too busy too soon. There's a lot to do in settling in. You also have to learn about your new country's position on the ground. It can look different close-up to what you learned in head office. Above all, you need time to 'press the flesh', meet staff, clients, local partners and suppliers. This may involve lunches and dinners.

- If your partner is not working or if your children are with you, it is important to make time in the evening to be with them. It is all too easy for them to feel left out while you are extremely busy.

4. Things to watch out for

- Hidden taxes: check for any regional, VAT, or additional services taxes which you didn't expect.

- Unexpected holidays: in addition to national holidays, different regions may have local holidays.

- Mobiles: do they call them 'mobiles' (UK), 'cellphones' (US) or something else? Get a local phone for in-country calls. It will save you a lot of money on international calls or 'roaming' charges.

- Servants: in many emerging countries, it is common to have house and garden servants, night watchmen etc. This is often embarrassing for new arrivals and it may feel like an invasion of your privacy. In fact, serving is a profession and many house servants have worked in the same property for many families for a number of years.

Once you get used to their presence, they can really save you time and trouble on basic shopping and maintenance, as well as security. And, as a profession, it is a respectable way to keep and feed your family.

- Protocol: meetings with officials and dignitaries may be much more formal than you are used to. Remember to show respect. Don't use first names until invited and if in doubt, always ask, 'How would you like me to address you?'

5. Making friends in the community

This is what it is all about – meeting people and making friends in the community. But each community has a different way of making friends. The Americans have the Welcome Wagon, the Brits the coffee morning, and other countries have, well, what? Here are some tips, gained from hard experience:

- **Don't ignore the expats**

  Many emigrants decide to go for total immersion and ignore the expat community. But what makes you think the locals want to know you? Although not every one of the expats may be to your taste, you will meet some who have integrated well into the local community. They will introduce you to the people you want to meet – the ones who are interested in you or your country.

- **Never refuse an invitation**

  Unless it is a sexual invitation you need to refuse or one that may lead to violence, accept. They are entries into local society and to refuse once is to reject the society. You may never get a second chance.

- **Be patient**

People often talk too much (maybe you do!). If you can hold your tongue and really listen, you will learn things. The other person will think you are interested and you will earn brownie points for being an interesting conversationalist.

- **Learn a bit about local affairs**

  If you can find something that local people are interested in, ask about it. It is a good ice-breaker.

- **Look for people to take an interest**

  It may be an interest in your language or in your country.

- **Never refuse a request for a favour**

  You may be unable to do it but always say you will try. The willingness itself will create the relationship, even if you can't deliver.

Remember Tool RADAR Five Alive. Whenever you encounter something odd, aggravating or just ridiculous, go through these five steps:

1. Identify. What's happening?
2. Compare. How different is it?
3. Empathise. Why is it different?
4. Manage. How can I best manage it?
5. Reflect. What have I learned?

As you encounter the challenges of settling in abroad, it will help you maintain a philosophical attitude to even quite uncertain situations, such as culture shock.

Culture shock

Barry's worked in over 60 countries and has a reasonably specialised knowledge of French-speaking countries. Mike has worked in Europe, the USA and Australia, and is also passionate about Latin America and Spain.

Both freely admit to experiencing culture shock – not just once but every time they go away on an international assignment for any length of time.

Nathalie spent 20 years in French-speaking West Africa but returned to France five years ago and now works as an office manager in a leading telecommunications company in Paris. She misses Africa and admits to a feeling of alienation. She no longer feels part of either country: France or the Ivory Coast, where she used to live.

Culture shock describes this feeling of alienation caused by being separated from family and friends and familiar routines when one is abroad, and is recognised as a medical condition. Twenty years ago, people abroad didn't like to admit they had culture shock: they feared their managers would think they were weak or suffered from 'lack of moral fibre'. It is a bit like the First World War when what we now know as shell shock was seen as cowardice. Culture shock won't get you shot, but it might cost you promotion opportunities or bonuses and even your job.

So how do people come to experience culture shock, and how can you avoid it?

The honeymoon

When you go abroad for a short (two or three months) or a long period (a year or two years), the first impression can be quite exciting. It's a new experience, a new life, new people, an exciting challenge. It's invigorating. Sometimes, the experience of being in a new country may seem infinitely superior to being in your own. Experts call this the honeymoon period. These honeymooners often criticise their own country severely.

Culture shock brings you up short. You wake up feeling unbearably depressed. You start crying for no reason. You hate the place you are living in and wonder why on earth you ever left home. The trigger may be loneliness, homesickness, or simply the air conditioning breakdown or some aspect of local bureaucracy that has upset you. This is the onset of culture shock and it can last for months.

When a leading British steel company moved to the Netherlands, the British migrants thought they were still in the UK: O'Neill's Irish pub every night and English spoken on the shop floor. But after six months their Dutch colleagues decided, 'OK, we have spoken English for six months. Now, it's Dutch.' And they started communicating uniquely in Dutch. For about a week. Culture shock! By the time the Dutch reverted to English, the Brits were ready to leave. But the message was delivered: 'Just because the Dutch speak English it doesn't mean you can take it for granted that we'll use it all the time.'

How culture shock manifests

Culture shock manifests in a number of ways. One is loneliness and homesickness. Another is lack of motivation and fear of underperformance. A third is burnout. You work every hour God gives, then you hit a brick wall and become completely demotivated. These are the symptoms of culture shock. You need coping strategies.

Coping strategies

First of all we agree it is easier to write about culture shock than to experience it. We've both been there more than once. And that's our first recommendation:

1. Expect it

Expect culture shock when you go abroad for any period of time over a month or so and expect it every time you do it.

2. Recognise it

When you get these feelings of loneliness, homesickness, depression or burnout, recognise it. Distance yourself from it. It's not you, it's the culture shock. Treat it like the flu. Go to bed for a day.

3. Get help if you need it

As we said earlier, managers overseas used to hide their experience of culture shock. They didn't want it on their record in case it prejudiced future promotion. Nowadays attitudes have changed. HR managers recognise the symptoms and know what to do. Let people know if you have a problem and if you need to see a doctor.

4. Keep in touch

Some people believe in total immersion in the new culture. Fine – but if you don't, keep in touch with people back home. Use social media, Skype and email to contact friends and family. Make it personal. Ever received one of those 'round robins' from the Tomalin or Nicks family telling you of their adventures abroad? Boring! A short personal note from time to time is all you need.

5. Keep in touch with HR

Let your HR and line manager at home know what progress you are making and how you are adapting. They may not reply but it will be important in the long term when you are preparing your return.

6. Take comfort items

Shut your eyes for a minute and think of yourself in the most comfortable room in your house or flat. Mentally look around the room. See what strikes your mind's eye. Does it give you pleasure? If so, can you take some part of it with you? We know people who take their favourite Star Wars duvet cover or a cushion from the sofa. One Danish couple even relocated to Britain with a complete kitchen table and chairs, handcrafted by the husband's father. If the budget allows, don't limit yourself.

7. Find comfort places.

Think what you enjoy doing for leisure. A Finnish colleague loved piano bars, so a weekly visit to a five-star hotel cocktail bar with the piano tinkling kept her happy. Another colleague in India liked visiting churches in the UK, but in India he started visiting Hindu temples and became an expert in architecture and symbolism.

If you belong to a club, see if you can find the equivalent where you are. The search is part of the fun.

8. Sport

Many people who do sport at home say, ' I'll pick it up over there when I've got my feet under the table.' And they don't notice themselves getting day by day less fit and more sluggish. On the contrary, the managers of a major fashion chain relocating abroad had one question when they arrived for a cultural adjustment session: 'Where's the best jogging track?' Find a way of getting exercise and keeping fit. It will make a difference to your mood and your productivity.

9. Keep a sense of humour

Culture shock isn't funny. It can make you feel awful. If you can, detach yourself. Observe it from the outside and don't take it too seriously. As you'll see as you read on, it's worse coming back to your home country!

Adaptation

By using these techniques you go through a period of adaptation. It's slow, with many shocks, but they become fewer or easier to absorb as time goes on. You learn to take things in your stride. And so, little by little, you become part of the national furniture and achieve ...

Integration

This is the point where you are at one with the country you are in. You are at ease with the people, the bureaucracy and the lifestyle. You may never 'go native', although many people do, but you feel as much a part of your temporarily adopted country as you do of your own. 'I could get used to this,' you say to yourself. And then...

Repatriation

Everyone agrees that coming back is much more traumatic than going out. Most organisations like to rotate personnel and send people abroad for between two or three years on long-term assignments. So why is coming back such a problem? Ask Claire Snowdon. She runs Expat Knowhow which specialises in 'counting them out and counting them all back'. In other words, relocation and repatriation.

When you get back home, she says, the first thing is that it's wonderful to see everyone again. Then you realise you've changed. And so have they. You're no longer on the same wavelength.

Then you go to the office. 'In Bangkok, were you? Nice there, was it?' And that's the extent of their interest. As far as they're concerned, you've been on holiday. All your painfully accumulated experience and knowledge of the mysterious East dismissed in one perfunctory question. Worse still, your colleagues have changed. Some have left, new people have come in. Other colleagues have been promoted. That corner office you once coveted has gone to someone else and no one quite knows what to do with you. In his amiable memoir, *Ever the Diplomat,* Sherard Cowper-Coles describes how ambassadors in far-flung posts did less well in the promotion stakes than those who stayed closer to home. Whatever the company policy, out of sight, out of mind, often seems to be the reality.

At home you find taxes have gone up, prices have doubled, you have to look after yourself (no servants), and the kids are having difficulty reintegrating into school. The syllabus is different and their English sounds funny. They and you feel lonely and out of place.

So what can you do to avoid repatriation shock or at least relieve the pain? In his book, *The Art of Coming Home,* the American author Craig Storti describes some of the techniques that people he knows use.

1. Don't assume

Don't assume you can just fall back into your country like you fall back into a comfortable chair at the end of a hard working day.

2. Keep in touch with the HR director

Three months before you leave post, make sure he or she knows your plans and can advise you on career and work once you get back home.

3. Keep in touch with office colleagues

If you do this, you'll know who is doing what and to whom.

4. Keep in touch with family and friends

Make sure they know your plans and that you know theirs. This will make the process of rebuilding contact much smoother.

5. Initiate a process of closures

Organise goodbye parties with the kids and also for yourselves and the friends you have made in the country. Do the same in your office.

6. Plan your repatriation

Make sure your kids' schools are in order. Check that the house will be ready to move back into. Make sure you have somewhere to stay. Make sure bank accounts are working smoothly. If your physical conditions are comfortable, you'll find it much easier to handle the psychological disruption.

7. Don't underestimate it

We used to pride ourselves on being able to fit into any city in the world within 24 hours. Nowadays, with families and responsibilities, it's not so easy. In addition, the world has changed. What used to be familiar surroundings are now weirdly different surroundings. You can adapt practically, but adapting psychologically takes longer – as much as a year in some cases.

What the HR director can do to help

The HR director has an important role to play in acclimatisation. The first thing is to recognise that things have changed and that the manager returning may not be up to speed. The second is to make sure the manager has somewhere to sit and a job to do. Take time to introduce the returning manager to new members of staff and to brief him or her on changes in the office. It may be helpful to appoint a mentor from among the returning manager's colleagues to be on hand to advise over the first month or so. Make sure the returning manager is happy with this before proceeding. Finally, it is worth making sure that the manager's overseas experience is captured before it is forgotten. Writing a cultural and market report will be valuable. He or she could even brief other colleagues in bite-sized internal workshops. In these ways the returning manager's experience in the field is valued and preserved for other managers to use in the future.

What happens if it all goes wrong?

Arthur was a highly experienced oil engineer. He had worked overseas in the Gulf and most recently in Angola. When he returned home after three years in the field, he was like a fish out of water. Travelling into the capital every day he hated the trains, the tubes and the city. His colleagues didn't understand him and he didn't understand his colleagues. Arthur wasn't married but was still young. He felt very lonely in his new environment. More than that, he felt unappreciated at work. No one was knowledgeable about the work he had been doing and even fewer were interested. Finally, after nine months, demotivated and dispirited, he took a redundancy package and left the company. Last we heard he was in Nigeria, in the Niger Delta.

Arthur's not alone. Statistics compiled by GMAC, the global relocation organisation, and by the National Foreign Trade Council Survey, show how many people leave their companies after repatriation. In 2005 the estimate was 23% of 'repartees' leaving their company in the first year and 40% after three years. The main reason was mismanagement or non-existence of a formal company repatriation programme. The cost? Millions of dollars a year in lost investment in the company's human capital.

Conclusion

Working abroad is a great opportunity and many international corporations consider it an essential element of career development. It can be both linguistically and culturally enriching but, as we have seen, it can also pose problems. Being aware of the possible problems and planning ahead as far as you can is a major step to ensuring that going away and coming back successfully is not a challenge but an enriching and rewarding experience for the executive and his or her family.

Five things to remember

1. Relocation isn't routine. You need to plan for it.

2. If appointed to a hardship post check terms and conditions, especially home leave and allowances. Check

security advice before going to a hardship post or an unstable environment.

3. Remember Tom's tips about what you need to know before you go, when you arrive, what to watch out for and how to make friends.

4. Be prepared for culture shock, not just for you but for your family. Learn the strategies for coping with culture shock for assignees and their families.

5. Make plans for repatriation three months before you leave. Keep in touch with HR at home to ease your reintegration into the company on repatriation.

Part Two
Market profiles

Tool 7: ECOLE

These market profiles use our unique ECOLE © organising principle. Relevant information can be hard to distinguish and difficult to organise. The secret is to know where to look.

The ECOLE © organising principle helps you both know what to look for and how to organise it.

If you know French, ECOLE means school. However, for us it is just an acronym. It stands for:

E Expectations

C Communication

O Organisation

L Leadership

E Etiquette

But that's not all. We also add an Overview with information about the place you will visit and the people you will meet, including their historical background. And we add Fast Facts with essential country information and a RADAR profile so you can compare your style to the default style of the country you are in.

We've included twelve key territory profiles in this edition but you can download others from our website:

www.worldbusinesscultures.com

Download the profiles. Add more information as you obtain it and use ECOLE © to create your own profiles.

Oh, and if you disagree with anything we've said, be sure to let us know. Information exchange is a key element in increasing cultural knowledge, awareness and sensitivity.

Arabian Gulf

Ways to succeed	Ways to fail
• Be courteous and polite	• Criticise Gulf ways of doing business
• Look for solutions not problems	• Stress problems and disadvantages
• Be patient	• Show interest in Gulf history and lifestyle
• Build the relationship over time	• Refuse a favour if someone asks – you must at least try
• Maintain formality until invited not to	• Criticise Gulf record on women's rights or crime

Overview

The Gulf is the term many people use to describe the markets of the Arabian peninsula, principally Saudi Arabia and the seven United Arab Emirates of Abu Dhabi, Dubai, Sharjah, Ajman, Fujairah, Ras al Khaimah and Umm al-Quwain, of which Abu Dhabi is the national capital. Yemen, Qatar and Oman are also Gulf states. Apart from Yemen, which is a republic, all the Gulf states are led by hereditary monarchies.

Once relatively poor countries dominated by desert, their economies have been transformed by the exploitation of oil and gas reserves, which they are now seeking to diversify into other industries. Even so there are huge differences in wealth between the different states, of which Saudi Arabia (the world's 13th largest country), Abu Dhabi and Dubai are the richest, alongside Qatar.

A characteristic of the Gulf states is that their immigrant population dwarfs their native population. You are likely to be working with Indians and Pakistanis, Brits, Americans and Australians, as much as or more than you are with Arabs, although ultimate authority and control is carefully guarded by Arabs. In the Gulf states, the royal families are the ultimate arbiters of everything that goes on and a connection, at some level, with a member of such a family is considered important to major business success.

All Arabs believe in *ummah*, the community of believers, the followers of Islam in the Arab lands. It is one reason for the resentment against foreign invasion or occupation and for the petty ownership and citizenship restrictions that exist in some states.

The Gulf states are primarily Islamic societies, with varying degrees of public and private devotion, but all adhere in principle to the five pillars of Islam. Islam means submission to God and is based on divine revelations given by the Prophet Muhammad (Peace and Blessings be upon him) in the Saudi city of Mecca around 610 CE (Christian era) and contained in the Muslim holy book, the Koran. The historical date usually attributed to the rise of Islam as a religion is around 633 CE.

The five pillars of Islam are:

1. **Belief in Allah** – Islam is a monotheistic religion of belief in one God, Allah, and in Muhammad as his Prophet. Muslims do not recognise the threefold divinity of the Christian Holy Trinity, but revere Jesus Christ as a Prophet.

2. **Prayer** – Muslims are expected to pray five times a day on their knees and facing in the direction of Mecca. In Western countries, this process is often sandwiched at

the beginning and end of the working day, but in Saudi shopping malls and offices, for example, there will be a series of 15-minute breaks as prayer takes place. In many cities you will hear the muezzin's call to prayer from the local mosque.

3. **Alms**– Muslims are expected to give alms to help those less well-off than themselves. This may amount to 10% of income.

4. **Fasting** – this happens for about four weeks once a year, but dates vary according to the Muslim lunar calendar. Between dawn and dusk no devout Muslim can eat or drink anything. This can affect energy levels and irritability, especially during the first week or so, and is especially testing during the longer days of summer and early autumn.

5. **Haj** – the pilgrimage to Mecca is something every Muslim should strive to undertake at least once in his/her lifetime. This involves visiting Mecca and Medina, the two cities most closely associated with the Prophet, and worshipping at his tomb, the Ka'aba in Mecca. Non-Muslims are not permitted to enter this area.

SUNNI AND SHI'A

As in Christianity, Islam also divides into slightly different approaches to religious belief and worship. The key distinction is between the Sunni (companions of the Prophet) and Shia (family of the Prophet) sects, but Saudi and Qatar also practise an austere reformed form of worship dating from the 18th century called Wahhabism.

SHARI'A LAW

Muslim states are governed under a legal system based on the Muslim religion known as Shari'a law. The strictness of the Shari'a law has earned it a bad press in the West, but its more extreme modes of punishment are rarely put into effect.

VARIATIONS OF BEHAVIOUR IN SAUDI

As the heartland of Islam, Saudi tends to be the strictest inter-preter of Muslim law and practice, but there are variations between Riyadh and the coastal cities of Jeddah and Ras Tanura, for example. In the other Gulf states, once again, the strictness of application of Muslim principles varies both individually and from state to state.

Expectations

Relationships

The Gulf states are very much a relationship culture and Arabs will take time to get to know you before doing business. So you need to take the time to visit, to maintain contact and build friendships with your Arab counterparts. As befits a relation-ship-oriented society, Arabs are normally calm and reserved to begin with but will become much more emotional as they get to know you. When they know you and trust you they will be extremely loyal.

Respect for authority

Arabs are very hierarchical and will be quite formal and reserved at first. Respect for authority is important.

Respect for Islam

Respecting Islam is a way of building good relations and acceptance. Show interest in Islamic faith and practice, dress modestly and do not drink or eat in public during the day in Ramadan. Make allowances for grumpiness and tiredness during Ramadan, and allow time for *iftar*, the breaking of the fast, at the end of the day before starting evening work.

Communication

The key to communication in the Arab world is personal relationships. These may be secured through third-party intermediaries (trade fairs, embassies) but must be built on by personal contact. This means that personalised arguments, persuasion and appeals to personal friendship are an important part of the business process. It also means that a personal favour should be acknowledged and reciprocated. Even if you can't accede to a personal request, you should always try and never reject it outright. Arabs, unless they are very much higher in authority, will tend to stand or sit closer to you than most Westerners and their body language will be more expressive. Politeness and praise are important in Arab society and you may find that 'bad' news may not be communicated to you direct.

Presentations

Arabs are interested in what will work for them, and in know-how. They look for a personal touch, and warm praise when due is appreciated. Stick to good news: introducing subjects such as illness, misfortune, accidents or death is demotivating for Arabs (and not much fun for anyone else either). Arabs can be impatient listeners, and are 'ping-pong' speakers – they will interrupt and tolerate interruption. Arabs equate raised voices with sincerity. Shy quiet speakers do not impress.

Meetings

Arab business meetings proceed at a leisurely pace. Depending on your status, you may be asked to wait for your appointment to start: take a good book or your laptop. Meetings may be interrupted by international calls or by visits from friends or relatives. Arabs are more tolerant of interruptions than Westerners. Meetings begin with polite conversation about families and business. It is best to wait until your host brings up the business discussion.

Before you arrive, your business contact will probably have sought out the people most likely to favour your proposal. Have lots of copies of your sales brochures available, as well as cards. They will be circulated to people outside the meeting.

Negotiation

Negotiators may agree in principle fairly quickly, although the decision may be communicated outside the meeting, but will bargain over details, especially price. This process can take a long time.

Networking

Ice-breakers	Ice-makers
• Polite contribution to any subject under discussion	• Criticism of human rights or the position of women
• Success of children	• Criticism of or jokes about Islam or Shari'a law
• Exchanging information about business and travel	• Religion, politics and sex
• Praise for Gulf achievements	• Showing interest in wives and families (unless you are a woman)

Organisation

Business hours

The Gulf climate is extremely hot and the working day may last from 7.30am to 2.30pm from Saturday until Wednesday. Friday is the Holy Day, equivalent to the Western Sunday. Banking hours are usually 8.30am to 12pm, and then from 5pm to 7pm. Most business appointments should take place in the morning. Remember also that Muslim holidays are based on the Hijrah 28-day lunar month calendar and may therefore vary from year to year. Many calendars have both the Gregorian and Hijrah (Arabic) dates. The pace of business is necessarily more relaxed and air- conditioning is a must.

Time

Time is elastic in the Arab world. It is more important to get things done in the right way. If this takes more time than budgeted – so be it. A key word in Arabic is *'In'sha'Allah'* (if God wills).

Teamworking

Arab teams work best under clear direction from a charismatic direct leader.

They need clear orders and instructions with clear deliverables to which they can bring their own creativity. If there is vagueness in team leadership the team will fragment, as it remains a group of individuals giving loyalty to its leader. To achieve and maintain that loyalty, the team leader must show personal interest in team members and their lives and be prepared to listen to professional and personal problems.

Leadership

Management style

Arab society is traditionally top-down with clear distinctions of authority. In getting any major decision, it is important to go directly to the top. A key person in the decision-making process is your sponsor, who should be both flexible and influential, with the ability to meet key decision-makers including, in the Gulf, members of the royal families. Remember that when Arabs say 'yes' it may mean 'possibly', and that saying 'no' to your face would be impolite.

Feedback

Feedback is usually given in private in order to protect and save face. However, negative feedback may not be given directly at all but be conveyed by absence of information or through a trusted third person.

Women in management

Highly regarded but carefully protected, the position of women in Muslim societies varies immensely in different states. Many hold leading positions in the 'humanist' professions of medicine and education, and also in administration, but in some countries, notably Saudi, they may not associate professionally or socially with men outside their families. Many Muslim women choose to wear the *hijab* (headscarf) and some wear face masks (*niqab*) or the full veil of the *burka*. The elegantly clad wife of a Muslim colleague who graces your reception in London may not meet you in Saudi and it may be considered inappropriate to ask after her.

Etiquette

Greeting and leave-taking

Use a soft handshake and strong direct eye contact. Arabs of the same sex sit closer to each other than foreigners do. Try not to move away – it signals coldness. Arabs touch each other as a sign of confidence. This varies among different Arab states. Take your lead from the people around you. You may be addressed by Mr or Mrs and your first name.

Dress code

Arabs are equally at home in Western or Arab fashions. Make sure you dress with the appropriate level of formality and modesty, but be prepared for the heat. Also be conscious that the air-conditioning in hotel rooms, cars and interiors can make the temperature quite cold. A light sweater may be useful.

Foreign women in Arab countries should not exhibit bare shoulders or upper arms and should wear knee-length skirts. In Saudi itself an *abaya*, or long-sleeved black tunic, may be worn although not all Saudi women wear the *burka* or full veil. In Saudi, women may not drive cars. If you are a man do not attempt to shake hands with, let alone kiss or hug, an Arab woman, although some more international Arabs may initiate this.

Gift-giving

Although Gulf traditions of hospitality are very strong, gift-giving is not an important part of the business process and gifts are not taken if you are invited to a home visit. There is a popular belief in the West that if you show appreciation of something it will be gifted to you. This is not usual, but if it happens it is exceptional generosity. Accept graciously and reciprocate when you can.

Great gifts	Gifts to avoid
• High-value scent (only for people who share or appreciate your taste)	• Silk and gold (for men)
• High-quality furnishings	• Anything for women (unless from a woman)
• Hallmark silver jewellery (only for close friends)	• Any gift for a colleague's wife must be from the wife, never from the man
	• Pictures of dogs or dog toys
	• Any pork-based products (for example, pigskin)
	• Products containing alcohol

Hospitality

Socialising is a very important part of Gulf business. It mainly takes place in hotel restaurants and coffee shops, but you may be invited to a wedding or celebration. These are very good opportunities to meet partners socially. Contrary to UK/US convention, talk and discussion takes place before the meal and people tend to leave immediately after eating. If entering a private house, expect to remove your shoes and also be prepared to eat with your fingers (the right hand is used only for touching food or passing serving plates). He who invites, pays. Reciprocity is the important thing. Remember that Muslims also observe two important food taboos, avoidance of alcohol and pork or pork products

Arabian Gulf: business style

Expectations of business relationships

1. Relationship driven									Task driven

2. Risk embracing									Risk averse

3. Equality									Hierarchy

Communication

4. Direct									Indirect

5. Formal									Informal

6. Emotional									Neutral

Management

7. Teams									Individuals

8. Time tight									Time loose

9. Top down									Delegation

Arabian Gulf: fast facts

Name	Arabian Gulf
Nationality	Arab (but many other nationalities work in the Gulf)
Population	Saudi: 28.5 million (inc. 5 million non-nationals) UAE: 4.8 million Oman: 3.15 million
Languages	Arabic UAE: Arabic and Persian (Farsi)
Capitals	Saudi: Riyadh (pop. 5.25 million) UAE: Abu Dhabi (pop. 921,000) Oman: Muscat (pop. 634,000)
Main cities	Saudi: Jeddah 3.4 million Mecca 1.6 million
Climate	Varies between seasons, parts can be quite cool in winter. Jeddah in Saudi is hot all year round.
Currency	Saudi: Saudi Riyal UAE: Dirham Oman: Omani Rial
Ethnicities	Saudi: Arab 90%, Afro-Asian 10% UAE: Emirati 19%, other Arab and Iranian 23%, South Asian 50%, other expats 8% Oman: Arab, Baluchi, South Asian, African
Religion	Muslim (various sects)
Internet code	Saudi: sa UAE: ae Oman: om
Phone country code	Saudi: 966 UAE: 971 Oman: 968

SOURCE: CIA WORLD FACTBOOK JULY 2013

Brazil

Ways to succeed	Ways to fail
• Build the relationship	• Consider them as Portugal's 'little brother'
• Dress your best – good clothes and accessories, clean and pressed	• Criticise Brazil or Brazilians as a nation
• Show your education	• Don't accept social invitations
• Show interest in Brazilian culture	• Be inflexible
• Stay in good hotels – style matters	• Be intolerant of local customs and lifestyle

Overview

Nearly everything about Brazil is vast. It has the largest economy in South America and the most advanced industrial sector in Latin America. It is the world's fifth biggest country in terms of land area and population. The Amazon basin covers some 60% of the country's surface, and contains 20% of the world's fresh water supply and the world's largest rain forest. Nearly 20 million people live in greater Sao Paulo, the largest city in the southern hemisphere and the seventh largest city in the world.

But not all of Brazil's statistics are so impressive. It is one of the world's most unequal societies with 5% of the population owning 85% of the wealth, and its economic growth rates have been weak compared to those of many Asian countries. Barriers to growth include poor infrastructure, low quality public services, corruption, social conflicts and government bureaucracy, while deforestation in the Amazon remains an environmental controversy. But Brazil also has vast natural resources and strong manufacturing and service sectors, and in recent years the government has had some success in redressing the country's imbalances.

Portuguese is the official language of Brazil. This makes it one of the few Latin American countries where Spanish is not the main tongue. It declared independence from Portugal in 1822 and became a republic in 1889. It has historical links with the UK, which was an early supporter of Brazil's independence, helped the country to build a railway system, and encouraged it to abolish slavery. Some three to four million African slaves were transported to Brazil during its colonial period, seven times the number taken to the US.

Economic development

With a GDP of over 2.5 trillion dollars (The Economist 2013), Brazil is the world's sixth or seventh largest economy and the B in the BRICS (the world's mega-emerging economies – Brazil, Russia, India and China). Brazil's advantages over India or China are that, despite great poverty in its slums or favelas, it has a better balance between town and country (86% of Brazilians live in towns), a better democracy (meaning easier adaptation to change), and low aggressive nationalism. It has also dealt with debt, inflation and democracy. Brazil's export wealth has come from commodities and the new Tupi oilfield is estimated to produce between five and eight billion barrels a year. Another, Carioca Sugar Field, may hold 33 billion barrels.

Expectations

Brazil and Portugal

Brazil is proud of its Brazilian-Portuguese identity. All references, business cards etc, should be in Portuguese and English, never in Spanish. On the other hand, Brazil is sensitive about its relationship with Portugal. Say Brazilian, not Portuguese.

Think big

Brazil is a big country: the biggest in Latin America and the fifth largest in the world. As a consequence, people like to think big – big plans, big projects and big ideas.

Think new

Brazil is also a young country. New ideas and original ideas tend to be greeted with enthusiasm and open-mindedness – a tribute, perhaps, to Brazil's multicultural style and flexible attitudes.

Personal contacts

Personal contacts are the way of doing business in Brazil: the time you spend socialising will greatly contribute to your success there. Brazilians respect social class, family and education rather than personal achievements, and will value your personal style, emotion and commitment.

Intellectual interests

You will also enhance your status by showing a lively interest in intellectual pursuits – some knowledge of Brazilian history, writers, architecture and music will help – and also Brazilian tel-enovelas – TV soap operas. Television reaches 99% of Brazilian towns and villages.

Emotions

On the other hand, Brazilians are a very emotional people, responding to memories and experiences, both happy and sad, and expressed in popular songs through the word *saudade* (nostalgia, or something missing).

Relationships

Brazilian society is very much relationship based, quite formal at first but moving towards informality fast as the relationship is established. Brazilians are relaxed about time (but less so in the big commercial city of Sao Paulo) and like to see the human side of the people they deal with. Brazilians are also very family-oriented. In Brazil, families come first.

Jeitinho culture

Jeitinho means literally 'little way'. It reflects the Brazilian belief that there is a way round every problem. Brazil has heavy bureaucracy and the Brazilian love of challenging authority means they will always try to find a way through, from paying minimum taxes to finding seats on full trains.

Individualists

Brazilians are primarily concerned with their own interests and those of their families and friends. This is because there is little social security and people are dependent on their own resources for survival.

Communication

Small talk

Chat first, then get down to business: that's the way things are done in Brazil. Brazilians need to feel that you appreciate them as a person. What Americans and Northern Europeans may consider unnecessary socialising is simply a Brazilian's way of feeling comfortable with you. Treat the office secretary as your new best friend: she will advise you on procedures, dress codes and a multitude of other details. A *cafezinho* (little coffee) is an opportunity to socialise at the beginning and end of a meeting.

Portuguese not Spanish

Brazil is proud of its Brazilian-Portuguese identity, so all documentation, including business cards and letters, should be in Portuguese and English, never in Spanish. Brazil is a multiracial, tolerant society. Treat it on its own terms and don't criticise Brazil.

Bold presentations

Brazilians consider the European mode of presentation to be rather overcautious, so be prepared to be bold. They are interested in ideas, so they will want to know your vision, supported by facts. But style, eloquence, expressiveness and body language are also important. Try to maintain strong eye contact, and show your human side. Keep your presentations short – around 30 minutes – and allow time for discussion.

Meetings

Make your appointments two or three weeks before and confirm them on arrival. 'Dropping in' without an appointment is discouraged. It's best to schedule only two or three meetings a day; remember that you must start them with coffee and socialising before you discuss work. A typical meeting might last around two hours. The seating plan in meetings is usually arranged on a hierarchical basis. The style of the gathering will be formal but structured so that more casual conversation is possible: Brazilians like to discuss and analyse situations from all sides. Expect the debate to be lively and overlapping: they don't mind interruption. Neither do they expect to keep to an agenda. They prefer to complete the business at hand rather than cut it short because of time schedules. Don't expect clear-cut yes or no answers, and don't try to impose tight deadlines.

Negotiations

Keep your negotiation team together – changes in personnel are considered bad practice. Brazilians trust the negotiators as representatives of the company. Brazilians are talkative, with lots of body language, and will be quite emotional. They are also quite analytical, preferring to take time to examine a case from all sides. Argument and debate are valued, but it's important to avoid direct confrontation in meetings: try and look for constructive solutions. If there is disagreement, it may be expressed in terms such as 'It's your money' or 'That's a cour-ageous decision'. Disagreements will normally be resolved face to face, without recourse to writing or to a third party.

Meetings usually end in a decision. However, that could be modified before it is implemented if circumstances are con-sidered to have changed. Demonstrating trust (while investigat-ing the reality of a proposal) and giving people the benefit of the doubt is important. Personal loyalty is the key to successful negotiation in Brazil.

Networking

Ice-breakers	Ice-makers
• Region	• Compare Brazil with Portugal
• General business	• Argentina (especially re football)
• Brazilian culture	• Ethnicity
• Football	• Personal matters (until you know people well)
• Music	• The term 'America' to refer to USA

Organisation

Business hours

Usually 9am to 5pm, with one or two hours for lunch. Senior managers may start and finish later. The best time for business meetings is between 10am and 12pm and 3pm and 5pm.

Time

Brazilians work very hard, but don't expect them to be on time. Employees usually are, but executives often arrive late and stay late, so slow down a little.

Team-working

Seniority and experience tend to be the criteria for team selection. The pace of work may be slow, although Brazilians do put in the hours. Deadlines are often treated as flexible. Highly structured business practices may work against a team, as does a degree of arrogance and bossiness often displayed by managers. Flexibility and pragmatism are the keys to success.

Leadership

Strong leaders

In Brazil, a team is a group of individuals bound together by a strong leader whom they regard as a superior. Brazilian managers will consult with key stakeholders, but the function of team meetings is often simply to give orders and instructions. The process can appear autocratic to Northern Europeans and Americans, but managers are also expected to demonstrate a duty of care towards subordinates, which means taking a personal interest in them.

Decisions

Expect some people to say one thing and do another in Brazil: your word is not regarded as an absolute bond. Always check the decision-making authority and get confirmation.

Feedback

Many large companies in Brazil have formal appraisal processes for employees but everyday feedback on performance or to raise issues is always done in private.

Gender and race in management

Although women may earn comparatively lower salaries than men, in the principal cities women are an important part of the workforce, less so in the more conservative interior. Woman own companies and are leading journalists, lawyers and doctors. Foreign women executives should not expect to encounter problems in Brazil.

Brazil is a multicultural, racially tolerant society but there may be some tension between 'white pride' and people of mixed race. If in any doubt, lead with your business card and make clear your position in the business hierarchy.

Etiquette

Greeting and leave-taking

Forms of address in Brazil can be quite formal, as Brazilians are used to distinctions of age and rank. Even if you are on first-name terms with someone, you will probably use a term of respect, such as *Seu* Pedro, Dona Ana or *Doutor* Francisco (for bosses). Address strangers aso *Senhor* or *o Senhora*. One of the key issues in Brazil is rank inequality within the population. This means that people will always be polite to foreigners but may appear quite rude to junior and support staff, in the way they give orders or criticise.

Dress code

Dress well: Brazilians are fashion conscious. In Rio, even if someone is dressed casually, their jeans and shirt will be fashionable and perfectly pressed. Businesswomen wear sandals with 'city heels' and often no tights. Men wear designer ties, good shoes and a good leather belt; a short-sleeved shirt with a tie will make you a figure of fun. Personal hygiene is considered very important.

Gift-giving

Gifts are not necessary although invitations to lunch or dinner are appreciated. Gifts may be given on social occasions, but keep them inexpensive and avoid personal items. Also avoid green and gold together (the colour of the national flag).

Great gifts	Gifts to avoid
• Scotch or champagne, something for the children for home visits	• Anything black or purple (associated with funerals), knives (the breaking of a relationship) or handkerchiefs (grief)

Hospitality

Lunch is normally a two-hour affair between 12pm and 2pm. Dinner starts from 7pm, but dinner parties may not begin until 10pm. Formal business entertainment usually takes place somewhere smart and prestigious. If you're entertaining a business associate, ask his secretary to recommend a restaurant. Business is usually discussed during coffee at the end of the meal. A couple of general points: punctuality is not important in Brazil; smoking is common.

Brazil: business style

Expectations of business relationships

1. Relationship driven — Task driven

2. Risk embracing — Risk averse

3. Equality — Hierarchy

Communication

4. Direct — Indirect

5. Formal — Informal

6. Emotional — Neutral

Management

7. Teams — Individuals

8. Time tight — Time loose

9. Top down — Delegation

Brazil: fast facts

Name	Federative Republic of Brazil Brazil
Nationality	Brazilian
Population	201 million (estimate: July 2013)
Languages	Portuguese (official) Spanish, English and French A large number of minor Amerindian languages spoken
Capital	Brasilia (pop. almost 4 million)
Main cities	Sao Paulo (20 million) Rio de Janeiro (12 million) Belo Horizonte (5 million) Porto Alegre (4 million)
Climate	Hot: July is midwinter; January is summertime.
Currency	Brazilian Real (BRL)
Ethnicities	White 55% Mulatto (mixed white and black) 38% Black 6% Other 1%
Religion	Roman Catholic (nominal) 73.6% Protestant 15.4% Spiritualist 1.3% Bantu/voodoo 0.3%,,other 1.8% Unspecified 0.2% None 7.4% (2000 census)
Internet code	Br
Phone country code	55

SOURCE: CIA WORLD FACTBOOK JULY 2013

China

Ways to succeed	Ways to fail
• Sincerity is most important in China	• Expect quick results
• Spend time building the relationship	• Lose your temper or get impatient – shows lack of control
• Show respect and consideration to senior people and older people	• Fail to keep in regular contact
• Show modesty in clothes, in eating and drinking	• Be extravagant or immodest in dress, behaviour or personal habits
• Doing favours is the way to build relationships. If you are asked to help, you should always try. It will be reciprocated	• Fail to reciprocate generosity or favours

Overview

When China began to reform its economy in the late 1970s, few could have foreseen the transformation and paradoxes that have swept over the country in four decades. China now exports more IT products and services than the USA, but poverty is rife in rural areas. It is the world's most populous country, but is also one of the most rapidly ageing, a partial consequence of its one-child policy introduced in 1979. It is ruled by a Communist government, yet only a third of the economy is now directly state-controlled.

China is now attempting to achieve a more balanced pattern of economic growth and fairer rewards for more of its population, and has to address some of the severe pollution issues caused by its surging expansion. But growth will continue, and business opportunities for foreign companies will flourish. For centuries, China's civilization was more advanced in the arts and sciences compared to the West, so it's not surprising that its people continue to believe in their superiority, despite the social and military problems that afflicted the country in the 19th and early 20th centuries.

Expectations

Confucianism and Daoism

A key principle in Chinese society is Confucianism, the code established by the sixth century BC philosopher, Confucius. He preached that the family is the basic unit of society, and praised the virtues of hierarchy and filial piety. Daoism is another strong force in China. It lays down a system of natural justice, first propounded by Lao Tse in 570 BC. Even 30 minutes absorbing the ideas of these two movements would benefit visitors to China.

The Chinese admire the work ethic, the power of the extended family and sincerity. They dislike losing face, immodesty, disrespect towards elders and extravagance.

Guanxi

The Chinese practice *guanxi* – gratitude for favours – and rely on the *danwei* unit, which regulates much of its members' working, social and community lives, although much less so than in the pre-reform era before 1978.

Face – *mianzi*

Mianzi, the giving and not losing of face (personal dignity) is very important and dictates how people act and talk, indirectly and with discretion.

Relationships

Chinese business is based on the development of good personal relationships over time. Duty, self-sacrifice, gentleness and wisdom are other traits admired by the Chinese. They consider that relationships are more important than tasks, and that the search for virtue is more important than the search for truth.

Communication

The Chinese don't use gestures and strong facial expressions, and are not tactile, so it's not surprising that they are often said to be inscrutable. Interpreters are often used in discussions, but never make the mistake of talking to the interpreter and not the boss. In discussions with the Chinese, check whether they're talking about today, tomorrow or several generations in the past or future. Unlike Indo-European languages, Chinese does not use verb tenses to differentiate between the past, present and future. Westerners must ensure that they clarify times and dates.

Presentations

Allow for an attention span of about 30 minutes. Stress the benefits of your proposal for China and the bottom line. The Chinese rarely say 'no', but instead will hint at difficulties, so be sensitive to this. Show commitment and enthusiasm to your project, and repeat your key points several times. Don't assume that silence means acceptance, and avoid asking for personal opinions.

Meetings

Agendas are adhered to in China, but expect slow, repetitious dealings. The Chinese like to establish general principles before moving onto detailed discussion. They also take the long view – sometimes extending over several generations. Be prepared to discuss problems at length, and be ready to understand their difficulties – these may be linked more to social matters or relationships than to the business. Don't push for information, and despite any irritation that you might feel internally, maintain a flexible but firm negotiation style. Your aim is to develop long-term mutual trust.

Negotiations

Be prepared to restate your position – several times. Be aware that 'yes' in China means 'I hear you' and not 'I agree'. A Chinese may also say 'yes' where Britons or North Americans would say 'no'. 'Is it ready?' Englishman: 'No, it isn't.' Chinese: 'Yes, it isn't.' Check what's really being said.

Subordinates in your team should not interrupt in meetings. Other tips: don't assume that a smile equals satisfaction, or that agreement equals understanding. Business cards are important, and it can be useful to have yours printed in Chinese on the back.

Networking

Ice-breakers	Ice-makers
• Chinese food	• What did your daddy do in the cultural revolution?
• Chinese art, literature and culture	• The Tiananmen Square massacre
• China's economic growth	• Taiwan
• China's achievements in the 2008 Olympics	• Tibet
	• Human rights in China

Organisation

Business hours

The new market-oriented economy has raised living standards for much of the population. But the Chinese continue to work relentlessly hard – for six days a week. Even government offices are open from 8am to 5pm from Monday to Saturday. Lunch in China is taken between 12 noon and 2pm, when everything shuts down. Office hours are usually 9am to 5pm with a half day on Saturday although the five-day working week is becoming more common. Many offices are closed in the week before and following the Chinese New Year.

China is a bureaucratic country, so things are unlikely to happen fast. Don't show impatience or anger: this is seen as a serious character flaw. Keep your schedule light to allow for long meetings. The Chinese appreciate patience, soft-spokenness, adaptability, humility and perseverance. They don't appreciate boisterousness, impetuousness or anger.

Time

Chinese people will always be on time for meetings and social occasions. Cancellation or lateness may be seen as insulting, unless good reasons are given.

Teams

Chinese teams are groups of specialists working under a leader, who is the acknowledged head of the group. He may not be a specialist but will have high seniority and links to the head of the company. Show respect to the team leader and refer issues to him in the first place. Any one-to-one contact between members of the team should be authorised by the team leader first. The Chinese like to achieve harmony within a team. Team members expect to see their view expressed in the outcome of a project, although implicit obedience to the team leader is also expected. The working pace tends to be slow and methodological, and deadlines are regarded as flexible. Emphasise the moral and social aims of the project.

Leadership

Organisational structures in China are vertical. A manager will seek consensus from his team, but will take personal responsibility for decisions. One potential difficulty for visitors is that a manager's authority is often based on his wealth and family background, rather than on his competence. Personal connections will also influence decisions. All of this, together with language difficulties, makes it hard for visitors to read meetings and negotiations accurately. In addition, family businesses tend to belong to trade groups, which also exert pressures.

Decisions are made slowly in China, but will have a long-term effect. Unlike many Western organisations, the Chinese are not obsessed by achieving short-term successes that may look impressive, but have not been fully thought through. Be prepared to invest time and money in visiting the decision-makers.

You'll find a difference in leadership style between older and newer organisations. The latter will tend to move faster and be less formal. Even so, don't be too forceful, and be careful not to express too many differences of opinion in public.

Feedback

If there is disagreement, manage the problem in private, and always use an impersonal approach. Say, 'Our partner was disappointed that the deadline was missed,' not 'You missed a deadline and now our partner is angry.' Stress harmony: 'Yesterday we won four new clients,' not 'Yesterday I negotiated deals with four new clients.'

Women in Chinese business

The position of women in Chinese society has improved dramatically since the advent of Communism in 1949, but they still hold only a few senior seats in government and business. Women visitors to China therefore receive special respect by virtue of being foreign.

It's important for a visiting woman to establish her credentials and expertise. One way might be to send an agenda, with brief biographies of your team members, before meetings. Dress conservatively – trouser suits are acceptable – and be prepared to be stared at – you're unusual. There will also be some unintentional rudeness in the form of cigarette smoke, or a door slamming in your face.

Moderation is expected of women in China, and many Chinese women don't drink at all. If you see women being treated in ways that you don't like, be cautious in your reaction. Women may be expected to be polite and respectful to senior men, which may be seen as sexist by some Westerners. Don't react to this: women have considerable authority in the domestic domain and individual women have considerable power in politics, administration and commerce, particularly in Hong Kong, China and Greater China (Taiwan).

Etiquette

Meeting and greeting

Introductions in China will be courteous and formal: expect to take a fair amount of time over them on your first visit. The highest-ranking member of your group should lead the way. You might be greeted by applause from your hosts, in which case the polite response is to applaud back. The Chinese are sensitive to titles, so use them whenever possible (for example, Director or Engineer). Don't address a Chinese person with the word 'comrade', a privilege reserved for Communist Party members. If you don't know a person's title, use Mr, Mrs or Miss until you're advised otherwise. In Chinese names, the surname comes first and the given names second. So Mao Tse-dong was known as Chairman Mao, not Chairman Tsedong.

Dress code

The Chinese appreciate conservative suits and ties, and dislike loud colours. Women tend to wear high-necked blouses and low heels.

Gifts

Gifts are important, as is the wrapping. Gold and red are good, but avoid black, white or blue (funeral colours). Offer gifts with both hands and don't open any that you receive in the presence of the giver. Make it clear that the gift is from your company to their company. Post-visit gifts – calendars, cards – are also appreciated. Unless you are invited to do so, don't take partners to official dinners and events.

Great gifts	Gifts to avoid
• Company pens, ashtrays, paperweights, books, whisky. Red is considered lucky.	• Flowers, chocolates, knives or clocks, which represent death or the end of a relationship. Avoid black, white or blue wrapping.

Hospitality

Chinese people tend to get up early and retire early, so expect to eat lunch around noon and dinner at about six for around two hours. Hospitality is an important tradition in China, and sharing the bill is unknown. You must reciprocate, however.

You'll probably be honoured with at least one banquet during your visit. Eat lightly – there may be a dozen courses. Use chopsticks, not your fingers, if you need to remove food from your mouth. The host will sit opposite the door, the honoured guest to his right. Speeches and toasts will happen. Remember *Gan-bei*! (dry glasses) is the common and expected toast. The evening will end when the host stands, usually soon after last course. The Chinese like to invite visitors to their homes, even though the conditions are unlikely to match your own domestic circumstances.

China: business style

Expectations of business relationships

1. Relationship driven   Task driven

2. Risk embracing   Risk averse

3. Equality   Hierarchy

Communication

4. Direct   Indirect

5. Formal   Informal

6. Emotional   Neutral

Management

7. Teams   Individuals

8. Time tight   Time loose

9. Top down   Delegation

China: fast facts

Name	People's Republic of China China
Nationality	Chinese
Population	1.4 billion (July 2013 est.)
Languages	Mandarin Yue (Cantonese) Wu (Shanghainese)
Capital	Beijing (pop. 20.5 million)
Main cities	Shanghai (23.5 million) Guanzhou (14 million) Tianjin (13 million) Shenzen (10 million)
Climate	Very diverse, ranging from tropical in the south to sub-arctic in the north
Currency	Remimbi (RMB)
Ethnicities	Han Chinese 91% Others 8.9%
Religion	Officially atheist Daoist, Buddhist, Christian 3-4% Muslim 1-2%
Internet code	cn
Phone country code	86

SOURCE: CIA WORLD FACTBOOK JULY 2013

France

Ways to succeed	Ways to fail
• Understand the free market vs social contract in France	• Do it all in English (and if you have no French, apologise)
• Make sure that French guests eat and drink well	• Ignore the French intellectual approach
• Be logical in your presentation and analysis	• Appear too familiar too soon or swear and drink too much
• Maintain a degree of formality in initial dealings	• Dig up the old clichés about France and the UK
• Be logical and consistent in negotiations and when you reach a decision, stick to it	• Decline lunch and buy a sandwich to eat at your desk

Overview

If you've ever felt a little overawed about the prospect of making a business trip to France, don't worry – your reaction is normal. The French can seem too cool and worldly, and sometimes aloof, especially to Britons and Americans. It's hardly surprising: they're great thinkers, and they value intelligence and eloquence. Philosophy is a part of French children's education, and logical thinking and a passion for abstract argument are inherent in the people.

This can cause problems for visitors from more pragmatic cultures, such as Britain and the USA, who often claim that the French are 'difficult'. But this simplistic dismissal ignores the contribution that the French have made to philosophy, literature, science and the arts over centuries. They are rigorous debaters, and they enjoy exercising this skill. Travel with a well-prepared proposition, think through the answers to all the awkward questions they could bring up, and learn from the experience.

The French are very conscious of the status of being French, and invest in big, imaginative projects aimed at increasing their international prestige. You see the architectural expressions of these ambitions every time you walk around Paris. The French also feel frustrated that their beloved language is rapidly losing ground to English in global business and diplomatic circles, so if you can talk at least some French, it will help to earn the respect of your new colleagues.

There are close links in France between industry and government, and the top echelons of both are educated at the *grandes ecoles*, graduate schools entered by competitive examination. To be an *énarque*, a graduate of the Ecole Nationale d'Administration, is to be marked as a future political or business leader. The structure of the state is mirrored by its major businesses, which are often centralised, ordered, legalistic and elitist.

France continues to struggle with the crisis of self-confidence that has affected its people in recent years. Its tax burden remains one of the highest in Europe, and unemployment has risen during the recession. Most French people accept that the country must adapt in the face of globalisation, yet no one seems to want to surrender the privileges bequeathed by their social system. While comfortably off Britons scour *la France profonde* in search of second homes, many younger French people openly express their admiration for Anglo-Saxon business models, and some 400,000 are said to be working in the UK. It's important to see France in context, however: it retains rich agricultural, manufacturing and service sectors, and claims one of the world's lowest poverty rates of only 6% (against 15% in the USA and 18% in the UK).

Expectations

Relationships

Building relationships is important in French business, and it's a process that French people do not like to rush. Lunches and dinners are important opportunities to develop these bonds. Although shorter lunch breaks are becoming more common, much of France stops work between 1pm and 2.30pm, and in August many firms close down for the annual summer break.

Civilisation francaise

The French believe that they have developed over centuries a civilised way of life which has contributed massively to European and world civilisation. They guard this ferociously. One key to this is the French language: elegant, logical and precise. It is very important that if you work regularly in France or with French people you learn some French. It is also important to respect the French way of life – food and wine, sport and leisure and intellectual pursuits.

The French way

The French often criticise the British for inconsistency – not following through on decisions and changing their minds after something has apparently been decided. In turn, the British accuse the French of 'selfishness' – acting in their own national and commercial interest at the expense of others. To succeed in doing business in France it is vital to escape these stereotypes, and accept that there is a French way of doing things to which the British need to conform.

French intellectualism

French education is very structured. There is an emphasis on logical thinking and presentation, building up of precise arguments in clear logical steps. They believe everything is interrelated. Therefore they like to examine a problem from every point of view. This can make French interventions in meetings quite long, thorough and quite academic-sounding, but practical in the end.

Rationality and emotion

Combining both northern neutrality and southern passion, France is a hybrid community combining rational thinking with a flair for passion and imaginative solutions.

Authority and individualism

French history has been punctuated by national outbreaks of violence and resistance. This illustrates the tension in France between the need for strong central control and the search for ways to express individualism.

L'exception francaise (the French exception)

The French believe they know what is best for them and for France, or more often what isn't best. They're good at complaining! This is why they can be very obstinate and stubborn in protecting what they see to be their own and France's best interests.

Overall, the French would describe themselves as relationship-oriented, formal, relatively relaxed about time and emotional in their dealings with others.

Communication

Presentations

The French love of logic and elegance means that you should be explicit and clear in what you are saying. Listen also for the logic behind the communication when a French person is speaking. Focus on the content of what you want to express, but remember that body language is also important in France. Demonstrate eagerness and enthusiasm for what you believe in, and use gestures for emphasis if you feel comfortable doing so. However, this is not an art that comes easily to most people from Anglo-Saxon cultures, so it's probably better to keep to your natural style rather than look like an overactive TV presenter.

The French are often categorical when they speak, and feel happy to express their disagreements directly and openly. Don't be put off by the Gallic *bouf!*, a dismissive snort or sniff that indicates dissent. Rely on factual evidence to prove your case, but demonstrate that you understand other points of view, even if you disagree with them. The French enjoy using wit in business discussions, but avoid criticising France.

Assume a relatively short attention span of about 20 minutes when you are addressing a French audience, so keep your presentation moving briskly. Stress the style, imaginative features and elegance of your idea or product, and expect active audience involvement and questions.

Meetings

The purpose of business meetings in France is coordination, briefing and allocation of tasks rather than to arrive at decisions. Given the French desire to debate intellectual propositions as well as practical points, you should outline the general principles of your proposal before you get into the details. It is considered rude to end a meeting if the business to be conducted has not been concluded, which can affect overall punctuality.

An agenda might be circulated, but no one will expect to keep to it. French meetings can be long and wordy, and the debate can become an intellectual exercise. The French believe that clarity of thought is achieved through intensive discussion, so it is important not to rush the proceedings. Expect to be questioned if there is imprecision in your proposition.

Meetings are usually formal occasions. Dress well, and expect a hierarchical seating arrangement. Surnames and formal introductions are used, and jackets are usually kept on. The style of the meeting will probably be polite and formal: use respect at all times.

Negotiation

French companies take time to reach decisions. They prefer to examine a problem or proposition from every angle. There is a stress on comprehensive, well-structured and well-written reports and studies. The French like to find out your position without revealing theirs until late in the discussion. Their approach will be perceptive, opportunistic but cautious. Rationality and logic are important to them: simply having a 'warm feeling' for something will not do, so go in armed with plenty of knowledge about your product, your market and its trends, and what the opposition is up to.

An important part of French management is systeme D (D = *debrouillard* or 'getting by'). This is a largely unspoken agreement or way of getting round complicated rules and bureaucracy in order to reach a satisfactory result. If there is a logjam in negotiations, ask or wait until someone suggests 'another way round the problem'.

Never take no for an answer. It may simply mean 'this is not the right time' but it sounds like an absolute refusal.

Networking

Ice-breakers	Ice-makers
• France's fascinating regions	• Compare French and UK unemployment rates
• Food and wine (including cheese)	• Ancient French/British rivalry (an outworn topic)
• Six Nations rugby football	• Why you've abandoned French wine for New World varieties.

Organisation

Business hours

French business hours are normally 9am to 5pm but may be extended as it is important to French workers to enjoy a proper lunch break to allow relaxation and networking. This may last an hour and a half to two hours. The French working week is legally 35 hours but many work longer. However, many French preserve a firm work-life balance and do not work at weekends.

Time

Although largely time conscious, the French are tolerant of lateness.

Teams

The principle criterion of selection is specialisation in a field required by the project. A strong leader is the focal point and teams are often characterised by competition rather than collaboration. Team members may act within their competence or remit (or even beyond it) without reference to others without group consensus. The authority of the team leader is essential in ensuring group harmony and completion of goals.

Leadership

It's important to be *correct* in style and manner and to be seen as *sérieux* (professional) in France. The PDG – *président directeur général* – decides the strategy, and managers draw up and execute the plan. The French say *'une entreprise n'est pas une démocratie'*– a business is not a democracy.

Feedback

Large companies have formal appraisal systems but general feedback may be given in team meetings. Personal feedback is normally done in private.

Women in management

Women occupy important positions in the cabinet and in business. Qualifications, not gender, are the way to executive power.

Etiquette

Greeting and leave-taking

The French are quite formal in public and preserve the distinction between the familiar *tu* and the formal *vous, two different ways of saying 'you'.* You should use *vous* with people you know until they invite you to use *tu.* Saying *bonjour monsieur* or *bonjour madame* is important in greetings: it preserves a degree of formality until you get to know people.

Gift-giving

Gifts are not expected but small personal gifts are appreciated. If offering food or wine, make sure it is from your country and of high quality.

Great gifts	Gifts to avoid
Flowers (but not yellow), chocolates or liqueur.	Wine (it may suggest they don't know their vintages).

Hospitality

Business entertaining in France is usually formal in style and takes place in restaurants. Check the dress code with your hosts: smart casual is increasingly acceptable. Smoking is a declining habit even among the French, although you'll often see people lighting up at the table, and certainly in the bar, without any embarrassment. Britons often see a visit to France as a reason to indulge in a little too much vin, but resist this. Drunkenness or overfamiliar talk after too many glasses is not seen as cool by the French. Likewise, Britons should leave at home those tired references to the supposedly ancient rivalry between England and France.

French people keep their private and public lives very separate, and tend not to invite visitors to their homes until real bonds have been established. Smoking is common in people's homes, but it's courteous to ask before you light up. Chewing gum at meetings and social events is considered rude.

France: business style

Expectations of business relationships

1. Relationship driven / Task driven

2. Risk embracing / Risk averse

3. Equality / Hierarchy

Communication

4. Direct / Indirect

5. Formal / Informal

6. Emotional / Neutral

Management

7. Teams / Individuals

8. Time tight / Time loose

9. Top down / Delegation

France: fast facts

Name	French Republic France
Nationality	French
Population	Country comparison to the world: 21
Languages	French (official) 100%, rapidly declining regional dialects and languages
Capital	Paris (pop. 10.5 million)
Main cities	Marseille-Aix-en-Provence 1.457 million Lyon 1.456 million Lille 1.028 million Nice-Cannes 977,000 (2009 est.)
Climate	Temperate climate with mild winters and hot summers in the south. A strong cold, dry wind called the Mistral also blows in the south.
Currency	Euro
Ethnicities	By law there are no official statements of ethnicities in France but market research estimates of first and second generation immigrants: Maghreb (North Africa) 1.23million Sub-Saharan Africa 1.08 million French West Indies: 757,000 Turkish: 250,000
Religion	Roman Catholic 83%-88%, Protestant 2%, Jewish 1%, Muslim 5%-10%, Unaffiliated 4%
Internet code	fr
Phone country code	33

SOURCE: CIA WORLD FACTBOOK JULY 2013

Germany

Ways to succeed	Ways to fail
• Demonstrate efficiency and punctuality	• Be disorganised and ignore due process
• Be straightforward and direct	• Promise and fail to deliver
• Do what you say you will do	• Do things without consultation
• Find out the rules and follow them	• Go over the heads of line managers
• Respect the management hierarchy	• Be overfamiliar with colleagues

Overview

Germany is the world's fourth largest world economy, and the leading economy and powerhouse of Europe. How Germany tackles the issues posed by globalisation will affect many other countries, especially its European Union partners, and its neighbours in Central and Eastern Europe.

The country has problems typical of Western European nations. Its social costs and taxes are high, and its population is ageing and unwilling to surrender privileges. In addition, Germany continues to modernise and invest in the east of the country, pumping millions into the former Soviet satellite territory. Jobs are beginning to disappear eastwards from its manufacturing sector, which is already suffering unemployment problems. The government is struggling to address these challenges, and it is hard to imagine that a country so rich in resources will not resolve at least some of its difficulties.

Geographically, Germany has three main areas: the lowlands in the north, the uplands in the centre and the mountains in the south. There are sixteen states, or länder, with the federal capital in Berlin. Like many parts of Europe, Germany preserves a cultural difference between its Lutheran north and its Roman Catholic south (Frankfurt and below). Southerners tend to be more expansive than their northern compatriots.

Although Germany is a varied country with considerable differences between business communities and firms north and south and east and west, there are a number of common features and trends. We have identified these in this profile.

Expectations

Efficiency

Efficiency is imperative to the Germans. In business they seek *ordnung* (order) and *klarheit* (clarity) to achieve an organised system, and they expect a strong work ethic, reliability and honesty from their employees and partners. Formality, punctuality, fairness and obedience to authority are other German characteristics. All of this means that the Germans excel at the detailed planning of projects, and completing them on time and to specification.

Separation of home and work life

Many visitors remark on the difference between German business and home life. The friendliness and cosiness (*gemutlichheit*) of German homes contrasts starkly with the utilitarian nature of much of their offices. For Germans the light conversation about everyday things (*unterhaltung*) is kept for the kitchen table. In bars a table is kept for regular clients to gather and drink and talk. Although it is changing, Germans still maintain a stronger separation between home and office than we do. *'Dienst ist Dienst und Schnaps ist Schnaps'* ('Work is work and play [drink] is play') is an important distinction in German culture.

Truth and duty

Truth and duty are important values for Germans. Germans are brought up to believe that using their language correctly and precisely is a point of honour and that to say what you mean and mean what you say is important. This leads to a degree of directness that can come across as rude or arrogant. This is rarely intentional. Germans, on the other hand, can find British indirect and non-committal communication quite hard to take.

Social responsibility

Germans also have a strong sense of social responsibility and citizenship. This affects everything from their attitude to organisation to their recycling of rubbish.

Although Germans, by and large, show tolerance for foreigners, they are prepared to remind them of their social responsibilities, such as how to put our rubbish, or when to wash or not wash cars, or when to make noise. What the British sometimes see as intolerable intrusion on personal liberty, the Germans simply see as being a good citizen.

Thoroughness

Doing things thoroughly (*grundlichkeit*) and in the right way is a German value.

Within limits, they would rather things happened later (as long as they are well-informed in advance) than with lower quality by taking short cuts.

Time consciousness

German and British cultural behaviour is broadly comparable and is different in degree rather than by type of behaviour. The British are equally time conscious, task- and systems- minded and reserved in their emotions. The one difference is that British business tends to be less formal in style and approach than German business.

Humour

The tone of many work environments can be serious and formal, which probably contributes to the misconception that Germans lack a sense of humour. But talk to foreign business people who have worked in Germany, and they'll give you a different version: when the Germans are off-duty, they can be plenty of fun.

Communication

Communication style

German communication style tends to be direct and to the point. This can sometimes appear abrupt and rude but is simply a style of speech and writing. There are differences in communication styles between different parts of the country. Bavaria, for example, is considered to be more effusive and expansive than the rest of the country.

Germans are interesting, intelligent conversationalists, interested in ideas and in the world around them.

Presentations

When you're presenting to a German audience, they will expect to hear the full technical details of your idea. They prefer logical arguments rather than emotional 'hunch' type proposals, and the content is more important for them than body language. The attention span in German meetings is usually long – up to an hour. They will ask detailed questions and expect in-depth answers. They also have a great respect for the truth as they see it, and this may lead them to appear unusually outspoken at times. As a rule, expect politeness but don't look for flattery. It's best to avoid jokes in presentations or formal discussions, and during office hours generally. Audiences are unlikely to interrupt you except to seek clarification.

It used to be traditional in Germany to follow up phone or e-mail communications with a written confirmation by conventional mail, but even German managers are now saying that life is too short to observe this at all times.

Meetings

Meetings in Germany are used to agree decisions and action plans, brief participants and implement action. The pace may be slow if technical issues are presented in detail, and the agenda will be followed in order. The discussion will seek consensus and common ground, reliable partners and long-term profit. Be punctual, dress formally, observe the hierarchical seating plan, and be serious in your approach.

Negotiations

In bargaining with Germans it is important to start with a real-istic 'first price'. A too high or too low bargaining position will raise distrust. German negotiators prepare carefully and are not easily moved from their prepared positions. They also take time to discuss with responsible colleagues before agreement. A German company may offer a small contract to a new supplier. Depending on performance and reliability, a larger one may follow. Once signed, contracts are non-negotiable.

Networking

Ice-breakers	Ice-makers
• Interest in German and European affairs	• Private life - Personal circumstances, children etc. Avoid overfamiliarity.
• Overseas travel and holidays – Germans are great travellers	• Germany's role in the Second World War
• Latest exhibitions, movies, events – not necessarily German	• 'Five-one', stressing the Anglo-German football rivalry
• Sport (especially football) – UEFA and World Cup	• Inappropriate jokes in business meetings

Organisation

Business hours

The office tone in Germany tends to be quiet and measured, and the working environment clean and well ordered. A clear desk is admired, and there's a tendency towards a closed-door culture rather than open-plan arrangements. Working hours in Germany tend to be from 8am to 5pm or 5.30pm. People often eat lunch in the office or the office café for 30 minutes or an hour. Note that most Germans leave work promptly and that the switchboard and, in some companies, even the server may be closed before work ends. Germans tend to consider late working as inefficient or evidence of poor job description.

Time

A key part of German organisations is delivery on or before time. Lateness is considered inefficient and evidence of poor planning. The only area where lateness might be considered is in order to improve quality. However, an important feature of German management is preparation and planning time. This can take much longer than business partners and clients expect.

Team-working

A typical team in a German company will be formed of individuals selected for particular technical competencies. Everyone will have a strong sense of their position in the organisation's hierarchy, and will conform to company procedures; they will also regard deadlines as fixed. Progress might be slow and methodical, but the leader will be expected to give firm and confident direction.

Leadership

Management tends to be by consensus and consultation, backed by a great deal of research. Juniors show seniors considerable respect. Equally, you should respect the hierarchy: never split or undermine superiors in German organisations, and do not bypass people by going higher to complain or search for decisions. Propose constructive alternatives rather than offering criticism. Differences of opinion are best dealt with in face-to-face discussions rather than via a third party or on paper.

German managers often spend more years at university than their counterparts in other countries, and may not enter the workforce until they are 27 or even older. German managers and business leaders may have doctorates, and the appellation Herr Doktor is not uncommon. Key factors in promotion in Germany are a person's education and qualifications, track record and seniority. Managers change jobs less often than their British and US colleagues.

Women in management

There is no distinction made between men and women in the management hierarchy.

Etiquette

Germany is still a surname culture. Although Germans may use your first name outside the office, in business meetings they will address each other, including women, by surnames alone. Naturally, they're experts at decoding when to switch between surnames and first names.

British and American visitors to Germany should forget the matey office culture that exists in their home countries, where employees are often encouraged to address even the MD or CEO by his or her first name. You'll look a bit of a cowboy if you do that in Germany.

Meeting and greeting

Shaking hands at the beginning and end of business meetings and the business day is essential. Good working relationships can be easily formed, but be careful not to lapse into over-familiarity. Formality is important in office dealings, and endearments and diminutives – using the short form of someone's name – are not acceptable. When addressing women, use *Frau* Schmidt rather than *Fraulein* Schmidt, except for young people.

Dress code

In many offices smart casual is the dress code. But for client-facing business a jacket and tie or a more formal top and skirt or trousers is preferred.

Gift-giving

Gift-giving is personal not business. Keep gifts, if you take them, small and take food or drink or maybe a personal souvenir typical of your country. Flowers are usually presented unwrapped.

Great gifts	Gifts to avoid
Unwrapped flowers	Lilies and chrysanthemums (funerals)
Chocolates and presents from your	Intimate gifts (perfume or jewellery)
region	Wine (unless of high quality)

Hospitality

Lunch is the main meal of the day. Germans normally expect to spend evenings with friends and family so don't expect invitations unless you are a close friend. If invited to a German house, never greet or give gifts across the threshold – either inside or outside, for good luck.

Germany: business style

Expectations of business relationships

1. Relationship driven — Task driven

2. Risk embracing — Risk averse

3. Equality — Hierarchy

Communication

4. Direct — Indirect

5. Formal — Informal

6. Emotional — Neutral

Management

7. Teams — Individuals

8. Time tight — Time loose

9. Top down — Delegation

Germany: fast facts

Name	Federal Republic of Germany Germany
Nationality	German
Population	81 milllion
Languages	German
Capital	Berlin (pop. 3.5 million)
Main cities	Hamburg 1.786 million Munich 1.349 million Cologne 1.001 million (2009 est.)
Climate	Temperate and marine; cool, cloudy, wet winters and summers; occasional warm mountain wind (foehn)
Currency	Euro
Ethnicities	German 91.5%, Turkish 2.4%, other 6.1%
Religion	Protestant 34%, Roman Catholic 34%, Muslim 3.7%, unaffiliated or other 28.3%
Internet code	De (Deutschland)
Phone country code	49

SOURCE: CIA WORLD FACTBOOK JULY 2013

India

Ways to succeed	Ways to fail
• Spend time building the relationship	• Be patronising
• Do things on the phone or face to face where you can – you will get better results	• Be overzealous about timing
• Explain very clearly what you want done – thought put in earlier to precise wording of tasks achieves better results	• Show no interest in Indian culture and family life
• Be friendly, smile and don't be afraid to show your human face	• Be intolerant if things don't happen exactly the way you expect
• Be more relaxed about time and schedules – things can happen very quickly when needed, but often not before	• Don't show your human side

Overview

India is a South Asian country with the second biggest population in the world after China (1.1 billion) and is scheduled to be the third largest economy in the world by 2050 after China and USA, according to Goldman Sachs.

Its population has a large and increasing middle class of some 300 million people. Indians are proud of the huge variety of their country, including the six metros (metropolitan cities) of Delhi, Mumbai, Hyderabad, Bangalore, Kolkata and Chennai, its 28 states, its 14 official and 300 minor languages, and seven major religions (Hinduism, Islam, Buddhism, Sihkism,

Parseeism, Jainism and Christianity). They are also deeply aware of the difference between the cities and the rural areas and the poverty and wealth that exists side by side in India.

Hindi is the official language and the majority of Indians (80%) are Hindus. English is the lingua franca of the country, including among Indians from different regions, but it is a particular variety of English – different in some respects from the English used internationally. There are 13 other official languages.

The famous caste system, which divided Hindus into four groups, Brahmins (priests), Tshatriyas (warriors), Vaishyas (merchants) and Sudras (clerks), together with the Dalits (untouchables), was outlawed in 1950 but still has some social values. India won independence from British rule in 1947 and became a republic in 1950.

Many Indians settled in Kenya and Uganda but came to Britain in the early 1960s.

India and the UK share many superficial similarities in the way they conduct business. Legal, banking and administration systems have many synergies with British procedures. This is not surprising, as many Indian business practices originated during the Raj, the era of British colonial domination from the 18th century to the country's independence in 1947. However, these apparent similarities mask significant cultural differences.

Indians think the British are much more formal than they really are, which accounts for their sometimes old-fashioned approach to us and the use of what has been called 'dictionary' English. Equally, Britons must be careful not to patronise. This is all too easy to do after the decades of *Carry On*-type films that caricatured Indian speech and mannerisms. The Indians you deal with will probably be highly qualified, and many have wide experience in a number of industries. Show respect for their abilities and point of view.

Expectations

Values and attitudes are the key to the way a community thinks, derived from parents, schools, education, social environment and media. These values and attitudes will be reflected in business behaviour.

Family

The first value for Indians is their family. They recognise a wide variety of relatives as immediate family, and it is common for different generations of the same family to live in a property together. The father is the absolute head of the household. First and foremost, Indians earn money to support their family. Foreigners are often unaware of the enormous pressures of family life, religion and environmental issues (such as the monsoon) on Indian working life. Don't assume that someone who is occasionally late or requests time off is slacking. This is usually made up for in other ways. If there are problems, be prepared to sit down and talk with people.

Relationships

In the first place, India is a relationship-based business culture, while the UK is, by and large, a systems-based business culture. The British don't have to be friends with you to work with you. Indians are different: they appreciate a family atmosphere at work, so take time to learn names – it's a sign that you care. Expect people to ask you a lot of personal questions: Indians are emotional, and they appreciate seeing the human side of the people they deal with. Kindness and empathy are key to success in India.

The guest is king

Indians show great politeness and consideration to guests, and they extend this courtesy to foreigners. You will meet politeness and courtesy and should be careful to respond in kind.

Devotion

Indians are devout and belong to a variety of different religions with different religious preferences. Hindus eat no beef and venerate the cow. Muslims will not touch pork or ham, Sikh men wear long hair under a turban and carry a ceremonial knife. Followers of Jain eat no root vegetables, such as onions, garlic and potatoes. Most Indians follow a mainly vegetarian diet with meat eaten occasionally.

Although India has no official religion, it is a strongly religious society with great respect for age, tradition and sacred symbols. Hindu and Buddhism are the two main religions, but there is also Jainism, Sikhism, Christianity and Islam.

Karma – fate

Indians believe in karma – your destiny as shaped by your actions in previous existences – and fatalism. They value the family, human warmth, gentleness and asceticism. They also appreciate the profit motive, creativity, and the importance of seeking compromises that will benefit all parties. They cherish democracy – India is the world's largest democratic state – and hate any suggestion of exploitation by Europeans or

Americans. Impiety, loss of face and personal criticism are also offensive to them.

Authority

India is very respectful of authority. This extends to not taking decisions beyond their immediate responsibility, not challenging instructions and not contradicting managers – even if they are wrong. It's important to check instructions have been understood and to follow up on implementation.

Respect

It is also important for Indians to protect personal dignity and they will go a long way to prevent you losing face and will want to protect their own. They hold respect for older people and people in authority and foreigners have a special position in Indian society. It is important to recognise that what may seem exaggerated politeness and deference in some cases is simply respect.

Communication

Regular contact by phone and email and frequent personal visits are important when you're doing business with Indians. If you try to communicate simply by sending occasional formal emails, no matter how detailed and clear they might be, you won't build the kind of relationship that is so prized in India.

Compliments

Flattery and compliments are an important way of putting people at ease when you're developing the relationship. Beware, though, that this inevitably means that people may say what they think you want you to hear rather than objective truths. The word 'no' has harsh implications. Evasive refusals are more polite, so say something like, 'I'll try' instead. Learn to develop a tolerance for ambiguity in conversation.

Indians value eloquence in spoken communication, which can lead to long speeches delivered with passion. They will normally present the reasons for doing something first and the conclusions afterwards, which may conflict with American and British approaches. The British and the Americans will tend to work the other way round, say what they want and then explain the reasons.

Humour

Indians may not always understand Western humour, but they appreciate charm and laughter, so rely on those approaches to get you through. Politeness and praise are important, and people often use 'we' rather than 'I'. Indian body language is generally expressive and important to communication – but don't be confused by the nodding of heads when people are listening to you. It says, 'We are paying attention', not 'We agree with you'.

Oral agreements are very important in India. The phone – and increasingly the mobile – is a vital communications medium. Telephone answering machines are often seen as impersonal, and may not be responded to.

Meetings and negotiating

Indian business is unhurried, and people take time to discuss the finer points of a project. But implementation can move extremely fast. So expect negotiations to take longer than you are used to: what you see as efficient time management may be viewed as aggressiveness or greed in India. Time spent at the beginning discussing all the points of the relationship will save time later. There will be a difference between managers who are used to working in the old family-run businesses and those who have experience of multinational companies. The latter will behave much more in ways that you are used to.

Indians are open to being persuaded. They appreciate eloquent speech and elaborate description, and it's also useful to outline your education, expertise and experience. Your audience will want to give feedback: allow time for this when you are presenting, and indicate when you will accept questions.

Respect for education and formality means that Indians use titles and surnames when they first meet you. Don't use first names unless you are asked to, although the younger generation gets on first-name terms much faster. Don't offer to shake hands unless your Indian counterpart does. You don't normally shake hands with women in India, but Westernised women will sometimes offer their hand.

Agendas are not strictly adhered to. The aims of a negotiation will be revealed early in a discussion, but the objectives may not be divulged till later. They may say what they want to achieve in general terms but the details may take time to emerge. Indians are usually flexible, patient negotiators, and they often use personalised and sometimes emotional arguments. They are usually willing to compromise, especially in the interests of forming good long-term relations.

Negotiations often involve large groups, although individuals may be given the responsibility to pursue discussions beyond initial meetings. Remember that contracts are often considered as statements of intent, which can be modified, an approach that can be confusing to Westerners. This is because the first and foremost aim of an Indian negotiation is to achieve an agreement on which the relationship can be built. The details can be managed later. Indians tend to see contracts as the beginning of a negotiation, not the end. But anything written will be held to and will be scrutinised carefully.

'Do and taboo' conversations in India

As a multicultural, diverse society Indians are very tolerant, especially of foreigners. When you get to know people you can discuss anything you would in the UK and the USA but the following guidelines may be helpful.

Networking

Ice-breakers	Ice-makers
• Business • Family • Region people come from • Local food and culture	• Politics: particularly Kashmir and China • Poverty • Sex and dirty jokes • Negative attitudes to Indians • Money and income

Organisation

Indians are masters of improvisation and flexibility, and their attitude to time reflects this. They believe in cycles – the equivalent of the saying, 'What goes around, comes around.' Adaptability is therefore a necessary skill for visitors doing business. Your pre-planning may not be acted on until you arrive, but when you do get there, it will be put into practice fast. So although the overall process of business is quite time-consuming and demands patience, individual actions will be accomplished very fast. Some say it's easier to see the CEO of an Indian company at three hours' notice than at three months'. Company organigrams are not fixed, and people may be given additional internal responsibilities in your absence or be transferred to you without notice. Be prepared for change when you arrive and maintain a relaxed attitude. Keep in regular contact with colleagues to stay up to date with changes in personnel responsibilities and job movements. Indian managers believe that the prime factors in winning promotion are connections, education and hard work.

Team-working

Indians often feel happier working together on tasks that Westerners would normally do on their own. For example, emails are often not acted on, as people feel more confident talking things through face to face, so be prepared to follow up requests with a phone call to discuss issues. A team is usually headed by a charismatic leader, who will often have family or trade group connections; remember that these may influence his decisions.

Team members will usually be selected on the grounds of seniority, experience and education. Decisions are reached by consultation, and team members will expect to see their view-point reflected in the outcome. The working pace tends to be slow, and deadlines are flexible. Although consultation is important, the team leader makes decisions, the most powerful ones with or without consultation. Try not to put the team under too much pressure, or be too openly competitive or ambitious. Don't attach personal blame: if something goes wrong, it's karma.

Leadership

Management style

Indian companies operate a top-down system of management and all major decisions will be taken at the top of the company, so make your approaches at this level. Indians prefer estab-lished processes, and new ideas will have to be sold convin-cingly to your new colleagues. Persistent persuasion and appeals to emotion are often more successful than hard logic or fact. Remember, too, that Indians appreciate a win-win situation, and compromise is therefore acceptable to them.

Listen carefully to proposed solutions. They may seem illogical to you, but will usually work in the Indian context. People do not express disagreement directly. Disagreements may be expressed in writing or face to face.

Gender

Women can occupy senior positions in business and adminis-tration in India. However, Indians generally are not accustomed to women in authority and may feel awkward dealing with senior foreign women.

Feedback

Feedback from senior to junior colleagues can appear quite abrupt and dismissive. Direct orders are common. However, feedback on performance is normally done in private.

Etiquette

Greetings and leave-taking

Handshaking is the normal style of greeting and leave-taking but wait for women to extend their hands first. The *namaste* greeting of hands joined in prayer at chest level with head slightly bowed is a traditional gesture of respect.

Dress code

Smart casual is common in offices and suits and ties or trouser suits for more formal occasions. Traditionally the head and the ears are viewed as sacred and the feet as dirty, so don't point your feet or touch another with your shoes (if you do so, apologise).

Gift-giving

Gift-giving is common, but if you receive one, don't open it in front of your visitor. Green, red and yellow are seen as lucky colours, but black and white as unlucky.

Great gifts	Gifts to avoid
• Chocolates • Flowers (but not frangipani – associated with funerals)	• Leather products to Hindus • Pork or pig products to Muslims • Dog toys or pictures of dogs (unclean to Muslims)

Hospitality

Don't refuse refreshment – it's an insult. It is customary to decline the first offer, but you should accept the second or third. Business lunches are preferred to dinners. Most Indian meals are vegetarian with a little meat on the side, but remember that Hindus do not eat beef and Muslims do not eat pork. People drink water (only from sealed bottles), soft drinks or beer. Evening entertaining is quite often done at home: if you are invited, arrive 15 to 30 minutes late. Wash your hands after a meal.

India: business style

Expectations of business relationships

1. Relationship driven — Task driven

2. Risk embracing — Risk averse

3. Equality — Hierarchy

Communication

4. Direct — Indirect

5. Formal — Informal

6. Emotional — Neutral

Management

7. Teams — Individuals

8. Time tight — Time loose

9. Top down — Delegation

India: fast facts

Name	Republic of India India
Nationality	Indian
Population	1,220,800,359 (July 2013 est.)
Languages	Hindi 41% (official language), English (subsidiary English language), 14 other official languages: Bengali 8.1%, Telugu 7.2%, Marathi 7%, Tamil 5.9%, Urdu 5%, Gujarati 4.5%, Malayalam 3.2%, Kannada 3.7%, Oriya 3.2%, Punjabi 2.8%, Assamese 1.3%, plus Kashmiri, Sindhi and Sanskrit (2001 census)
Capital	New Delhi (pop. 21.72 million)
Main cities	Mumbai 19.695 million Kolkata 15.294 million Chennai 7.416 million Bangalore 7.079 million (2009)
Climate	Varies from tropical monsoon in the south to temperate in the north
Currency	Rupee
Ethnicities	Indo-Aryan 72%, Dravidian 25%, Mongoloid and other 3% (2000)
Religion	Hindu 80.5%, Muslim 13.4%, Christian 2.3%, Sikh 1.9%, other 1.8%, unspecified 0.1% (2001 census)
Internet code	in
Phone country code	91

SOURCE: CIA WORLD FACTBOOK JULY 2013

Italy

Ways to succeed	Ways to fail
• Business is strictly personal; build good personal relationships and keep in contact	• Criticise or belittle Italy
• Show appreciation of Italy and especially your partner's region	• Remain solely on a business footing
• Remember the top man/woman makes the decisions	• Refuse invitations to eat or drink with your hosts
• Dress carefully and in a coordinated fashion for all meetings; in Italy, clothes *do* make the man (or woman)	• Fail to present as good and as stylish an image as you can

Overview

With some 90% of its inhabitants Italian-speaking native Italians, Italy remains a remarkably homogeneous population. However, that is threatened by two issues: one long existing and one more recent. The long-existing one is the division between the north and south. This is often expressed as the tension between the richer more industrial north of Italy and the *Mezzogiorno*, the traditionally more rural and poorer south. A feature of post-war life in Italy was the migration of southern Italians to the industrial cities of the north, such as Milan. In fact in the post-war years, the south has benefited from considerable national funds and, since Italy became a founder member of the EU in 1956, of European funds for infrastructure and development. Even today there are differences in lifestyle and perceived wealth between the two regions. A more recent fear is that of immigration, particularly from Romania, Albania and from Libya, once an Italian protectorate.

Mini-states

It's important to remember that as well as the well-known boot of the Italian mainland, the islands of Sicily and Sardinia both form part of the country. Italy also contains two self-contained mini-states – San Marino and the Vatican State. The Principality of Monaco, ruled by the Grimaldi family, also considers itself to be Italian, despite being surrounded by France.

Regionalism vs nationalism

Italy is a Mediterranean country but extends upwards into the Alps in the northwest and Austria in the northeast. The people of Trieste, Turin and Milan have more in common with each other than any of them do with Rome or Naples.

Since Italy was a collection of city states loosely held together under the rule of the Austro-Hungarian empire until 1861, when Italy was unified, the regions jealously guard their cultural independence. Indeed, Italians embrace the concept of *campanalismo*, loyalty to the sound of your local church bell or campanile. Some say the only time the country gets together is to celebrate the success of Azurri, the national soccer team!

Economic growth

While many Northern Europeans dream of owning a house in the Tuscan sun, Italians get on with daily life in their country – and that's not always easy for them. Italy shares some problems with other 'old European' countries – an ageing population, high welfare costs and labour-market rigidities. But Italy also has to contend with its own unique difficulties. In common with the European Union recession, its growth has generally been slow. In addition to this, Italy has to cope with the north-south divide – unemployment is high in the agricultural south, high levels of organised crime, and controversy over immigration – even though the industrial north clearly needs labour. Tax avoidance is a national pastime, and experts claim that the underground economy accounts for between 15% and 27% of GDP. On top of all this, Italy has to import around 75% of its energy needs and most of its raw materials.

Small firms

A distinctive feature of the Italian economy – and what gives Italian products so much charisma – is its huge number of energetic small firms, many of them family owned. Around 90% of Italian businesses have less than ten employees. However, this vibrant SME (small- and medium-sized enterprises) sector is vulnerable to competition from lower-cost Asian products.

Cultural heritage

None of this detracts from the sheer fascination of being in Italy and in interacting with Italians. Their cultural heritage is vast and varied, from the Roman Empire to the Renaissance, to contemporary motorised emblems such as Ferrari and Ducati. Now they must find a direction for their future development.

All this being said, Italy remains one of the top ten world economies by GDP.

Expectations

Family first

An Italian's most immediate loyalty is to the family. Family ties are more important here than in any other country, with the possible exception of Spain, and mean far more to an Italian than political rules and regulations or company policy.

Pride

Italians are proud, and sensitive about their world reputation. A critical article in the *Financial Times* or *The Economist* can turn into a national event, responded to and discussed in the national press and on TV. They appreciate that their country is justly famed for its cuisine, wine, art, architecture and quality of life, but they are also intensely aware that its bureaucracy and business administration do match the standards of other European countries. Italy also remains sensitive about its Fascist period in the 1930s, especially when the movement experiences recurrences, and by the extremes of wealth and poverty in the north and south of the country.

Hierarchy

Keep in mind all these things when doing business in Italy, and remember also that Italians respect age, seniority and power. This means that the business structure is very hierarchical.

Relationships

The Italian cultural style is to build relationships, from which business can grow. This involves eating and drinking with business partners and getting to know each other's families. The business relationship remains quite formal and quite top down with decisions being taken at top level. Doing the business and taking the time needed is more important than bending the business to the time for Italians and they are not afraid to show their human side when they trust their business partner.

Communication

Intuition and emotion

Italians are driven by intuition and emotion, which is often the opposite to how business is conducted in many Northern European countries and in the USA. They will want to know you before they do business with you, so be prepared to chat about your family and personal life, your experiences in life and your impressions of Italy, without being obviously gushing. Your demeanour and the way you open up could have a major influence on the outcome of any dealings. They will want to feel that they can trust you.

Presentations

Because Italy is synonymous with style and elegance, ensure that any visual material you hand out or show, including audio-visual presentations, is well designed. It's also useful to have your card printed in Italian on one side, and to have your title clearly expressed. Include details of a relevant degree, if you have one.

Italian presentations tend to be short, 30 minutes is ample. Listeners are interested in your vision and style and in the presentation quality. They like a moderate to hard sell and a discussion of market opportunities. Allowing time for discussion is important.

Meetings

Don't expect to reach decisions in an initial meeting with Italians. At this stage it will be about finding out who you are and seeing if a relationship can evolve. If you push too hard at this stage, you will appear brusque – and it will weaken your eventual negotiating position. You may find that even at subsequent meetings no actual decisions will be reached: these gatherings are more to encourage debate and constructive criticism, while the boss rules on the outcome later. If your proposal involves dealing with the Italian bureaucratic or legal systems, expect to suffer lengthy delays and build that into your schedule.

Italians cut across one another during meetings, and their discussions may become very heated. Don't be alarmed by this as it's quite normal and not seen as at all rude by the participants.

Negotiation

Italians have had centuries of successful negotiation and are excellent at negotiating in detail. Italians see contracts as ways of building long-term relationships. They may accept secondary objectives as a way to achieve primary ones in the long term. Be aware that discussions on details may change the nature of the contract. Check the other side's promises. Can they deliver what they promise? Take notes so you can check.

Networking

Ice-breakers	Ice-makers
• Conversation about your family and background	• 'I used to have a Fiat but it rusted to bits'
• Italian culture, food and wine	• 'Your football hooligans are worse than ours'
• Sport, especially football	• 'Italy is dominated by the Mafia'
• Italian art, music and films	• Religion, politics, Second World War
	• Asking 'What do you do?' when you have just met
	• Sexual jokes

Organisation

Flexibility

Protocols, rules and procedures are often ignored in Italy, where managers focus on getting the essentials done without principles or rules getting in their way. This may be unnerving to visitors from cultures with more fixed patterns, but you have to learn to adjust to it in Italy.

Team-working

Teams are groups tasked with implementing policy. All decisions are taken at the top. Task leadership is delegated to trusted individuals.

Leadership

In an Italian company, the *presidente* is assisted by a board of directors (*consiglio d'amministrazione*) and an MD (*amministratore delegate*). A *direttore* is a departmental manager. Other titles tend to be meaningless: power lies with the boss and things are done well only with his or her personal supervision or involvement. Organigrams are usually for foreign colleagues, and may have no relevance within the organisation. Your best move as a foreign business person is to find out who is the prime decision-maker in a company.

Hierarchy

True hierarchies in Italian firms are based on networks of people who have built up personal alliances across the organisation. The primary attributes of a manager are flexibility and pragmatism; different departments will have different management styles depending on the boss.

Feedback

Appraisals and job descriptions are rarely used, and the key indicators monitored in Italian businesses are cash flow, turnover and gross profit.

Women In management

Women are highly respected in the home but less so in the workplace. Courtesy is important but so may be flirting. Make clear your position in the company and make sure your junior colleagues defer to you.

Etiquette

Greeting and leave-taking

It's normal to shake hands with everyone when you enter someone's office or when a meeting begins and ends, and to establish good eye contact. You may sense that it's appropriate to wait until a woman offers her hand before making the first move. Italians are generally punctual, especially in the north, so get to appointments on time.

Dress code – *la bella figura*

La bella figura means the way you present and conduct yourself, and the image you create. This includes the way you dress, so pick the best clothing from your wardrobe for both formal and casual wear. If necessary, buy something in which you feel really good before you go. You're never going to match the inherent style of the Italians, but at least you should leave behind those scuffed shoes and the bad ties that don't match your shirts. Italians, apparently, are Europe's biggest spenders on clothes and shoes.

Gift-giving

It's appropriate to take wine or chocolates if you are invited to someone's home for dinner. Make sure that it's a decent bottle, because Italians know their wine. If you're taking flowers, avoid red and yellow – the former implies secrecy, and the latter jealousy.

Great gifts	Gifts to avoid
• Small gifts of real quality, alcohol, delicacies or crafts from your country or maybe flowers or chocolates for junior personnel • Italian companies often give glossy coffee table books • Make sure flowers are odd numbers	• Gifts branded with a company logo • Chrysanthemums, handkerchiefs and brooches – sometimes associated with funerals • Black or purple wrapping (mourning) • Knives or sharp objects (breaking of friendship)

Hospitality

Timekeeping is a little more relaxed for social events than it is for business, so you can arrive between 15 and 30 minutes late for most of these functions. Italians tend not to exchange business cards at social events, but instead carry a calling card, which bears their contact details. If you're in Italy for a short time you may have no option but to rely only on business cards, but anyone settling there for a while, or even making frequent visits, should consider using a calling card.

You may find it difficult to pay the bill in a restaurant as the Italian host will normally expect to pay and men would normally expect to pay for women in the group.

Italy: business style

Expectations of business relationships

1. Relationship driven — Task driven

1. Relationship driven   Task driven

2. Risk embracing   Risk averse

3. Equality   Hierarchy

Communication

4. Direct   Indirect

5. Formal   Informal

6. Emotional   Neutral

Management

7. Teams   Individuals

8. Time tight   Time loose

9. Top down   Delegation

Italy: fast facts

Name	Italian Republic Italy
Nationality	Italian
Population	61,482,297 (July 2013 est.)
Languages	Italian
Capital	Rome (pop. 3.5 million)
Main cities	Milan 2.962 million Naples 2.27 million Turin 1.662 million Palermo 872,000 (2009)
Climate	Predominantly Mediterranean. Alpine in the far north; hot and dry in the south
Currency	Euro
Ethnicities	Italian
Religion	Christian 80% (overwhelming Roman Catholic with very small groups of Jehovah's Witnesses and Protestants), Muslims (about 700,000 but growing), atheists and agnostics 20%
Internet code	it
Phone country code	39

SOURCE: CIA WORLD FACTBOOK JULY 2013

Japan

Ways to succeed	Ways to fail
• Spend time building a good relationship	• Forget you are part of a team
• Be a good team player – consult	• Try to rush things
• Work hard and earn trust	• Ignore collective negotiation process
• Show loyalty to boss and to organisation	• Fail to build trust
• Value karaoke and socialising as a chance to get to know people personally	• Fail to deliver on time and to required standard

Overview

The development of Japanese society has been influenced by two factors: population density and isolation. On Japan's islands, 3% of the world's population live in just 0.3% of the world's landmass. Moreover, three-quarters of the landmass is mountainous and two-thirds forested, so only about 3% is habitable. Japan therefore has one of the world's highest population densities.

For two centuries, from 1648 to 1853, Japan was cut off from Western and other Asian trends. This isolation, together with the crowded living conditions, has produced a society with carefully evolved social rituals marked by high degrees of politeness and consideration.

After Japan began to modernise, a strong work ethic, a mastery of high technology and a comparatively small defense allocation (1% of GDP) helped it advance with extraordinary rapidity from

1955 to 1989. Then its bubble burst, and stock market and prop-erty prices slumped. The country remains, however, the second most technologically powerful in the world, and the third largest in economic terms behind the USA and China.

Expectations

Web society

Japan society is based on the principles of Confucius, the Chinese philosopher who taught that the family was the basic unit of society and that the father was its leader. From this developed a social model which includes these values:

- We are members of a group, not individuals
- The father is the leader, and relationships are unequal
- Save, stay calm, avoid extremes and shun indulgence – maintain moderation in all things

Senpai-kohai

The Japanese respect age and experience. Listeners are careful not to disagree with teachers or presenters, and the relation-ship between a mentoring manager, or *senpai*, and the learner, the *kohai*, is important in Japanese business.

Gaman

Gaman is the quality of endurance, of which the Japanese have great amounts. It implies following orders without question, and not complaining but 'gritting it out' and getting on with the job. This quality in the workplace explains the culture of long hours and sacrifice of 'me time' to the group.

Tatemae and honne

As in many countries, there is a difference between reality and façade. *Tatemae,* the art of diplomacy, indirectness and avoiding controversy and conflict, refers to the façade. As the Japanese get to know and trust you, they will reveal their real feelings – *honne* – and be more direct and honest. *Honne* often happens not in the office, but at social events. It's important to take every opportunity to attend these.

Face

The Japanese are extremely sensitive to what others think of them. They value a good image, and harmony with those they deal with is important. They achieve this by being obsessively polite and by showering you with compliments. You can return the compliment by being polite and respectful to them, especially in the early stages of a relationship.

The Japanese have a dread of losing face. To lose face means that you cannot be trusted. Extravagant gestures, loud voices and aggressive behaviour are signs of a lack of control and can cause loss of face. It's not good to be critical of colleagues or managers. Much Japanese reticence with foreigners is due to the fear of them losing face through Western unawareness of their culture. If you lose face by failing on a task or deadline, simply apologise: explaining the reasons is seen as making excuses. Accept responsibility, and work hard not to repeat it.

Communication

Indirect communication

Communication in Japan is subtle and much is left unspoken, although it is perfectly understood by the Japanese. It's easy for Westerners to cause offence where none is intended, so until you are attuned to Japanese nuances always check that you've clearly understood instructions.

Neutral style

The Japanese think it is wrong to get emotional or lose your temper. Rather than saying 'no' outright, they will convey disagreement through silence, hesitation, or responses such as 'Yes, but ...' or 'The situation is delicate'. They often refuse by saying, 'Thank you. We'll study that.'

Presentations

The presentation style tends to be quiet, and the presenter should be soberly dressed. The Japanese are polite and attentive listeners. They avoid steady eye contact, and maintain an impassive expression. Some may adopt a posture of deep concentration, and may appear to be asleep, although they're not. They prefer hard facts rather than emotional persuasion, visually presented. The Japanese take time to consider, and are comfortable with silence for reflection, which can unnerve Western visitors. If the room falls quiet, resist the urge to burst into speech. Signal any questions you wish to ask before you ask them.

Don't assume that because Japanese managers are hesitant in speaking English, they do not know the language. The Japanese can usually read and write it, but they can't always speak it or understand spoken English. Find ways, unobtrusively, of helping them to understand you. Give them more than one opportunity to grasp your message by using different ways to say the same thing, and always support any oral presentation with written backup.

Meetings

The Japanese are less concerned with what you say (they can read that) than with who you are. As a result they set a high value on *haragei* (belly talk), the art of reading feelings through silent meditation and observation. Senior Japanese managers sit in on meetings but rarely speak. They prefer to listen in a state of deep concentration. *Ishin-denshin*, heart-to-heart communication, is important in revealing the internal state of partners, expressed through tone of voice, facial expression and posture. The Japanese say, 'We hear one thing (the content), but understand two', (content and your feelings).

Before you enter a meeting, prepare a short introductory statement explaining why you're in Japan and how long you'll be there, the sort of people you're seeing, and your previous contact with the country. Decide on the five or six crucial points you want to make, and repeat them at each encounter. The Japanese believe that everyone who is in the loop needs to be at meetings, so these they can be quite large. The most senior person may say little, but to learn who that figure is, watch who is served tea first!

The amount of time spent on a meeting is less important than the procedure, so expect these sessions to be quite long.

Formality and the sequence of events matter. Don't use first names unless you're asked to. Use the suffix *san* for both men and women (for example, *Suzuki-san*). Never corner people or make them lose face. Don't seek final decisions in meetings – they're for gathering information or stating positions. Don't expect instant feedback: the Japanese prefer to question and clarify. Check what is verbally agreed, and follow it up with a written minute.

In a meeting with a new manager don't open business immediately, but let him do so. Your remarks will be taken seriously. How you express things is as important as what you say.

Negotiation

The Japanese negotiating style is impersonal and unemotional. But emotion lurks just below the surface, and logic alone will not work – the Japanese manager must like and trust you. It is important for the Japanese to establish the status of the person they are dealing with in order to know how to talk. This means that they may ask personal questions about your job, your responsibilities and your reporting structure. The exchange of business cards at the beginning of meetings is an important way of establishing this status for the Japanese, and should be carried out with proper respect.

Networking

Ice-breakers	Ice-makers
• General business	• Home and household – until you get to know people well
• Japanese language and culture	• The Second World War and Japan's role

Organisation

Business hours

The Japanese value hard work and long hours. Working hours are from 8am to 6pm and although Saturday working doesn't exist everywhere, many executives go in on Saturday to get noticed or to put themselves in line for promotion. It is considered respectful to leave the office after the boss. Executives usually have a one- or two-hour hour commute, and leave home early and get home late. They often don't see their children until the weekend.

Time

Punctuality is essential in Japanese culture, and suggests organisation and respect.

Team-working

A Japanese team is a group of individuals who work as a group for the wider good of the company. The group is therefore superior to individual wishes. Harmony is crucial: avoid open confrontation, or criticising superiors or subordinates. Allow all parties to save face, and reject nothing bluntly.

The team leader will make decisions, but will not act independently without internal support. The process tends to be slow to allow for consensus to emerge, and team members will be modest and self-effacing. It's important to keep to schedules, but deadlines can be extended if necessary.

Leadership

Team decision-making

The Japanese consult at all levels within a group before they reach the decision-making stage: this is called *nemawashi*. They then seek universal consensus – *ringi-sho* – to arrive at a decision. Japanese managers like to understand the background and reasons for decisions and proposals. Be patient – *nemawashi* and *ringi-sho* mean that they may be slow to decide, but once they do you can expect fast implementation.

The Japanese desire to save face becomes evident when they deliberate carefully and avoid taking risks in their statements and actions. Be patient in trying to get decisions: even routine issues may be subject to extensive discussion. Look for a contact who can keep you up to date informally on progress.

Feedback

Japanese managers rarely give direct orders: they hint at what is needed instead. Courtesy for the other person controls all their dealings. They use polite, indirect forms of English such as the passive voice: 'The company has decided' rather than 'We have decided'. They also rely on impersonal forms of speech: 'It has been found necessary to cancel' rather than 'We are cancelling'. Formal appraisals in international firms exists. However, feedback is usually personal but not always private. Japanese managers may criticise in public to demonstrate a lesson or to make an example.

Women in management

Japanese women tend to have separate lifestyles to men, and control the household. They still tend to give up work on marriage, and promotion for them is therefore restricted as they are not expected to stay in the workforce. This may change with the younger generation adopting more of an American lifestyle and the end of the job-for-life 'salaryman' tradition in Japanese business, leading to a greater need for double-income families.

Etiquette

Greeting and leave-taking

Japanese managers often introduce themselves by identifying their company, their department and finally their name. This is because they think of themselves as a 'we' society and not an 'I' society. They have a strong group mentality, which shows in their social life in the way they get together after work, and in their working life through collective decision- making. So use 'we' and not 'I' when talking about your department or company, and socialise with your Japanese colleagues after work when you can.

Contrary to a widely believed myth, bowing is not necessary for foreigners, but the business card ritual is. Offer your card so that the receiver can read it, study his card, keep it on the table while you're talking, and then put it in a business card holder, not your pocket. Your card should carry your company's name, your name, your job title and department. It should be in Japanese as well as in your own language.

Dress code

Office dress is quite formal, usually a dark suit, white shirt and dark tie. Women tend to wear dresses or a suit.

Gifts

Gift-giving and the creating and resolving of obligations is an important consideration. Gifts should be carefully wrapped and will often show the brand name. These are practical examples of *giri*, which manifests itself at a much deeper level between people as a debt of honour for favours received.

Great gifts	Gifts to avoid
Good quality branded goods especially local drink, whisky and golf-related items (the packaging is as important as the gift)	White chrysanthemums (funeral), even numbers (for example, four golf balls)

Hospitality

Evening hospitality offers an opportunity for personal revelation and more relaxed conversation, when you can discuss things off the record and reach decisions. Karaoke nights are important in team building: grit your teeth and go for it, and have a popular song ready to perform if you're up for it. You might also be invited to expensive restaurants, and if you're the MD of a reasonably sized company, you'll be expected to reciprocate. Entertaining usually takes place immediately after work. Midweek entertainment may stop at around 9pm to allow for the long commute home. Keep alcohol under control: the Japanese may get drunk to let off steam, but they don't expect it of Westerners. If Japanese colleagues get drunk in evening drinking sessions, no mention is made of it the next day.

Japan: business style

Expectations of business relationships

1. Relationship driven   Task driven

2. Risk embracing   Risk averse

3. Equality   Hierarchy

Communication

4. Direct   Indirect

5. Formal   Informal

6. Emotional   Neutral

Management

7. Teams   Individuals

8. Time tight   Time loose

9. Top down   Delegation

Japan: fast facts

Name	Japan
Nationality	Japanese
Population	127,253,075 (July 2013 est.)
Languages	Japanese
Capital	Tokyo (pop. 36.507 million)
Main cities	Nagoya 3.257 million Fukuoka-Kitakyushu 2.809 million Sapporo 2.673 million (2009)
Climate	Varies from tropical in the south to cool temperate in the north
Currency	Yen
Ethnicities	Japanese 98.5%, Koreans 0.5%, Chinese 0.4%, other 0.6%
Religion	Shintoism 83.9% Buddhism 71.4% Christianity 2% Other 7.8% (Note: many Japanese follow both Shintoism and Buddhism)
Internet code	Jp
Phone country code	81

SOURCE: CIA WORLD FACTBOOK JULY 2013

Russia

Ways to succeed	Ways to fail
• Be patient	• Criticise Russia
• Be very firm in your negotiation procedures, even tough – leadership and firmness are important business values in Russia	• Compromise too early in a negotiation
• Respect the Russian calendar. Their meeting times may not be the same as yours	• Fail to show unity in the team
• Pay attention to the hierarchy. It is important to give due respect to the boss	• Fail to check what lies behind the prosperous front
• Show personal warmth – Russians build business on personal relationships	• Use 'hard sell' rather than 'academic sell' tactics in negotiating

Overview

If you're going to be dealing with Russia, you'd better first consider the great topic of *dusha*, the Russian soul. Note that we said consider, and not understand, because even the Russians and some of their greatest writers continually debate the subject. Russians are certainly different from Westerners: they themselves claim that they are more spiritual. The vastness of their land, the harsh winters, and the country's tragic-glorious history have all contributed to the forging of the Russian soul.

Remember that Russia lost tens of millions of people – some historians claim 40 million – during Stalin's purges in the 1930s, and up to 27 million in the Second World War. From all this, Russians maintain a sense of endurance and faith in life, and they do not seem to make the clear distinction between hard logic and emotion that is prevalent in many Western business cultures. They often value intuition more than rationality. Certainly, Russians will want to feel that they like you before they do business with you.

Destiny now appears to be rewarding Russia's fortitude. Oil and gas revenues have transformed its economic situation and world standing after its loss of superpower status in the 1990s.

There is an expanding middle class, and a consumer economy thrives – at least in major cities. However, for the business community, Russia can still seem a daunting prospect. The country derives the bulk of its export revenue from commodities, which can leave it exposed to fluctuating prices. It must modernise its manufacturing industry, reduce corruption and crime and make its banking and other business infrastructures more welcoming to foreign investors. Even so, Russia is now enjoying greater stability than at any time since the momentous dismantling of the USSR in the 1990s.

Expectations

Money and community

Billionaires who can buy British Premiership football teams with the cash in their back pocket may have given a false impression of what Russians are really like. Most of them share a highly communal and collective spirit. This dates not just from the decades of Communist rule in the 20th century, but from long before the industrial era, when agrarian life was dominated by village communes and the traditional *artels,* cooperative associations of workers.

Traditional values

The analyst and former Russian Minister of Economics, Yevgeny Yasin, notes the following traditional values among his countrymen:

- An emphasis on spiritual principles and moral laws
- A propensity for teamwork based on a history of collectivism
- *Sobornost* – the community of the individual will and the endeavours of the people
- The joy of working
- A tendency to make far-reaching plans and sweeping actions

Some of these can have unfortunate reverse implications – collectivism can lead to the suppression of individuality and the creep of authoritarianism – but overall he believes that the Russian people's qualities can enable them to adapt to their challenges.

Importance of relationships

Russian business depends on good relationships and starts off formally, although the business will only develop if good informal relationships are developed. Russians would

describe themselves as relaxed about time. It is more important to complete the business in hand rather than to stick to strict timetables. Initially, Russians may appear reserved but they are happiest in an environment where they can freely express their emotions.

Communication

Relaxed approach

Good speaking skills are valued in Russia, but they will also note your tone of voice and body language. Russians appreciate a warm, relaxed approach, and will often ask you personal questions about your family and life in your home country. They can be quite tactile with people they regards as friends, but they are also direct and blunt, and mean what they say. This is unlike most relationship-focused countries, but learn to appreciate their candour rather than fearing it.

Presentations

Russians are interested in establishing the credibility of the speaker in terms of experience, qualifications and knowledge and you must establish this. Russians have a moderate attention span of 30 to 45 minutes. They will not appreciate you starting off with a joke, so keep your presentation serious, and include facts and technical details. But given what we've already said about the Russian personality, you can feel free to inject some emotion into your proposals. Russians enjoy looking at new ideas, but they distrust anything that sounds too official. Avoid words such as 'aggressive' and 'compromise': instead, talk about meeting each other halfway, or propose actions that depend on equal concessions from both sides.

Meetings

Meetings in Russia tend to be long, and often followed by meals. They're also quite formal, reflecting the hierarchical structure of Russian business, although it is important to preserve *uravnilovka*–- egalitarianism, or the idea that nobody is better than anybody else. You should respect this formality in your style and dress, especially at first encounters. Russians may start and finish late, so be flexible in timing. Meetings may also be subject to interruptions.

Negotiation

When it comes to negotiating in Russia, good personal relationships are what get you through. Your counterpart should like you and trust you. Russian business depends to some extent on *blat*, a network of contacts and favour. Although it is less strong than it was once was, it will help if you can operate in the spirit of *blat*.

Most business is done face to face, so frequent visits or phone calls to Russia are important. Russians have a variable negotiation style ranging from extreme patience – sitting you out – to strong confrontation. Stay calm: patience is also the strongest card that you can play. Russian negotiations may proceed by concession, so it's important to build some into your proposal and offer them at appropriate moments.

If there is disagreement, try to show that you understand their difficulties. Be direct and straightforward. Share in their soul searching of what is wrong or causing problems. Talk in terms of personal recommendation rather than of direct orders or regulations. Build up trust through clarity of action, keep your inner circle small and at all times aim to build trust.

However, it is important to monitor subsequent performance. Don't put facts before feelings and don't be sophisticated or devious because Russians are privately quite straightforward.

Russians often send a written confirmation after an agreement has been reached to protect themselves. They are, however, prepared to renegotiate the fine print of a contract after it has been signed if it seems appropriate.

Networking

Ice-breakers	Ice-makers
• Russian culture, literature and art	• Chechnya
• Russian achievements	• Criticism of Russia (even if Russians do it)
• Russian business	• The Communist period
• Families and regions in Russia	• Mafia/KGB (FSB) etc.
• Second Word War (the Great Patriotic War in Russia)	

Organisation

Business hours

Business hours are 9am to 5pm Monday to Friday. It's important to allow plenty of time for appointments. They start late and run much longer than planned. Punctuality is not generally a Russian virtue.

Time

Russians vary in their attitude to time according to location and the importance of the event. However, you should expect delays due to heavy traffic (especially in Moscow), and the tendency for meetings not to start until the arrival of the meeting leader.

Teamwork

Teams need to be built on individual trust, so it's important to establish a personal link with each member of the group you're dealing with, and to know them well. Asking advice is important, and is not seen as a weakness. Once people cooperate with you, it is then important not to disappoint them. Make sure the working process is highly organised and structured, and that you and they know who is responsible for what. Unofficial channels and processes are as important as official ones, and can cut through red tape.

Team strengths in Russia tend to be their ability to forge relationships, and come up with imaginative solutions. They're less strong on implementing and completing tasks. Team members are selected primarily on their competence for the role, although educational qualifications and family connections can also be influential. The team leader makes all decisions, and is usually well connected to other decision makers.

Leadership

Importance of hierarchy

It's important to bear in mind that Russia only began to evolve from its combination of traditional patterns and Soviet coercion in the early 1990s, so it's hardly surprising that Russian business tends to be hierarchical. The top man in the company makes all the decisions, which has two corollaries: it slows down the process, and it means that you must make sure that you're negotiating with the right person.

Feedback

This is usually given in private. Large international companies have formal appraisal processes but small companies prefer personal feedback.

The position of women

Although women have equal status to men in many areas of business, especially in academia and administration, top-level posts are still mainly held by men. Women visitors may be subject to 'old world' courtesy and gallantry but may also feel patronised as senior Russian businessmen are less used to dealing with women executives on an equal basis.

Etiquette

Greeting and leave-taking

Strong eye contact is important, and you should shake hands firmly. It will help if you have your business card printed in two languages – yours and Russian. Take your cue from your inter-locutor as to whether to use surnames and titles or first names. If in doubt, go formal, but no real business takes place until a more informal relationship has been established. 'Bear hugs' and kissing on the cheek are reserved for close family and friends.

Body language

People shake hands on meeting and leave-taking (older men may kiss a woman's hand). Smiling on greeting is not automatic (it helps explain the tradition of surly Russian service in restaur-ants, shops and hotels). Shaking fists and the US A-OK gesture is considered rude. Russians are sensitive to what they consider *nyeculturny* (uncultured) behaviour.

This includes swearing, not depositing outer garments in the clockroom, lounging and standing with hands in pockets, shouting or laughing loudly in public and whistling indoors.

Dress code

Russian senior managers tend to dress to impress, both men and women, and to observe some formality in dress and public behaviour. You should do the same.

Gift-giving

Don't go empty-handed. Gifts may be exchanged with a foreign visitor if a meeting has gone well. Russian executives appreciate the offer of good quality business gifts, especially showing a well-known logo. On the other hand, a small business gift may not be treated seriously.

Great gifts	Gifts to avoid
Good quality logo products, popular products in demand. Flowers, alcohol or a luxury food item are appreciated when invited home.	Poor quality items. The days of second-hand jeans, tights or magazines are 30 years out of date.

Hospitality

An invitation to a Russian home is something to be prized. You should definitely accept. Dinners tend to take place early (at around 6pm) and it is good to have prepared the words of a few toasts as toasting the host, the country and the relationship is common.

In a meeting, the table may be laid with *zakuski* (snacks) and even vodka. If so, eat and drink sparingly. If you are holding the meeting it will be appreciated if you provide some snacks, but alcohol is not necessary. Don't assume the vodka culture. Many Russians don't drink it but prefer wine instead.

Russia: business style

Expectations of business relationships

1. Relationship driven   Task driven

2. Risk embracing   Risk averse

3. Equality   Hierarchy

Communication

4. Direct   Indirect

5. Formal   Informal

6. Emotional   Neutral

Management

7. Teams   Individuals

8. Time tight   Time loose

9. Top down   Delegation

Russia: fast facts

Name	Russian Federation Russia
Nationality	Russian
Population	142,500,482 (July 2013 est.)
Languages	Russian (official), many minority languages
Capital	Moscow (pop. 10.5 million)
Main cities	Saint Petersburg 4.5 million; Novosibirsk 1.4 million; Yekaterinburg 1.3 million; Nizhniy Novgorod 1.25 million (2009)
Climate	Short summers and cold winters, in European Russia Siberia sub-arctic tundra climate Southern steppes cold climate with short summers Black sea coast more temperate
Currency	Rouble
Ethnicities	Russian 79.8%, Tatar 3.8%, Ukrainian 2%, Bashkir 1.2%, Chuvash 1.1%, other or unspecified 12.1% (2002 census)
Religion	Russian Orthodox 15-20% Muslim 10-15% Christian 2% (2006 est.) From the Russian revolution to 1989 religious worship officially banned
Internet code	ru
Phone country code	07

SOURCE: CIA WORLD FACTBOOK JULY 2013

South Korea

Ways to succeed	Ways to fail
• Be friendly	• Fail to respect the business card exchange ritual
• Respond to personal questions openly	• Avoid personal questions
• Do what you say you will – fast	• Make people lose face
• Take time to build a good relationship	• Make unfavourable comparisons with Japan and China
• Use your connections to help people	• Fail to respect age, status and rank

Overview

The 'land of the morning calm', as it is known, has the third highest population density in the world after Bangladesh and Taiwan. It is also one of the highest urbanised populations, with half its people living in the six largest cities. There is considerable rivalry with Japan, who occupied Korea from 1910 to 1945, a memory which still causes bitterness. In 1945 Korea divided into North and South, the North going with the then USSR (they were liberated by the Soviets) and the South with the USA (they were liberated by the Americans). In 1950, North Korea attacked the South, leading to the three-year Korean war, involving both US and British troops. After the war, which was won by South Korea and its allies (although peace has never been formally declared), South Korea's economy grew incredibly fast between the 1950s and 2000, mainly due to the development of industrial conglomerates or chaebols such as Samsung, which have a close relationship with government. Leading manufacturers have driven South Korea in 50 years from a poor war-torn state in 1953 to a major world economy.

Expectations

Confucian values

Like China, Korea is a community driven by Confucian values. The five pillars of

Confucianism are:

- Have respect for age and authority.

- Have respect for the collective – the basic unit of social organisation in the country and the company is the family. The family must be consulted and their needs considered.

- Behave virtuously – work to give face to others and to save face. Be sincere in your feelings and in your actions. Be modest about your achievements.

- Work hard and learn hard – value education and hard work.

- Moderation is all things is good – frugality, saving, calmness, avoiding extremes and being indulgent are all important qualities.

By embodying and practising these qualities as a foreigner, you will be able to build the relationships that are basic to successful business in Korea.

Hahn – trust

In Korea trust, *hahn,* is not given automatically but has to be earned. That is part of the reason why creating good relations with Koreans so that they can trust you is of vital importance to successful business in Korea. If you make mistakes in business with Koreans it is important to admit it, apologise and discuss how you can learn from them not to make the same error again.

Kibun– inner face

Part of the *hahn* comes from the need to protect your *kibun,* your 'inner face' or sense of personal dignity. Koreans are extremely protective of their *kibun* and, if they feel it is threatened, they may unofficially designate the person who endangers it as a 'non-person'. This means that people will continue to be polite and will keep you informed of essential developments, but you will have no involvement in or influence on any decisions or actions being taken. Effectively, you become invisible. As Richard Lewis points out in *When Cultures Collide,* 'Pay great attention to protecting their *kibun* – loss of face in Korea is more serious than anything else.'

Communication

Making contact with potential Korean business partners is relatively straightforward but is usually done through a third party contact, such as an embassy, trade mission or trade fair, as well as personal contacts. Meetings are usually booked well in advance although short meetings in hotel coffee shops are also common. Seniority is important in Korean meetings. Matching levels of authority is important and your business card should have your company title clearly marked – if you can translate the back into Korean, you should. The senior person should always enter a meeting room first and will normally sit in the centre. If in doubt, always ask before sitting down. Korea is a relationship culture. As the entrepreneur, Johnny Kim, said, 'Build the relationship and business will follow as day follows night.' A consequence of this is that your Korean colleagues will want to get to know you and may ask quite personal questions. This is not intrusive curiosity but an attempt to find things you have in common and also to determine your age and status, both of which are very important in Korean society. It's important to answer these questions in a positive way, even if diplomatic, and always to deliver negative information or news with an apology. Even more important is never to boast about your status or achievements. Keep it tight. Koreans do like you to get to the point.

The aim of early meetings is to establish a good relationship and recognise that several meetings may be necessary before both sides agree to close a deal.

Presentations

Like their Asian colleagues, Koreans are respectful listeners. Unlike their Asian colleagues, they are happy to give feedback and ask questions. Be prepared to answer them and also be careful to show appreciation of both the questioner and the question in order to give face. Keep your presentations to the point and always suggest win-win ways to profit. The interest is in the bottom line as much as product quality and detailed technical specification.

You can make your presentation more acceptable by breaking it up into small segments and inviting questions after each segment. This will promote extensive discussion and will allow you to gauge the interest of your audience. Avoid jokes and funny stories. It suggests you are not serious about the topic and don't respect your audience. Keep your language clear and simple. You might also use circles rather than triangles to describe process and organisation. Triangles symbolically have negative connotations in Korea.

Meetings

It is important to remember that although a Korean's reading and writing knowledge of English may be very good, their speaking and listening skills may not match up. This doesn't mean they are bad at English but that they are unfamiliar with foreign accents. Take things a little slower, allow time for absorption and response and if in any doubt, use an interpreter.

Business cards will always be exchanged between new contacts. Study the card you are given carefully and do not stuff it in your pocket or flick it in your fingers and above all do not write on it. By the way, writing in red ink suggests death. Avoid red ink pens.

Meetings will normally be led by the senior figure present but be prepared for your Korean colleagues to jump around the agenda and to ask lots of questions, many repeated in order to check information received. Maintain calm, never show impatience or lose your temper, and maintain a fairly formal style.

Negotiation

In negotiations, Koreans often begin with a very high start point. You should do the same but leave plenty of room in your opening bid for compromise. Flexibility in negotiation is favoured by Koreans and it is important to remain cool and calm. They will want to move fast and may try to hustle. Be firm about your requirements but never lose respect.

You'll find that Koreans dislike saying no. Dissent may be shown by sucking in air. Also remember that nodding may indicate polite attention rather than agreement.

As with many nationalities it is important to judge any promises made by Koreans against past performance. There is a tendency to make commitments that can't be delivered and to say that things have been done that haven't. This is why relationships are important to ensure loyalty and trust. With this background you may feel it is better to suggest short-term agreements, which are performance-based, rather than long-term exclusivity agreements. However, when you and your Korean partner feel you have a long-term relationship, then trust and loyalty will become the basis of the negotiation.

As in many Asian countries, a contract is seen as establishing a relationship and an expression of intent. They may suggest renegotiation if the circumstances have changed as long as the spirit of the contract is adhered to. You may do the same.

Networking

Ice-breakers	Ice-makers
• South Korean culture and business success • K-Pop, fashion and design • Sport • Personal hobbies	• Politics • Personal questions (apart from general enquiries about health and well-being)

Organisation

Business hours

Korean business hours are 9am to 5pm and the five-day week is increasingly the norm, but your best times for meetings are mid morning or mid afternoon. Mid July to mid August is the annual holiday season and the two great lunar festivals are the Lunar New Year in January or February and the Moon festival in September or October. Check Korean calendars for precise dates – each festival may last a week.

Time

Punctuality matters in Korea. Be on time for meetings but accept that Korean bosses may be a little late due to pressure of work. Similarly, delivery times are important. Ensure that delivery times are clear and if there is any slippage, inform people immediately and put things right as soon as possible.

The pace of business in Korea tends to be faster than you might expect in a society dominated by respect for age and status although slower than the US or Northern Europe. However, when the business opportunity appears, Koreans like to do things fast and, if they sense a lack of commitment or interest on your side, will quickly move on to other deals. It is important to do what you say you will do when you have stated, to keep in regular contact and to show commitment to your Korean colleagues.

Teams

As a Confucian society, Korea operates in a collectivist fashion under a strong leader who nevertheless has his/her team's interests at heart. This means that issues will be debated and discussed within the team and that task allocation and checking will be carefully controlled. There is a strong work ethic in Korea and group consensus, loyalty and deference to the group leader is important. The group leader should always be the first port of call on any issues regarding progress, organisation, delivery and so on.

Leadership

Management style

One of the characteristics of Korea has always been a cadre of leading families.

Family name, wealth and the power of the chaebol in which you work determine your social status in business. This means that in a company, respect for the boss is very important. One result of this is that Korean employees are very protective of their bosses and will hide bad news until an appropriate moment, especially at the beginning of the day.

Korean business is 'top-down' and the president of the company or the board of directors rule on any major initiatives. Be prepared for the fact that this may take time.

Etiquette

Greetings

Koreans normally bow when meeting each other, junior person first, and always exchange business cards. Wait for the senior person in the exchange to offer their hand first. Koreans prefer a softer handshake and in business a nod of the head is quite sufficient. The full bow is not necessary. Koreans maintain much stronger eye contact than the Japanese unless the person they are greeting is very senior.

Dress code

Dress-wise in meetings, dark clothes are preferred although brighter clothes may be the case for entertainment. Trouser suits are fine for women but pay attention to tight skirts in case you are asked to sit on the floor in a restaurant.

Gift-giving

This is part of building the business relationship but need not be expensive. It demonstrates thoughtfulness and considera-tion. The most successful gifts are those from your own country or region. Common gifts are items with the company logo. By the way, it is considered good form in Korea to be reluctant to accept gifts at first. Don't be put off.

If invited to a Korean home, chocolates, fruit, flowers or some-thing for young children would be appreciated. You should always aim to bring a gift.

If you give or receive a gift, do it with both hands and DON'T open it in front of the giver. They may lose face if you react inappropriately. Gifts should always be reciprocated at the same level, if not immediately, on your next visit.

Great gifts	Gifts to avoid
• Something with your company logo • Something from your country (Make sure that gifts to senior people are of higher value)	• Avoid too expensive gifts (reciprocity can be a problem) • Avoid too cheap gifts (particularly from developing countries unless a souvenir or piece of artwork)

Hospitality

Hospitality is an important part of the business process and should always be reciprocated at the same level. The rule is who invites, pays. You may find, however, that the invitation is limited to business colleagues and that spouses and partners may be excluded from the invitation. Much hospitality will be offered in hotels although, exceptionally, a friend may invite you home.

Take your shoes off inside the apartment or traditional eating place and point your shoes away from the inside, towards the door. When putting your shoes back on at the end of the evening, try not to have your back to your fellow guests. Traditionally, you pour someone else's drink, not your own, and if your glass is empty it will be immediately refilled. The standard toast is 'Gun bae'.

South Korea: business style

Expectations of business relationships

1. Relationship driven   Task driven

2. Risk embracing   Risk averse

3. Equality   Hierarchy

Communication

4. Direct   Indirect

5. Formal   Informal

6. Emotional   Neutral

Management

7. Teams   Individuals

8. Time tight   Time loose

9. Top down   Delegation

South Korea: fast facts

Name	Republic of Korea South Korea
Nationality	Korean
Population	48,955,203 (July 2013 est.)
Languages	Korean (Hangul)
Capital	Seoul (pop. 9.75 million)
Main cities	Busan (Pusan) 3.439 million Incheon (Inch'on) 2.572 million Daegu (Taegu) 2.458 million Daejon (Taejon) 1.497 million (2009)
Climate	Temperate, with rainfall heavier in summer than winter
Currency	Won
Ethnicities	Korean
Religion	Christian 31.6% (Protestant 24%, Roman Catholic 7.6%) Buddhist 24.2% Other or unknown 0.9% None 43.3% (2010 survey)
Internet code	kr
Phone country code	82

SOURCE: CIA WORLD FACTBOOK JULY 2013

The United Kingdom (UK)

Ways to succeed	Ways to fail
• Deliver on time, without drama	• Boast about your achievements
• Arrive at meetings punctually	• Talk for an hour in a presentation
• If you're having difficulties, ask advice immediately rather than risk missing a deadline	• Phone people in the evening about work
• Check at the end of a meeting exactly what the Brits expect of you	• Let a colleague down once he or she believes they can depend on you
• Join them for a beer after work, or in the gym (many Brits now avoid alcohol)	• Be patronising to women

Overview

A group of northwest European islands, and a member of the EU since 1973, the UK is a monarchy that never seems quite sure whether its key alliance lies with Europe, the USA or the Commonwealth. It has always resisted joining the Eurozone, maintains sterling as its currency and opts out of much of the European Union's Common Agricultural Policy. It claims a 'special relationship' with the USA that extends back to the two countries' common roots (the Pilgrim Fathers sailed from Plymouth, on Britain's southwest coast, to America in 1611), and remains a leading member of the Commonwealth, a loose association of countries that were formerly part of the British Empire. In some of them (Canada, for example) the British monarch is still considered Head of State.

Its 60 million population and common language (English) conceal quite deep social divisions. First there are the four main nationalities: English (the majority), Scots, Welsh and Northern Irish. Then there are the main migrant groups who have settled in the UK from Commonwealth countries, principally the West Indies, India and Pakistan and, most recently, the Central and Eastern European arrivals from the new EU entrants in 2004. Finally, within England itself there is a traditional rivalry between the old industrial north and the more affluent south.

Britain claims that it is a multicultural country with strict laws against discrimination by race, religion, gender, age, disability and sexual orientation, as well as respect for human rights. This policy has, however, been thrown into question by the 7/11 terrorist bombings of 2005 and debates about religious dress and separatism. Economically, the UK is placed seventh in Goldman Sachs' forecast of the world's richest countries in 2050. Its strength lies in the City of London's financial services sector and in Britons' personal wealth in a buoyant property market.

You would imagine that a nation whose language has become the global business language would be easy to understand. But this is not always the case with the British. They remain an idio-syncratic island race: frustratingly insular, reluctant to display overt emotion, and ambiguous in what they say.

The British are often uneasy and nervous when dealing with other people, even amongst themselves. Perhaps this explains their reliance on their notoriously unpredictable weather as a subject of small talk. It's a shield to save having to talk about – heaven forbid! – one's personal life or feelings. Americans get exasperated by the British fear of not saying clearly what they feel and what they want, and this impassive, undemonstrative approach also confuses many other cultures. You should, of course, remember the differences between the UK's four different cultures: the Scots can be healthily frank, while the Irish and Welsh regard themselves as far more open and passionate than the English.

Despite these drawbacks, combined with the devastating economic blows of two world wars and the loss of empire in the 20th century, Britain has emerged into the 21st century as one of the world's major trading nations. The Brits themselves exist in a curious mix of regret for a lost idyllic past, when life was supposedly less tense and less violent, and a relaxed contemporary hedonism.

Expectations

Privacy

Just like any other culture, Britain is full of paradoxes. On the one hand, the British continue to believe in the values of tradition, caution, restraint and fair play. They support the underdog, tolerate eccentricity (often by ignoring it), and think that taking part is more important than winning. Modesty and politeness are also important to them. This, combined with their zeal for personal privacy, can produce bizarre effects such as a reluctance to say what they actually do in their working life. If asked at a party what his job is, a Briton might say, 'I'm in advertising,' when in fact he's the high-performing CEO of a major advertising agency.

Humour

The British are also famous for their legendary ironic and self-deprecating humour. They find it useful as an ice-breaker at meetings, to defuse tension and cover potentially embarrassing moments. The difficulty for visitors is that they just don't get what's being said or, even worse, take it literally. Britons working internationally, or dealing with foreign clients in their own country, should develop more awareness of this pitfall and modify what they're saying or writing accordingly.

Informality

What has changed in Britain in recent decades is that the country has become much more informal in its social and business customs, and has shed much of its former respect for institutions, title and age. In this it follows the American model. People use first names very quickly, even to bosses, and the words 'Sir' and 'Madam' are now mainly used only by sales assistants in shops. Britons do, however, maintain a generally high level of respect for the law and for procedures, which largely explains the absence of corruption in British business and politics.

Systems

Britain is a systems-based society, very much governed by a strong legal system and a principle of fair play. The job comes first, the relationship second, and professionalism comes before friendship or relationship. Once renowned for its formality, Britain has become one of the most informal business communities in the world with all levels of society on first-name terms. This informality is crucial to successful communication, and many foreign business people, used to the stereotypical image of an English male from the 1950s in bowler hat and pinstripe suit, carrying a rolled umbrella, still fail to recognise it.

Communication

Coded communication

This combination of tradition and rapid change can make life confusing for the foreigner in Britain. The secret is to watch and listen carefully, and to learn to read between the lines to try and establish what the British are really saying. In this respect Britain is closer to some Eastern cultures than Western ones. It can take years to fully decipher British codes, but this is also true of any culture where much of what is truly meant remains unspoken.

Relaxed approach

As we have already seen, Britain has copied many social and business mannerisms from the USA. People use first names almost immediately: many bosses actively encourage their staff to call them by their first name. This informality even extends to those you are dealing with purely by phone or email: the person you have just contacted responds using your first name even though they may know nothing about you. The practice is uncomfortable to many foreigners, and has one very obvious drawback. If the relationship goes wrong and disagreement sets in, you are left in an uncomfortable position: having to address someone in a friendly way when you are feeling any-thing but that.

Friendly but detached

British style is to be courteous and friendly but detached. It's polite to shake hands at the beginning and end of meetings. However, if you're a frequent visitor to a company, you will not be expected to shake hands with everyone in the office, only with those with whom you're dealing directly. You'll receive a limp, tenuous handshake from a surprising number of Britons: it's their nervousness at confronting someone new, combined with the British reluctance to reveal too much emotion too soon.

Practical

The British are practical, empirical people, and distrust too much theory, philosophising and idealism. So pack your presentations full of attainable objectives, concrete detail and provable statistics. Time your presentation to last around 20 to 40 minutes, depending on the gravity of your proposal, and allow opportunity for debate and questions. People will concentrate more on the content of what you say than on how you say it or your body language. Remember that even if your audience is wildly excited about your project, their response may be muted: it's that British reserve at work, that fear of being seen to be too enthusiastic. If your audience is highly divided, the discussion is unlikely to be heated: a sense of calm and proportion usually prevails in British business.

Presentations

Britons are happy to listen for 40 minutes, especially if the presentation combines humour with information and is well organised. Expect interruptions to ask for clarification or repetition depending on the formality of the occasion and always allow time for questions at the end.

Meetings and negotiations

A formal business meeting in Britain will generally run to an agenda. If the discussion wanders too far from it, the chairperson may feel uncomfortable and try to drag everyone back on line. If important new matters arise in these digressions, the chair will often suggest that they are put on the agenda at the next meeting, or, if urgent, addressed rapidly by a sub-group of people outside the meeting. Meetings generally end on time.

Following the American example, British meetings can be highly egalitarian affairs. Managers are often happy to sit beside staff and not at the top of the table, and will try to draw everyone into the discussion. The ideal is to achieve consensus so that everyone feels that they 'own' the decision. The British like to arrive at decisions and action points in their meetings, which managers are then expected to follow up. The focus is on action rather than going through an exhaustive discussion of options.

In debates the British tend to avoid dogmatic and absolute statements, and use words such as 'perhaps' and 'maybe' to imply that alternative points of view might be valid. In negotiations they are often willing to compromise to achieve a win-win situation in which both parties can feel that the agreement offers a reasonable deal and prospects of further cooperation.

Networking

Networking is an important business skill and exchanging business cards in an informal way and following up is quite normal.

Ice-breakers	Ice-makers
• British weather – it never fails.	• Religion, politics and immigration
• Property prices – but don't ask someone directly what theirs is worth.	• People's salaries and personal worth
• Laments about traffic, parking and public transport	• 'Why do British people put their parents in homes?'
• Respect for taking someone's time	• Raising your voice
• Being courteous – using 'please', 'thank you' and 'sorry'	• Boasting about yourself or your country
• Remembering and using names	
• Gentle use of understatement and irony	

Organisation

Business hours

The business day is usually 9am to 5.30pm, excluding Saturdays, and appointments are best scheduled for around 10am or 11am or for early afternoon at around 2pm. Most appointments are scheduled for one hour but may go on longer.

Teamwork and motivation

Operating in management teams is a basic principle of British business. This includes sharing information, regular briefings and teams taking credit for success (or getting angry if the boss does so without crediting them). Team members are chosen for their experience and qualifications, but also on the basis of 'usefulness'. The team leader is responsible for setting the objectives and tasks, but team members take responsibility for implementation: delegation is an important principle of British management.

Consultation is important, although team members will normally abide by majority decisions. However, the way of giving feedback can sometimes be quite adversarial. Criticism should not be seen as an attack on personal competence.

Time

The British are known worldwide for their punctuality, so ensure that you're there on time. Some British managers can get agitated if someone is as little as two or three minutes late. Road congestion and rail disruption are common in Britain, but true business pros take that into account and leave extra early for key appointments.

Leadership

Management style

American management approaches and methods have also influenced this area of British business. Power is often devolved downwards, and people are expected to 'champion' and to take responsibility for their particular projects. Britain operates on a time-tight environment, so managers are also expected to deliver on schedule, or have a pretty good reason for why it's not possible. The more enlightened companies welcome input from any member of staff, no matter how modest their experience.

British managers often have fewer academic and technical qualifications compared to their equivalents in other countries, but tend to compensate for this by having more on-the-job experience. Some cultures regard British practices as unprofessional and slack: 'muddling through' is the British term for pulling everything together in the end, but this approach does not impress the Germans, for example.

The general management attitude in the UK is warm but detached, and relationships tend to be functional rather than personal. If confrontation emerges, it will be resolved face to face by focusing on the issues rather than on the personalities.

Feedback

Formal yearly appraisals and six-monthly updates are the norm in British business but informal personal feedback is normally given in private.

Women in management

There is no formal bar to women at any level of management but there is still felt to be a 'glass ceiling' with many women still paid less than male equivalents and fewer women at board level, despite women constituting 50% of the workforce.

Etiquette

Greetings and leave-taking

The British are informal right from the start and use first names (but not nicknames). Shaking hands on first meeting is common but not necessarily on leaving or on meeting a second time.

Dress code

Unless stated that you need to 'dress up', dress codes are fairly informal. It is always worth checking what the dress code is for any social occasion but 'smart casual' is mostly accepted. This might mean a smart blouse or top for women with skirt or trousers and an open-neck shirt and trousers for men. Jeans, unless very fashionable, are considered casual.

Gifts

Gift-giving is not necessary to the business process: it is more common to invite people to a good lunch to express appreciation. If you wish to offer a present, something from your country is always acceptable: remember that the British tradition is to open gifts immediately so that both giver and receiver can share the pleasure.

Great gifts	Gifts to avoid
Wine, chocolate, a speciality from your own country	Most presents are acceptable. Maybe ask a florist about appropriate flowers – red roses or white lilies may send the wrong message

Hospitality

'Going for a pint' after work is common in Britain. Join in: it's a good place to make friends and get to know the Brits, and you don't have to drink alcohol. Despite their reputation for reserve, the British are quite quick to invite visitors to their homes for dinner or for lunch at the weekend. If you are asked, don't arrive more than 15 minutes late, or you risk disrupting the hosts' timing. The evening will probably finish by 10pm or 11pm. Take wine: Britain is not a major wine-growing culture, so 'bringing a bottle' is an accepted convention. You may also want to take flowers or some chocolates for your hostess. Dress is almost always smart casual on out-of-office occasions.

UK: business style

Expectations of business relationships

1. Relationship driven — Task driven

2. Risk embracing — Risk averse

3. Equality — Hierarchy

Communication

4. Direct — Indirect

5. Formal — Informal

6. Emotional — Neutral

Management

7. Teams — Individuals

8. Time tight — Time loose

9. Top down — Delegation

UK: fast facts

Name	United Kingdom of Great Britain and Northern Ireland (Great Britain = England, Scotland, Wales)
Nationality	British (English, Scottish, Welsh, Northern Irish)
Population	63.5 million (July 2013 est.) England 53.5 million Scotland 5.25 million Wales 3 million Northern Ireland 1.8 million
Languages	English Also regional languages –Scots (about 30% of the population of Scotland), Scottish Gaelic (about 60,000 in Scotland), Welsh (about 20% of the population of Wales), Irish (about 10% of the population of Northern Ireland), Cornish (some 2,000 to 3,000 in Cornwall) (2012)
Capital	London (pop. 8.615 million)
Main cities	Birmingham 2.296 million Manchester 2.247 million Leeds/Bradford (West Yorkshire) 1.541 million Glasgow 1.166 million (2009) Edinburgh 496,000 Cardiff 325,000 Belfast 286,000
Climate	Temperate, moderated by prevailing southwest winds over the North Atlantic
Currency	Pounds sterling
Ethnicities	White 92.1% (English 83.6%, Scottish 8.6%, Welsh 4.9%, Northern Irish 2.9%) Black 2% Indian 1.8% Pakistani 1.3% Mixed 1.2% Other 1.6% (2001 census)

Religion	Christian (Anglican, Roman Catholic, Presbyterian, Methodist) 71.6% Muslim 2.7% Hindu 1% Other 1.6% Unspecified or none 23.1% (2001 census)
Internet code	uk
Phone country code	44

SOURCE: CIA WORLD FACTBOOK JULY 2013

The United States of America (USA)

Ways to succeed	Ways to fail
• Have a positive mental attitude	• Emphasise problems
• 'Can do' approach	• Be overcautious
• Deliver within time and budget	• Don't deliver what you promised
• Present in easily grasped images and explanations	• Criticise the US
• Emphasise benefits not drawbacks	• Be indirect or long-winded (Cuttothechase.com)

Overview

The USA and the UK, and to some extent Western Europe, have what is known as 'a special relationship' based on ties of language and shared experience. Increasingly however, that relationship is being tempered by the need to build Pacific relationships with China and the Far East. Britons and Americans do business easily and immediately, on the whole, but there can also be a real clash of misunderstandings, made even more confusing by the fact that Britain and the USA speak the same language and the USA and Western Europe share a common culture. Why can't we all get on better?

A 'new' country

The problems start in part with the fact that Europe is an old continent, and America is still new and shiny. Many Europeans carry a touch of cynical world-weariness about them. Their countries are overcrowded and over-expensive, the infrastructure creaks, and the weather is increasingly variable. The British, in particular, have characteristics – admirable in some circumstances – that Americans just don't get. Among these are self-effacement, understatement and an acidly sardonic line in humour. Britons hoping to make an impact with Americans should 'bin' – to use an American expression now current in British English – all three. For non-native English speakers, either the British or American variety of English is recognised and accepted worldwide.

Expectations

The American Dream

Despite the difficulties that the country has suffered in recent times, Americans continue to believe fervently in the American Dream. They believe in their legendary 'can do' attitude – though this can lead to huge errors, as the bursting of the dot-com bubble vividly demonstrated – and they believe that individuals can transform their lives by hard work. They like to think big, and are impressed by statistics that suggest that a project will be the biggest ever of its kind, or the first, or the finest.

America first

For foreigners, the USA can feel very parochial for a world power. You need to understand that there is enough going on in a large country of over 300 million people to make European or world news very far away – unless it affects the USA directly. Most Americans don't have passports and foreign travel is less than in Europe, for example. News services, such as CNN, have global reach although the approach may be American in interest and style.

Religious

Many more Americans than Europeans – especially Britons – express religious feelings and attend church. So visiting Brits should edit out of their speech the mild religious profanities and the swear words that pass as acceptable in the UK, at least until you're sure of usages within the group you're working with. Remember, too, that the USA is a nation of immigrants – these days more a salad bowl of races and cultures than a melting pot. At around 40 million, the Hispanic population was due to overtake the black population in numbers in 2006.

Politically correct

It's illegal in the US to ask the age, marital status or number of children of a potential employee, and endearments such as 'honey' are not acceptable.

Positive mental attitude

So, to do business with Americans it's a case of chest out, shoulders back, head up and stand tall. Be proud of who you are and what you do. Think positive and optimistically. Say what you mean plainly and clearly, and delete from your speech pattern that wickedly corrosive Brit humour – it will only lead to blank faces, and possibly downright irritation.

Generous

Things have become more complicated post 9/11. America's leadership and foreign policy have won it few admirers around the world (although neither has Britain's), and there is an undeniable – if often unspoken – anti-American sentiment in the air. But whatever your feelings about this, remember that American people themselves are extraordinarily generous and openhearted. And they really have a soft spot for Brits.

Communication

Confident communicators

Americans can appear so damned self-confident to many Europeans. They tend to speak louder than Europeans – very much louder, in some cases – use exaggerated body language, and manage to sound almost jarringly optimistic. They also talk in phrases that create mini-pictures: 'He's right behind the eight ball' (he's on top of his job or project), or 'I'm not going down that route' (I'm not going to talk about that, or pursue that course of action).

If you try to imitate American characteristics, you will end up looking and sounding like the worst kind of mid-Atlantic European. But you should project your voice confidently, address *all* the people in a meeting or group instead of mumbling to the chairperson, and sound positive about what you're proposing.

Informal approach

Americans may use first names almost immediately, even from the first handshake. But don't be deceived: this will not prevent them from subjecting your proposals to hard questioning. Focus on the bottom line – American business is very much systems-oriented, and always wants to see how much money can be made, and when. You will often hear the phrase, 'Are you hitting your numbers?' (are you achieving budget?). The numbers are sacrosanct in the USA, and those who don't hit them might experience a rapid farewell – still with that confident eye contact and the use of your first name as you are given that final handshake.

Direct

Although Americans can often seem very direct, to the point of appearing rude, remember that their use of language is just different to that of British English. When an American says, 'Pass that file!' it's just her way of saying, 'Could I trouble you to just pass me that file, please?' They're not being discourteous: Dutch, Scandinavians and Spanish people tend to have the same speech patterns.

Presentation style

Allow for a moderate attention span of 30 to 45 minutes in a presentation, and build in plenty of time for debate. Americans appreciate an informal style and humour, but make sure that your jokes and lighthearted asides don't drift into that area of dark Brit humour that can provoke blank stares. Relevance is very important – use simple, direct expressions, conveyed quickly with short pauses. If your pitch is going down well, expect categorical responses: 'Absolutely!', 'Definitely!', 'Fantastic!' – all of which reflect their can-do, achievement-focused attitude. If you are fortunate enough to have the kind of personality that allows you to entertain your audience while delivering a winning proposition, they will appreciate that even more.

Meetings and negotiations

Meetings in America are for making decisions, rather than for gathering views or simply sounding out people. The pace is brisk – 'Time is money' – and you should be open about your aims from the start. People are not always well prepared for meetings, and papers are not always read beforehand, but this won't stop them from commenting on your proposals. The dress code and seating are usually informal, and the discussion will follow the agenda.

Argument and debate are considered constructive and are highly valued. A tough negotiating style is often used, which can appear rude to non-Americans. Americans are willing to express disagreement frankly – 'You must be kidding!' – but it's part of what can be a rough and tumble atmosphere. Show humour, say what you think (even in front of seniors), and be ready to forget everything and start over if you lose the debate.

Try not to appear old-fashioned or slow, or get into too much detail. Negotiations are usually finalised quite quickly, and will often centre on figures. Concessions may be agreed when time is running out, whereas in other cultures there would be a break for reflection and a subsequent meeting to try and reach a conclusion. Equally, decisions may initially be made in principle, with everyone happy to settle the details later.

Networking

Ice-breakers	Ice-makers
• Job-related discussion	• Politically incorrect jokes and remarks
• American personal kindness	• Religion, politics and controversial subjects
• Sport (baseball/ American football/ basketball)	• Mention of health care and socialism can fragment a dinner party
• American TV and movies/music/food/ books	• Asking women if they are married (as opposed to questions about children and husbands)

Organisation

Business organisation

Business hours are from 8.30am to 5pm or 6pm Monday to Friday but overtime and Saturdays are common. For most Americans, work comes first. You'll be expected to work long and hard, show energy and enthusiasm, and volunteer for anything that you feel you can complete. Understand the aims and motivation of other team members, but be there and fight your corner, and make sure that your individual contribution is recognised in this highly competitive environment. Being overly modest or submissive doesn't work in the USA.

Time

Punctuality is crucial, because time is equated to money. Start and complete tasks quickly and respond to emails and voicemail messages promptly, and certainly within 24 hours. If they are out late, many Americans often check emails before going to bed – a practice that stress management experts would not recommend as a means of achieving a good night's sleep. They tend to take short holiday breaks, and fewer of them than Europeans. Even then, they will often check emails every couple of days.

Teams

Teams in the USA are usually selected on the basis of an individual's competence, a passion for trying new things, and a reputation for getting results. There is also an emphasis on equality of opportunity regardless of age, gender or race. Team members themselves often place their personal goals first, but they align these to the company's aims. Competition within the team is encouraged because it is said to release creative tension. Team members expect to be consulted and to have their view influence the outcome. Deadlines are regarded as fixed, and overtime to complete a project on time is common.

Leadership

Inspiration not autocracy

American managers are expected to lead in a way that generates confidence in the workforce. Tough leaders who get results are particularly admired. On the other hand, managers are expected to arrive at decisions only after consulting their teams and colleagues, and to convince them by logic rather than by feelings or intuition. An autocratic style is not liked: inspiration is what really wins followers.

Goal oriented

Executives are usually focused on goals, action and the bottom line, which can lead to short term-ism. Failure doesn't automatically carry a stigma if the manager was seen to be acting boldly, perhaps in an untried market or with new processes. Consistent failure to deliver will surely lead to dismissal, however.

Feedback

Set high targets for yourself and others, and give clear orders and opinions: Americans feel very uncomfortable with what they see as British timidity in telling people what they need to do or in expressing disagreement. Don't be pessimistic or hesitant. Take responsibility for initiating implementation, be prepared to disregard everything and start again, and be open about mistakes, failures and delays.

Women in management

In the US there is no formal bar to the advancement of women in any trade or profession, and the two sexes receive equal pay for equal work. There are many women executives, especially in fashion, cosmetics, arts and the media.

Etiquette

Greetings

First names, informality and humour are valued in the USA, although the terms 'Sir' and 'Madam' are often used with strangers as a mark of courtesy. Handshaking is common when Americans arrive at work or enter a room at the start of a meeting, and a friendly approach in general is considered important. It's part of America's 'Have a nice day' culture.

Dress code

Dress will be smart-casual or informal, especially on the more laid-back West Coast.

Gifts

Gift-giving is personal but not expected in business. Some people may send gifts by mail.

Great gifts	Gifts to avoid
• Wine • Flowers • A good Scotch used to be appreciated, but many Americans now drink less, or prefer lighter spirits	• Most gifts are acceptable but avoid gifts that may be considered politically incorrect or (for children) gifts considered inappropriate by the family such as toy guns or video games

Hospitality

Like many other aspects of American life, business entertaining and socialising is usually informal. Americans often eat early, with lunch at around noon and dinner at six. The USA used to be famous for cocktail-fuelled lunches, but the 'two-Perrier' lunch is increasingly the norm, and working lunches over sandwiches in the office are common. Heavy or enthusiastic drinking is frowned on amongst Americans.

If you smoke, you will increasingly feel like a pariah: if you need to, join those who step outside, or ask if it's OK if you're at all unsure.

Americans are quick to invite you to their homes. Arrive on time, as you should for all appointments in the US, and have the host's phone number in case you're running late or get lost. Think about leaving by 10pm: many Americans go to bed early and rise early.

The USA: business style

Expectations of business relationships

1. Relationship driven — Task driven

2. Risk embracing — Risk averse

3. Equality — Hierarchy

Communication

4. Direct — Indirect

5. Formal — Informal

6. Emotional — Neutral

Management

7. Teams — Individuals

8. Time tight — Time loose

9. Top down — Delegation

The USA: fast facts

Name	United States of America United States (USA or US)
Nationality	American
Population	316,668,567 (July 2013 est.)
Languages	English 82.1% Spanish 10.7% Other Indo-European 3.8% Asian and Pacific island 2.7% (2000 census) Note: the US has no official national language, but English has acquired official status in 28 of the 50 states; Hawaiian is an official language in the state of Hawaii
Capital	Washington D.C. (District of Columbia) (pop. 4.421 million)
Main cities	New York-Newark 19.3 million Los Angeles-Long Beach-Santa Ana 12.675 million Chicago 9.134 million Miami 5.699 million (2009)
Climate	Mainly temperate Tropical in Hawaii and Florida Arctic in Alaska Dry in the great plains in the west and the southwest North east is affected by cold and snow in January and February Hurricanes and tornadoes accompany storms in the mid-west in spring
Currency	US Dollar
Ethnicities	White 79.96% Hispanic est.15.1% Black 12.85% Asian 4.43% Amerindian and Alaska native 0.97% Native Hawaiian and other Pacific islander 0.18 (July 2007 estimate)
Religion	Protestant 51.3%

	Roman Catholic 23.9% Mormon 1.7% Other Christian 1.6% Jewish 1.7% Buddhist 0.7% Muslim 0.6% Other or unspecified 2.5% Unaffiliated 12.1% None 4% (2007 est.)
Internet code	us
Phone country code	01

SOURCE: CIA WORLD FACTBOOK JULY 2013

Further Reading

- Brian Hurn and Barry Tomalin Cross-Cultural Communication: Theory and Practice, Palgrave Macmillan 2013

- Craig Storti The Art of Coming Home NB Books 2001

- Richard D Lewis When Cultures Collide NB Books 2011

- Richard D Lewis When Teams Collide NB Books 2012

- Roger Fisher R and William Ury 'Getting to Yes' Penguin 1991

- Sherard Cowper-Coles Ever the Diplomat Harper Press 2012

Index